*f*P

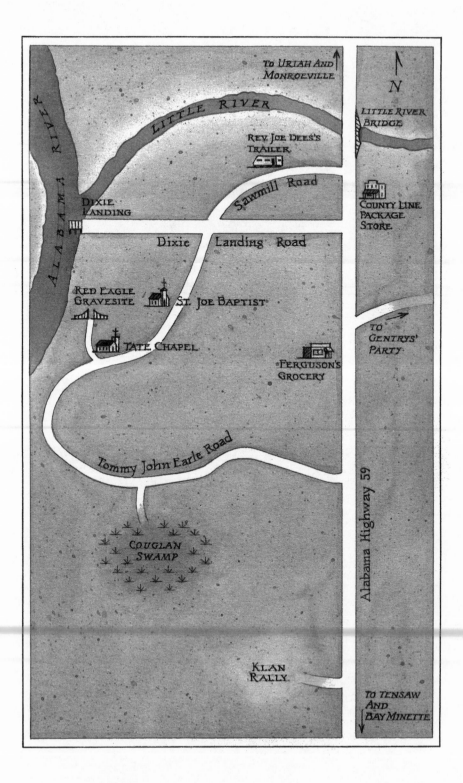

The Ballad of
Little River

A TALE OF RACE AND RESTLESS YOUTH
IN THE RURAL SOUTH

_____

PAUL HEMPHILL

THE FREE PRESS

NEW YORK LONDON TORONTO SYDNEY SINGAPORE

*f*P

THE FREE PRESS
A Division of Simon & Schuster Inc.
1230 Avenue of the Americas
New York, NY 10020

Grateful acknowledgment is made for permission to reprint the excerpt from
Let Us Now Praise Famous Men. Copyright 1939, 1940 by James Agee.
Copyright © 1941 by James Agee and Walker Evans.
Copyright © renewed 1969 by Mia Fritsch Agee and Walker Evans.
Reprinted by permission of Houghton Mifflin Co. All rights reserved.

Map © 2000 David Cain

Book design by Ellen R. Sasahara

Manufactured in the United States of America

10   9   8   7   6   5   4   3   2   1

Library of Congress Cataloging-in-Publication Data is available

ISBN 0-684-85682-4

FOR WALTER D. JONES

Mentor, friend, gentle soul

CONTENTS

_____

Small wonder how pitiably we love our home, cling in her skirts at night, rejoice in her wide star-seducing smile, when every star strikes us sick with the fright: do we really exist at all?

—James Agee, *Let Us Now Praise Famous Men*

A Spin in the Country

"BANANA? SAUSAGE BISCUIT? V-8? Got some tomato juice back there somewhere, if you can find it under the worms and crickets and stuff. Long ways between grocery stores around here. Gotta be prepared. Speaking of which, if you don't mind my saying, looks like you can't afford to be missing any meals. What you need is a woman to cook for you." Wearing sandals and gray double-knit slacks and a gaily embroidered white guayabera he had picked up somewhere in his travels since retirement, jawbone clopping away like Howdy Doody, teeth rattling like castanets, fingers lifting in salute to the drivers whizzing past, James Witherington was manhandling his big white Chevy pickup truck over the wild landscape where he had been born nearly eighty years earlier. He had called at daybreak to say he had some time if I wanted to go for a spin, get the lay of the land, and so now we were off on a bone-rattling tour of the Alabama swamps on this steamy morning in early spring.

Rushing past old cemeteries and barns and cornfields and freshly plowed furrows just seeded with cotton, slowing only to give wide berth to the monstrous logging trucks careening in both directions on the undulating macadam state road or to point out some site of historical interest stuck back on dirt roads the timber companies had gouged through the forests, he was singing in his high nasal twang like a tour guide on speed. "The battle of Shomo Creek was about as close as we got to the Civil War, and there wasn't much to it. My grandpa was a teenaged scout for the volunteers, and when they heard some shots they turned and ran like hell, and that was about the size of it. . . . Funny how everybody claims to be kin to Red Eagle, the Creek chief, man that tried to kill off the white folks . . . Lord, I don't see how some of these niggers can stand living like that . . . Lot of the problems with the sorry whites is cousins marrying cousins. There's one family with eight kids you might call 'slow,' and that's a lot of welfare checks every month. The daddy was asked to go count the hogs one day. Can't read or write, understand. Came back and told the boss, 'You got a bunch' . . . This one old boy claimed he had the biggest dick in Baldwin County, kept this nigger whorehouse in business, back in the forties, accounting for some of the half-breeds you see . . . Look at that pile of trash, would you, old mattresses and refrigerators, right on the side of the road. People don't have much pride anymore . . ."

It went like that for three hours. To a city boy like me, fresh on the scene, visions of Tobacco Road and Yoknapatawpha County flashed through the windshield of James Witherington's pickup as it bumped along the back roads of northern Baldwin County in the dank southwest corner of Alabama. It didn't take a dreamer to conjure up black folks bent over rows of cotton, redneck yahoos stirring corn mash in black kettles beside fetid streams, humpbacked old grannies in sunbonnets hoeing their pea patches, George Wallace thundering from a flatbed trailer about "pointy-headed intellectuals that can't park their bicycles straight," or crude kerosene-soaked crosses blazing in the night. If not for the late-model pickups and the television satellite dishes sprouting like pop-eyed toadstools in the rich black earth, this could have been the 1940s; or earlier, even, back to the Depression years of *Let Us Now Praise Famous Men,* which, in fact, was centered little more than a hundred miles north of here on land much the same as this.

As THE MILLENNIUM approached, in an age of computers and intergalactic travel and maybe even the cloning of human beings, I was curious about what life must be like deep in the American outback, in some little hardscrabble corner of the most powerful and advanced nation in the world. I had completed what one critic glibly referred to as my Bubba Trilogy, accounts of country music and stock-car racing and truck driving, and now I was threatening to stretch my Southern *oeuvre*, as it were, to a tetralogy if I could find the right place. It had to be distinctively Southern, blue-collar, thoroughly isolated from the mainstream of American life, and there had to be an issue involved to merit my going there—a *story*—as my lost colony was dragged into the twenty-first century.

It was in the summer of 1997 that I first heard of Little River, Alabama. Not much had happened in those parts since the massacre of five hundred settlers and slaves in the early 1800s by renegade Creek Indians, but 1997 had turned out to be something else. The short version was this: A young black man had been killed while trying to break into a white family's trailer, then a black man had nearly bludgeoned a beloved white store owner to death, and finally a marauding band of white kids had torched a black church and vandalized another during a drunken night of caterwauling only forty-eight hours following a rare Ku Klux Klan rally. This seemed to be the place, all right.

The nearest motels being thirty miles away, I had rented a stuffy little two-bedroom house refitted as a hunting and fishing cabin, with bunk beds, a pool table, heart-of-pine walls hung with stuffed buck heads and wild geese and largemouth bass. It was a weekend retreat where James Witherington's middle-aged son and some of his friends could shoot pool, drink beer, talk about women, and instruct their boys in the manly arts during the hunting season. My plan was to make the three-hundred-mile drive from my home in Atlanta to Little River about twice a month, trying as nearly as possible to blend into the scenery; becoming, as Marshall Frady once fancied it, "just another citizen who happens to have this secret eccentricity to write . . . getting up every morning and pretending to write letters to Dickens and Shakespeare and Balzac and all the rest, as though to say, 'Here's what went on around here yesterday.'" To know the past, I figured, would be to understand the present; specifically, I might discover what circumstances had created an atmosphere that would allow the destruction of a church and severely alter the lives of five young people.

Would they talk to an interloper? Rural Southerners are notori-
ously hostile toward outsiders, and I heard, early on, that the blacks
in the area were asking if I were "the Klan," while whites suspected
I was a federal agent of some sort. Any reluctance they might have
had dissipated in due time, and indeed, I soon began to imagine that
they had seen me coming and were putting me on; had observed this
writer hanging around, had held a meeting at, say, the Dixie Landing
Cafe, and had come up with a plan. *Lookie here, now, y'all, we might get
a sit-com out of this thing, one of them* Dukes of Hazzard *deals, start gettin' checks from Hollywood instead of Washington. . . . George, how 'bout
you spendin' the summer tryin' to get your 'crazy checks'? . . . We need a
jealous husband to set fire to his wife's boyfriend's trailer. . . . Want y'all
women lollygaggin' around the tannin' salon at Peanut's while the men are
out workin' . . . Oh, yeah, and Raymond, tell him 'bout the shootout at
Butterfork Hill. . . . We gotta give 'em what they want: Klansmen, moonshiners, pot growers, itchy wives, the whole shebang. Hell, we pull this thing
off, we may never have to work again.* In fact, most of those events
would actually come to pass on my watch during the spring and
summer of 1998. A friend in Los Angeles, after an exchange of letters, opined that the book really ought to be called *Midnight in the
Garden Primeval,* a droll spin on the title of a best-selling book about
the goings-on of the artsy classes in Savannah, Georgia.

But this was serious business, and everybody knew it. The racial
composition of the Little River area was evenly divided between the
races, and the two cultures had gotten along in relative peace for
much of the twentieth century. Now, though, there were open sores
that showed no signs of healing. For the aging blacks of the Jim
Crow and Klan era, who had wanted little more than to live out their
days with some modicum of serenity, this onslaught against two of
their churches had been the ultimate indignity and proof, again, of
what their white neighbors *really* thought of them. The whites, on
the other hand, were in full-blown denial, much more interested in
fending off any notions that they were racist than in offering anything that resembled an apology. Meanwhile, the penniless congregants of the church that had been destroyed were drifting from one

meeting place to another on every third Sunday, their pastor getting nowhere in his attempts to rebuild, and the five kids were headed for prison.

NOT SINCE THE DEATH in the eighties of my father, an over-the-road trucker from Birmingham, had I heard such cavalier use of the word "nigger" as came from the mouth of James Witherington. My old man had even managed to coin a word that would cover all of his prejudices in one breath—"NiggersJewsCatholics"—and Joe Witherington, James's thirty-eight-year-old son, was having no more luck than I in curing his father of the habit: "I'll say, 'Daddy, why don't you stop using that word? It's ugly.' And he'll say, 'That's how I grew up and I can't help it.' He *will* say there are '*good* niggers' and '*bad* niggers,' that he'd rather hire a 'sorry nigger' than a 'sorry white,' but he just can't make himself quit."

That aside, I found James Witherington, like my father, to be an honest, hardworking man, even in retirement, and probably the most knowledgeable person alive in matters pertaining to Little River and its environs. Born in 1920, in a big farmhouse that once stood amid cotton fields on the ridge above the cabin I was renting, he had sold cars in direct competition with the family of Nelle Harper Lee up the road in Monroeville, locus of her novel *To Kill a Mockingbird;* gotten badly wounded during the Second World War and spent sixteen months in prisoner-of-war camps; served for nearly two decades as the tax assessor for Monroe County; and, thanks in no small part to inside knowledge gained on that job, amassed nearly six hundred acres of timberland scattered all over the place. He had no cash-flow problems.

And he knew just about everything about everybody who lived in the seventy-mile stretch between the county-seat towns of Monroeville and Bay Minette. "That one might be a little too 'widdy-waddy' for you," he said of a black man in his eighties, a derivative of "wishy-washy," meaning that his mind waffles off onto tangents. He remembered the desperate efforts to eradicate the boll weevil during the Depression: "There was a gadget called 'Sur-Kil,' or something like that. You'd get it in the mail. There'd be a little hammer and a rock and some instructions. Said, 'Step One: Place weevil on rock and strike firmly. Step Two: Place *another* weevil on rock . . .' Lord, there might be a million of those little devils on one acre of land." So many people had died or been forced to leave Little River in order to find work, he said, that "there's a hundred times as many people below ground as there are on it." And the law wasn't exactly welcome in those parts: "It takes 'em so long to get here, by the time they show up it's already been 'settled,' for better or for worse, usually for worse. It's a wonder there aren't signs that say, 'Keep Out! Prosecutors Will Be Violated!'"

WE WERE HEADED back to the cabin now after our serendipitous wanderings through northern Baldwin County. "Tell you the truth, though, if it wasn't for [his wife] Louisa having to be near a hospital with her asthma, I'd be living down here instead of in town. Monroeville's all right, been home for a long time now, but it's not like living in God's country."

"You ever see Harper Lee around town? That's a great novel she wrote."

"Maybe."

"You either see her or you don't."

"Maybe she wrote it, maybe she didn't."

"Oh, come on now."

"She never wrote another one, did she?"

"Well, hell, James—"

"Lot of folks think that prissy cousin of hers, what's his name—"

"Capote. Truman Capote."

"Yeah, that one. *In Cold Blood.* He wrote a lot of books. Probably wrote *Mockingbird,* too."

There would not be much literature spoken during my stay, I could see, unless I could manage to flag down the county's bookmobile on its fortnightly rounds, but I could run back home to Atlanta for that and the *New York Times* in the driveway and restaurant meals featuring something other than the good old boy's four major food groups: salt, grease, ketchup, and beer. A journalist friend, Lee May, once referred to these dislocations as "parachuting into strange towns, looking for bad news." Another pal, a novelist named Terry Kay, noting that I might be getting too old for this traveling at sixty-two and with a wife back home alone, asked why I didn't "do like I do, just stay home and make up stuff." But no. The job, the adventure, was right here amid the streams and the forests and the swamps of northern Baldwin County. Besides, as my perambulations would soon reveal, some of the "stuff" I would come across in Little River would be stranger than any fictions I might concoct.

"Well, sir," Witherington said as he dropped me off at the cabin, "hope I got you going."

"I'll say. I need a tape recorder to keep up with you."

"Let me know if you need anything."

"I'm all right."

"And you be careful, now, you hear?" He revved the engine of his truck and clicked the transmission into gear. "There's some mean folks down here in Little River." And then he was gone.

PART ONE

The Heart of a Distant Forest

———

ONE

Lost Colony

———

FROM SHORE TO SHORE, the shortest length between national boundaries in the continental United States is the north-south route, a fairly straight shot of about nine hundred miles on Interstate 65, connecting the icy Great Lakes and the tropical Gulf of Mexico. There are more scenic drives in the country. By the time travelers have reached Montgomery, Alabama's capital city, they have seen about all of the rolling farmland a body can bear on one trip: Indiana's endless cornfields, Kentucky's white-fenced bluegrass country, Middle Tennessee's knobby little hills. The monotony breaks, though, and fairly abruptly, once the road has passed tired old Birmingham's battened steel mills to finally reach Montgomery, the "Cradle of the Confederacy." There are woodlands and pastures and farms there as well, but the change is more in *attitude,* for Montgomery is the jumping-off point for the vast forested no-man's-land of south Alabama. This is the Black Belt, so named for its rich black loam and the people who once slaved in the cotton fields, a broad band stretching from the coastal plains of the Carolinas to the piney woods of the Big Thicket in east Texas, and the motorists who might forsake the interstate for the sleepy back roads soon find themselves in the very bowels of the Deep South. HEART OF DIXIE, proclaim the state's vehicle license tags, and indeed it is.

This is the land of Bear Bryant and George Wallace, of tar paper shacks in the shadows of white-columned neo-plantations, of roadside fightin'-and-dancin' clubs and whoop-and-holler Pentecostal

3

churches and trim little high school football stadiums, of magnolia and dogwood and mimosa and honeysuckle, of pine forests and farm ponds and pastures, of 4-H and VFW and Rotary clubs, of junkyards and sawmills and decaying barns swallowed up by kudzu. On the square at Enterprise: a statue playfully "honoring" the boll weevil, whose devastations early in the twentieth century forced the South to abandon cotton in favor of other crops. At Georgiana, south of Montgomery on the lonesome road to Mobile: one of the many childhood homes of Hank Williams, a wild urchin who sprang from the sawmills and logging camps to become the quintessential country singer and songwriter. "I'm So Lonesome I Could Cry," was his most plaintive tune, released soon after his death in the fifties, from whiskey and pills, at the age of twenty-nine, and the song's morbid sentiments perfectly suit the isolated nature of this part of the American outback, where all news is local. There might be an old geezer left in Pine Apple who remembers the terse mention in the Personals column of the weekly newspaper announcing a favorite son's triumphant return, bearing medals, from the 1932 Olympic Games in Los Angeles: "Percy Beard has returned home from California, where he participated in a footrace."

Most tourists not bound for the port city of Mobile, or on beyond to New Orleans, exit south on Alabama Highway 59 and make a beeline for the oceanside resort of Gulf Shores, the westernmost point of what Alabamians insist on calling the Redneck Riviera: a marvelous strand of sugar-white beaches, among the most beautiful in the world, sort of a good old boy's sandbox of cut-rate motels and bars and seafood diners, with miniature-golf courses and makeshift amusement parks for the kids. The Redneck Riviera lies eastward for more than a hundred miles along the coast of the Florida Panhandle—"L.A.," they call it, for Lower Alabama—and although the 1990s saw the coming of expensive condos and gated vacation communities (on the Alabama portion of the Riviera, a stretch of less than thirty miles, about eighty high-rise condominiums require more elevators than does all of Birmingham, the state's largest city), it remains a workingman's playground; a place where three generations of Bubbas have gone for their initiations into manhood: to get drunk, sunburned, laid, and thrown in jail.

"My sheriff is Jimmy Johnson, built like a football player, wears a cowboy hat and boots, fancies himself as John Wayne." David Whetstone, Baldwin County's longtime district attorney, was holding forth one day at his office on the square in Bay Minette, the tidy little county seat, gussied up with park benches and oleanders and whitewashed storefronts. "He and his wife went off to France for a vacation one year and everybody was dying to know what he thought about the Riviera on the Mediterranean. 'Well,' he said, 'the nekkid ladies was all right, but the beaches ain't near as good as the *real* Riviera.'"

Whetstone—fifty-five, balding, pugnacious—marvels at the diversity of the southern portion of Baldwin, the largest county in area east of the Mississippi River, bigger than the state of Rhode Island and nearly the size of Delaware. "Because of the port at Mobile, we've got all of these ethnic towns. Daphne is full of Italians, Malbis is Greek, Elberta German, Silverhill Scandinavian, and a lot of 'em speak the languages from the old countries and have festivals every year. It seems like there's a new culture every ten miles. Northern Baldwin, now, that's another matter. There's these two towns on either side of the same exit off the interstate, Rabun and Perdido, settled by mountain folks, and they carry on feuds like the Hatfields and the McCoys. We've prosecuted ten homicides up there in the past twenty-five years. The patriarch of one clan always shows up in court wearing a black felt hillbilly hat, and one side always leaves a silver-handled knife as a calling card even if it was a shooting. Northern Baldwin keeps me in business."

By all means. Were the traveler to turn north instead of south off of I-65, he would be entering another world. Once past Stockton, a neat little village quickly gentrifying these days into an upscale Republican enclave for comfortable whites who commute to their jobs in downtown Mobile, a half-hour drive on the freeway, Highway 59 begins its run into the heart of a distant forest. Along the forty miles of road between Stockton and Uriah (pronounced *YOU-rye*), the first town of any size in southern Monroe County, there are no speed-limit signs and only a single blinking caution light to slow the traffic. Of Baldwin County's total population of about one hundred thousand in the late nineties, fewer than three thousand people were living in the piney expanses of the upper one-fourth. Between Stockton and the bridge over the Little River, marking the Monroe County line, there are but four hamlets denoted by green highway markers—Latham, Tensaw, Blacksher, Little River—with most of the people living on bulldozed or asphalted dead-end roads far from Highway 59, known locally as "the road," in house trailers or plain brick homes or tin-roofed shacks or prefabricated Craftsman and Jim Walter homes that have survived since the forties and fifties. The racial makeup in that part of the county is roughly fifty-fifty, black and white, with a lot of high cheekbones indicating Creek and Choctaw Indian blood on both sides, and the demographic profile is one of a society barely hanging on. A startling percentage of the people are old, sick, disabled, or simply idle (the unemployment rate is 20 percent, four times higher than the rest of the county, and the per capita income is less than $11,000 a year before taxes); and the younger ones who have chosen to stay—but not to risk their lives and health, as did their fathers and grandfathers, by logging in the forests that dominate the landscape—must drive for nearly an hour each way to reach menial jobs in textile mills, warehouses, factories, or shopping malls.

MOST OF THE history of northern Baldwin County is measured by small mileposts noted only by the locals: first school, first church, first doctor, first steamboat, first paved road; the coming of electricity, county water, plumbing, telephones; sawmills, cotton gins, slaves, Ku Klux Klan, boll weevil; radio, newspapers, television. The land belonged to the Creeks and Choctaws until the late 1700s, following the Revolutionary War, when white settlers began drifting in from Virginia and the Carolinas on the westward movement to stake out homesteads in what was then known as the Mississippi Territory. It was wild, forbidding swamp country—teeming with poisonous snakes, alligators, bears, deer, wild boars, mosquitoes, scorpions, chiggers, beavers, raccoons, 'possums, rabbits, squirrels—and black slaves, human cargo from the Gold Coast of Africa, were bought at auction on the docks at Mobile in the late eighteenth century to help with the carving out of a civilization in the wilderness.

The British naturalist William Bartram first drew attention to the land when he sent home specimens of exotic subtropical flora he had found around the time of the Revolution, and Aaron Burr was finally tracked down in those parts and arrested for treason in 1807 after his duel with Alexander Hamilton. But the only newsworthy event in the entire early history of northern Baldwin County was the Creek massacre at Fort Mims in 1813. Trouble had been brewing for years between the resident Native Americans and the settlers, prompting a prosperous farmer named Samuel Mims to build a stockade surrounding his land near what is now Tensaw as a line of defense against an unyielding branch of the generally benign Creeks, the "Red Sticks," who were rumored to be stockpiling weapons and laying plans to rout these interlopers. The Red Sticks were led by a thirty-three-year-old mixed-blood named William Weatherford but known as Red Eagle, a product of his Scottish father's marriage to a Creek princess named Sehoy. On the last weekend of August in 1813, feeling an attack was imminent, Mims summoned to his "fort" about 550 settlers, slaves, "half-breeds," and militia from a nearby military post. Some of the soldiers were still drunk from an all-night party when Red Eagle and about a thousand of his Red Sticks rushed the fort at noon that Monday. When the sun fell, the fort now a pile of smouldering ashes, some five hundred had died and no more than fifty had escaped from what is still recorded as the bloodiest such massacre in the history of the United States. It brought immediate outrage across the nation and led to the beginning of Andrew Jackson's "Trail of Tears," the deportation of all Native Americans to Indian Territory in what is now Oklahoma. One hundred and eighty-four years would pass before the outside world would hear again of northern Baldwin County, Alabama.

As soon as the land was cleared of Indians, the settlers dug in and began to whack out a crude society in the woods. Alabama gained statehood in 1819, not long after the Fort Mims Massacre, and life there was much the same as in the other frontier states joining the Union as it expanded beyond the Mississippi River. Huge tracts of virgin hardwood were cleared, the timber used for log cabins and outbuildings, the land plowed and planted in corn and cotton. It was backbreaking work, requiring large families (the more strapping sons, the better), but with the abundance of game and the rich soil, nobody starved who was willing to work. They were self-sufficient out of necessity, and proud of it, and except for the staples they had to barter for, all they needed could be taken from the land: food, housing, furniture, the clothes on their backs.

In steady increments, decade by decade, a semblance of order and civilization was wrought. Horse paths were widened to become turnpikes for stagecoaches; canoes and rafts and then rough keelboats and finally steamers turned the Alabama and Tombigbee and Little Rivers into highways for moving cotton and timber down to the docks at Mobile; taverns and inns and boat landings appeared; and schools and churches and barns and trading posts. Here and there one might see a gaudy mansion on the hill, built by men who had cleared massive fields for cotton and bought slaves at the auction in Mobile. One of those planters was David Tate, Red Eagle's stepbrother, whose "last will and inventory" upon his death in 1829 listed 150 slaves whose values ranged from twenty-five cents to $600. But most of the people were simple dirt farmers trying to survive the natural scourges around them—violent weather, diseases, wild animals, sheer loneliness—as best they could. They hunted and fished and plowed for sustenance, made their own whiskey for comfort, settled disputes with guns and knives and fists in the absence of organized law, found solace in a God who accepted no excuses, got so accustomed to being alone that the only people they trusted were kinfolks. Except for the handful of cotton planters, moguls with a vested interest in retaining slavery, the Civil War meant little to the simple men in the woods; Admiral David Farragut might have been steaming into Mobile Bay in August of 1864 in the largest naval engagement of the war ("Damn the torpedoes, full steam ahead!"), but northern Baldwin County's only involvement was the non-skirmish involving James Witherington's grandfather, Ausphera Bryant Myles, that same year on some meandering little stream known as Shomo Creek.

THE EMANCIPATION PROCLAMATION meant that slavery was abolished as a formal way of life, but most of the African-Americans whose ancestors had been bought at the slave auction in Mobile chose either to hire out as sharecroppers to their former masters or to accept the government's offer of forty acres and a mule and to homestead nearby in the woods and swamps on inferior land not already claimed by the pioneer white settlers; to build a society of their own that would be separate but by no means equal; and to become a dark, brooding presence that soon would attract the attention of the new Ku Klux Klan, the white South's response to Reconstruction. Whippings and house-burnings and lynchings by night-riding packs of hooded Klansmen were not uncommon sights in a harsh land where brute strength and intimidation and the power in numbers took precedence over fairness and intellect and formal rules of law. Then, as now, life in that part of the country boiled down to survival of the fittest, and everybody tried to take it in stride. Upon the news that the Gulf Florida & Alabama railroad was laying lines through there, it was said that GF&A stood for "Gophers, Frogs & Alligators."

When the boll weevil infested the cotton fields all over the South, in the early 1900s, practically finishing off what was left of the antebellum plantation society, the people in upper Baldwin County had to look no farther than the surrounding woodlands to find an alternative means of making a living. Huge forests of virgin hardwood were everywhere, and so that was where the men would go, both black and white, to spend all their waking hours in the deep woods and marshes, fighting off mosquitoes and alligators and timber rattlers as they drew turpentine from the pines and brought down the towering oaks and cypress that would be floated down the series of waterways to brokers in Mobile Bay, who would buy these "forest products" to make everything from houses to telephone poles to newsprint.

For the next half-century, through the First World War and the Great Depression and the Second World War, right up until the development of the Redneck Riviera as a tourist destination in the late sixties, the rich forests of northern Baldwin accounted for the bulk of the entire county's income, and thus its tax base. Many men of both races would go off to serve in the Second World War, where they would develop skills in carpentry and welding and construction, but most of them would return home to take jobs with the big timber companies that had begun buying up great chunks of woodlands, doing the same backbreaking work as before, but this time with a salary and benefits. For the women, in this booming postwar world, there were dull jobs in windowless mills or as clerks and waitresses in the towns of Monroeville and Atmore and Bay Minette.

Forget amenities. Lacking any sort of political clout due to its sparse population, the northern end of Baldwin County was the last to get such necessities as paved roads, electricity, telephones, even county water. Most of that came in the early forties—especially the paving of Highway 59, needed as a pipeline to haul turpentine and lumber to Mobile in the war effort—but then all of that stopped, once the war had ended, and the communities of Tensaw and Blacksher and Little River were abandoned during a period of unprecedented growth through the rest of the nation. The interstate connecting Montgomery and Mobile was laid out some thirty miles away. Oil was discovered near Atmore and Monroeville—oil in the cotton fields!—but not in Baldwin County. That neck of the woods had received none of the basic services that most American taxpayers had come to expect during this, the American Century: schools, libraries, town halls, playgrounds, small factories, white-collar jobs of any kind. The young left as soon as they could get a driver's license and wheels, leaving behind their parents and grandparents to scrape along on whatever savings they might have or on government checks of all sorts. About the only outsiders who knew much about that part of Baldwin County were the lawmen who responded to outbreaks of random violence, the loggers who came to haul the lumber away, the paramedics who carried off the sick and the dead, and the sportsmen who came in from the towns and cities to hunt or fish or simply escape civilization by holing up in their getaway cabins or trailers on streams and ponds in the deep woods, where bullfrogs and cicadas and foraging wild animals ruled the night.

ONCE HIGHWAY 59 has cleared the blinking caution light at Tensaw, the turnoff for the sad remains of the pinepole fort where the Creek Massacre occurred nearly two centuries ago, it begins an undulating roll northward toward the bridge over the Little River that marks the Baldwin and Monroe County line thirteen miles away. There is little to distract the motorist except road signs riddled by gunshot and fervent evangelical warnings hand-lettered on scraps of tin or lumber nailed to pine trees (HE THAT BELIEVETH NOT IS CONDEMNED ALREADY and REPENT OR BURN IN HELL), but it is, nonetheless, a perilous road as it twists and rises into woods thick with orderly rows of pine planted for harvest. Deer are everywhere, likely to bolt across the road at any moment; and vultures, picking over flattened armadillos and rabbits and squirrels and other hapless roadkill; and, out of nowhere, somebody riding a horse along the shoulder of the road. Most treacherous of all, though, are the ferocious logging trucks, Peterbilts and Freightliners and Macks, *big mothers,* belching smoke and changing gears, careening wildly, their ragged loads swaying behind, stirring the dust and fluttering the leaves as they hurtle on a pell-mell rush to the nearest lumberyard.

Finally, three miles south of the river bridge, the last stop in Baldwin County, there is the community of Little River. As they say of the thousands of little black-dot hamlets spread across the vast American outback, nobody goes there without a purpose; and on the cusp of a new century, in the summer of 1997, Little River had taken on the feel and look of a Lost Colony. The nearest Baldwin County schools were thirty-seven miles away, by yellow school bus, in Bay Minette (although high schoolers had the option of attending J. U. Blacksher High in Uriah, seventeen miles up Highway 59 in Monroe

County); the nearest doctors and dentists and full-service grocery stores nearly an hour's drive; the one remaining movie house twenty-two miles off in Atmore; the only public diners between Stockton and Uriah a pair of catfish-and-hamburger eateries open mainly on weekends, when the hunters and fishermen came around. The only jobs in the immediate area involved logging or clerking at the convenience and package liquor stores out on the road. The only time the residents of the community ever came together as a body, it seemed, was in the early afternoon of the first and third days of each month, when the government checks arrived, bringing swarms of old or disabled people to the gravel parking lot of the post office, a whitewashed fifteen-by-thirty-foot cinder-block affair squatting beside the road under a scraggly grove of trees. It sat next to the only place that could be called a community center in all of Little River, except perhaps for the boat launch at Dixie Landing on the Alabama River: Ferguson's Grocery, a combination country store and gas station where one might cash a check or buy limited groceries or make a call from a pay phone or simply catch up on the gossip.

Little River was on the earliest maps of the area, due to its post office and its proximity to the boat landing, but its stuttering growth has been haphazard at best. Now there are only two paved roads spinning off of Highway 59—the four-mile Dixie Landing Road, leading to the boat launch, and a stretch named Gantt Road that turns to dirt and winds into the woods after about a mile or so—and all of the other thoroughfares, if they can be called such, are widened old logging trails or newly bulldozed roads named after current or past families of some note: Couglan, Phillips, Boone, Cumbie, Earle, Gantt, Haywood, Benjamin. The lines separating the communities of Tensaw, Blacksher, Little River, and Chrysler are blurred, but the population of what is known as Little River is generally agreed to be about two hundred, spread over an area of some fifty square miles of swamps and bogs and hummocks and tangled woods and wandering streams.

The populace is a Faulknerian huddle of fairly exotic proportions. There is a thick, horny good old boy who would do anything for his wife, a temptress who knows it and drives him wild with jea-lousy; an ageless cantankerous black couple who embark from their trailer back in the swamp each afternoon for a trip to "the store," for supplies and companionship, driving twenty miles an hour on the dirt road and on Highway 59 alike in their duct-taped vintage car; at least one drunk and one well-to-do cotton baron and one strapping patri-arch who has been drawing disability checks for most of his life; a chatty postmistress, a bully, a hermit, a kid who has spent half his life in jail, moonshiners and pot growers, married cousins who have pro-duced damaged children, a shadowy Klansman who lives alone behind locked gates guarded by German shepherds, and on and on and on. The community's leading citizen goes by the name of Peanut. There is a hell-raising dandy named Doll, a black named Bubba, a sheriff's deputy lyrically named Murray January, and another called Hoss because he looks like the character from the old *Bonanza* television series, an L.B. and an H.L. and a John Wayne Boone (to distinguish from his cousin John John Boone) and an aging spinster named Bobbie Lee Gantt. Their lives are as thick and intertwined as a flavorful gumbo.

Whites live mostly on the paved roads, blacks in ragged areas back toward the woods in places known as Sawmill Road and Couglan Swamp, but they share a landscape dotted with modest fields of cot-ton and corn and kitchen gardens known as "pea-patches." In the yards beside most residences, whether brick homes or patched-up board shacks or trailers, there are television satellite dishes and pickup trucks and flat-bottom fishing boats and stanchions holding clusters of gourds that house flocks of voracious insect-gobbling martins. There are nearly a dozen churches in "metropolitan Little River," as some drolly refer to the place, most of them with congregations numbering little more than twenty, one of them (the black All-Seeing Eyes Holiness) with a hand-painted directional sign out on Highway 59 of a pair of stark, watchful eyes, raised eyebrows and all, remindful of the ominous optometrist's billboard in *The Great Gatsby*.

Over the years it has been a dangerous, violent place, where if the backbreaking labor or an errant piece of machinery doesn't maim or kill you, a neighbor might. It seems, at times, as if there is a shotgun under every bed. The family histories, and the files down at the county courthouse in Bay Minette, are brimming with tales of man's impatience with his fellow man in Little River: out-and-out killings in shoot-outs, tire-iron beatings just for the hell of it, bloody fist-fights, drug-turf wars, burglaries and robberies, and such simple acts of meanness as letting the air out of a man's tires just because he's pissed somebody off. Marijuana and cheap forms of cocaine, in addition to the old standbys beer and whiskey, had entered the mix during the seventies and become the curse of the latest generation.

And Alabama, like the hardscrabble countryside of Ireland and Scotland whence came most of its white citizens' ancestors, has been roundly denigrated by most of the larger world that it refuses to join. There is an apocryphal story about the airline pilot who came in over the intercom system, on a flight from Atlanta to Montgomery, to remind his passengers of the change from Eastern to Central Standard Time: "So don't forget to set your watches back . . . *twenty years.*" And there is the line that Alabamians like to use before some Yankee beats them to it, "Thank God for Mississippi," for Alabama would be dead last among the fifty United States in a long list of important rankings, from education to per capita income, if not for its even poorer next-door neighbor. Everybody needs someone to look down upon, and in the era of genteel political correctness at the end of the twentieth century, the only group of Americans not immune from ridicule were the rural poor white Southerners, the Bubbas, the Good Old Boys. They were roundly dismissed as "white trash," the lowest of the low, at the bottom of the social ladder, and their prickly awareness of what others said of them conspired to keep them there. Their favored novelty vehicle license plate showed a caricature of a curmudgeonly graybeard in a Confederate Army uniform, snarling, "Forget, hell!"

TWO

Peanut

_____

IF THERE WERE a need for an official city hall to serve Little River and, for that matter, the whole northern end of Baldwin County, it would already be in place: Ferguson's Grocery, known to locals as "the store" or simply "Peanut's." It is housed in a rectangular forty-by-hundred-foot whitewashed cinder-block building fronted by a buckled asphalt parking lot, large enough to accommodate ten fully loaded logging rigs, and sits beside the matchbox post office near the seventy-eight-mile marker on Highway 59, denoted only by a SPUR sign. Anybody who has traveled the back roads would know in a glance that the place is in the grand tradition of country stores all across rural America, a wondrous cramped emporium overflowing with about everything a family might need or want to make it through another week: canned and boxed and frozen food, milk and soft drinks and fruit juices, limited amounts of fresh meat and seafood and vegetables in season, beer and smokes and popsicles, hunting and fishing licenses and bamboo poles, videos and magazines, mousetraps and mops and brooms, toilet paper and tampons and Kleenex, sunglasses and cigarette lighters and motor oil. There are two rest rooms and three gas pumps, and a package liquor store tucked out back, and even, in a converted storage room, a "tanning salon" that had paid for itself in its first year of operation.

The store is the heart and soul of Little River, the place where locals go to cash checks or make phone calls or place special orders to be picked up the next time the owners go to "town" (a newfangled fishing lure or some shotgun shells or even a light switch from stores in Monroeville or Atmore or Bay Minette) or, more often than not, simply to see another human being. The school bus departs the store at daybreak for Bay Minette; loggers leave their rigs idling in the parking lot while they zip inside for a carryout snack and something to wash it down; hunters and fishermen stock up on gas and beer and victuals before heading for the woods or the water for the weekend; sheriff's deputies stop by to see who's been naughty or nice; voters drift in to argue politics and cast their ballots on election days; and those who had to emigrate to find work make it their first stop when returning for long holiday "homecoming" weekends. The store opens at five o'clock in the morning, for the sportsmen and commuters, and stays open as late as ten-thirty on weekend nights.

Come around looking for one William Spencer Ferguson, you'll get laughed out of Little River. It's been "Peanut" Ferguson since the day he was brought home from the hospital where he was born, in 1945, and the family's black maid, Lulu Reece, from the squalid black settlement known then as Benjamintown, took one look at the squawking little bundle and said—what else?—"Why, he ain't nothin' but a little ol' peanut." The first Ferguson to arrive in this part of Alabama was a soldier from South Carolina who took a liking to a girl from Latham and the promising virgin land when he passed through during the Revolutionary War and soon returned ("Went home for a change of clothes," Peanut reckons) to homestead in the wilderness and settle in. The store in its various incarnations has been in the family since the maternal grandfather shared by Peanut and his cousin James Witherington, Ausphera Bryant Myles, the teenager involved in the Civil War non-skirmish at Shomo Creek, set up a trading post in the swamps during the 1920s. Leonce Wilmer "Buddy" Ferguson, Peanut's father-to-be, took over the business during the Depression, trading animal hides for staples with men working the rivers from flat-bottom merchant boats. The store had been moved to its current location and was thriving, much as it is these days, when Buddy Ferguson suddenly died of blood clotting at the age of fifty-nine. That was in 1964, when the war in Vietnam was about to bust loose. Peanut had completed high school and was about to get drafted into the army, having already gone through his Selective Service tests at Maxwell Air Force Base in Montgomery, but his father's death changed everything. Since he was the only son left at home to care for the store and support his mother, his three older brothers having left Little River for white-collar careers in nearby towns, he was exempted from the draft at the last minute. At nineteen, having seen little of the world beyond Little River, Peanut had the course of his life forced upon him.

"I guess I was meant to run the store," he was saying, with a shrug, during a lull in business on a summer's day in 1997. He really isn't a "peanut" anymore, nor anything near the robust specimen like most of the loggers and farmers and construction workers seen around Little River; rather, he is a smiling, drawling, squint-eyed, kind and *gentle* man, standing perhaps five-ten and weighing about a hundred and sixty pounds, a stoic who has spent most of his life enduring whatever comes his way. "There was no way to afford college. I'd finished school, but I didn't exactly have any plans for myself. Mainly I was just helping with the store, waiting for the draft, and now here I was in charge of it. My daddy died in debt, and it's all I can do to hold it together." Peanut tugged at the checked flannel shirt that is every man's uniform in Little River, winter or summer, toed the linoleum floor with his work boots, and grinned sheepishly. "My daddy didn't believe in alcohol, but I had to start selling it to compete. Monroe County's dry, see, but we aren't. As much liquor as I've sold here, he's probably rolling over in his grave. My wife doesn't think much of it, either, seeing as how her father's the pastor of the Holiness Church down the road."

LIKE ALL OF the other natives who grew up in Little River during the postwar years, Peanut spent his childhood fishing, hunting, sneaking filched smokes and beer in the woods, swimming in "wash holes" at the river, flinging basketballs at hoops nailed to pine trees, playing "war" and cowboys-and-Indians (using real and willing Indians, in fact, given the proximity of the Creek reservation), spending nearly three hours each day being hauled in a yellow school bus back and forth to Stockton for elementary school and later to Baldwin County High School in Bay Minette. His was a tight family of four boys and a girl, offspring of parents who spent all of their waking hours on their feet at the store, eking out a living. In such a small community, your friends were where you found them and race wasn't an issue. "Colored or white, it didn't matter. We swam together, played together, did yard work together, and got into trouble together. Everybody was stuck down here being poor together, too, both colored and white, so that stuff didn't matter. We didn't know much about the outside world. Heck, I didn't even see my first television until 1958, when I was thirteen." As throughout the South, and the rest of the nation for that matter, that innocence began to crack when a white kid reached puberty and was grimly advised by his parents that there was a "difference" between blacks and whites. "Come to think of it, I can't say that colored kids ever entered a white house through the front door before that, but when we got to be thirteen or fourteen we just sort of stopped hanging out together as much. We suddenly realized that they'd been going to different schools all this time, and using separate rest rooms and water fountains, and now we were being told there was a reason for it." The N word was never used around the Ferguson household. "The rednecks said it and still do, but I've always said 'colored.' I still can't say 'black,' but nobody seems to mind."

Having lived under the cloud of segregation for so long, the black kids in the fifties and sixties tended to mind their manners; but the white ones, particularly some members of the two separate clans of Boones, who dominated the population, were a violent lot. "It was a long ride to school in Bay Minette, about an hour and a half each way, and that gave lots of time for trouble to come up on the school bus," Peanut says. "One day, about nineteen-fifty, when a fellow named Drew Phillips was the bus driver, there was the usual fighting and cussing and pigtail-pulling going on in the back when they were coming home in the afternoon, and Drew stopped the bus and went back there to break it up. He started to reach for one of the Boone girls' arm, to make her come sit up front and behave, and she said, 'If you touch me, old man, I'll tear your arms off.' He got 'em home, and then he quit." Peanut took over the driving soon after, at the age of sixteen, and the experience still pains him: "It was a rough bunch. I was still sort of small for my age, and some of the Boones and Cumbies were football players, guys who could pick me up by the neck with one arm if they felt like it, so there wasn't much I could do about 'em. After I'd dropped off the little kids at the elementary school at Stockton, we'd all light up our cigarettes, me included, and fill the bus with smoke for the last seven miles to the high school in Bay Minette."

Generations of kids from Little River had built a fearsome reputation over the years. *Watch out for that bunch if you're going to Little River,* was the warning given kids from the more civilized towns such as Monroeville and Atmore and Bay Minette, even serene little Stockton and Uriah, if they intended to visit there. It was a lusty band of snot-nosed tatterdemalions, the free-spirited sons and daughters of log-truck drivers and woodsmen and farmers and sharecroppers, not to be messed with. "They were mean as hell when they got together and traveled in packs," says a carpenter named Larry Weaver, who lives with his wife in a trailer at a tiny crossroads in southern Monroe County called Mineola, "but you found out pretty quick that they weren't so tough when you got 'em out somewhere alone." (That lesson was drilled home during the seventies, in a most grisly manner, when a Little River lad who had been romancing an Indian girl from the reservation, about twenty miles away at Poarch, near the I-65 exit for Atmore, was confronted there one night by a gang of Creek teenagers who resented whites messing with their women. They reamed his rectum with a tree limb, leaving his innards maimed for life.) Few white teens from Little River had any plans beyond marrying their own and following their fathers and mothers into the woods or the kitchen. When it was deigned that high schoolers from Little River would be given the option of attending Monroe County's J. U. Blacksher High School in Uriah, only seventeen miles from Peanut's store, rather than taking the long bus ride to Bay Minette, the Baldwin County school superintendent expressed great relief during a press conference he soon regretted. "They've been tearing up our buses for years," he said—knifing seats, starting fires, spilling drinks, smoking, spraying graffiti—"so as far as I'm concerned, those kids can *walk* to school. They don't *deserve* a bus."

Oddly, school desegregation went smoothly when it came to northern Baldwin County in 1970. This was darkest Alabama, where George Wallace ruled and even the Ku Klux Klan still had its follow-ers in a land with a high percentage of poor blacks who could take away a white man's job in a blink if given a fair opportunity, and the worst was expected. But then when the day came, Peanut recalls, "about the only change was that everybody got on the same bus that morning and rode off to the same school together. There never was a problem that I know of." Racial relations in the Deep South have always been complicated, especially in sparse rural areas, where the races have interacted so closely for several generations dating back to slavery, but Peanut wasn't surprised when desegregation came with barely a hitch. "Sure, we'd seen on television what was happening at other places, with the bombings in Birmingham and Wallace's stand in the schoolhouse door at Tuscaloosa, and the assassinations and such, but it's like that was *their* problem. I mean, my colored customers kept on using what had been separate rest rooms here even when they weren't separate anymore. Anyway, there weren't but four or five [black] families back on Sawmill Road, in what was called Benja-mintown, with kids who got on the school bus that day. The good [white] people thought it wasn't right, wasn't neighborly, to suddenly get ugly with people they'd known all their lives. There might have been some folks who wanted to build a separate school for whites, one of those private academies, but there wasn't any money for it. Besides, the rednecks never cared about schools in the first place. Their kids were never going to amount to anything, anyway."

AFTER THE DEATH of his father, now in charge of the store and his mother's welfare, Peanut hunkered down and began the long trudge that would become his life. He built the current post office for his mother, who had been serving as postmistress out of the store since 1953. He planted cotton and corn on the thirty acres surrounding the store, tried to forget that he had missed out on enjoying the normal years of teenhood, and in due time he got married to a local girl and they had three children. The first and third, Bridget and Scott, were normal and healthy, but the middle child, Tracy, contracted spinal meningitis at three months and was left deaf and brain-damaged. Having been raised to do the right thing, Peanut found the money to enroll her in the expensive Helen Keller School for the Deaf in Talladega, about two hundred miles away in east Alabama. To make things more difficult, the woman he had married was ill-suited for the life she had been thrust into—the draining days and nights of tending the store, the same faces and the same problems every day, the utter lack of any sort of excitement—and she "about went nuts," according to one of the Peanut-watchers in Little River. She had what the country singer Merle Haggard once called "hungry eyes," a need for fun and dancing and pretty things, anything to break the monotony.

It was the most frenetic time of Peanut's life: one severely damaged child to be nursed, two others he intended to send to college, an unhappy marriage, mountains of debt. He was doing everything he could—minding the store, keeping the kids out of trouble, making the weekly runs to markets in Pensacola and Mobile for meats and vegetables and other supplies, selling the fish he caught and the game he shot, tending the modest crops of cotton and corn in his field behind the store—and for one five-year period he sold life insurance up and down the byways from Stockton to Uriah and to Atmore. "Let me tell you, that was some experience. I sold policies for Woodmen of the World. Right off, they said I'd have to fly to Omaha for a week or so of training. I was scared to death just thinking about it. Begged 'em to let me drive, but they said that was foolish, I'd have to fly. Turned out to be the first and last time I ever got on a plane. And those folks didn't believe in selling to colored, said they were a bad risk and couldn't be trusted to pay the premiums, but I did it anyway, since half the folks in my area were colored people I knew. So I just didn't put down anything where the form said 'race.' The customers would get this monthly magazine from Woodmen of the World, with lots of pictures of happy customers, all of 'em white, and my colored policyholders kept asking me when *they* were gonna show up in the magazine. For five years, I kept telling 'em, 'Oh, they'll get around to it, just be patient, they've got millions of customers all over the country. Trust me.'"

The marriage ended after nineteen years, "way too long" (the first wife has "been married and divorced twice since we broke up," and now lives alone down the road toward Stockton), and in 1983 Peanut married Virginia Sue Roberson, a daughter of the pastor of the Little River Holiness Church about a mile north of the store on Highway 59. This was more like it. Sue had learned to accept hard times—her father, before his conversion, had lost both legs as a teenaged Marine home on leave in 1941 when he left a rowdy bar near Rabun and got involved in a hellacious car wreck—and she had the temperament to be the wife of a country storekeeper. They settled into the tawny brick three-bedroom ranch-style house Peanut had built right behind the store, and in 1990 she gave birth to twins they named Shane and Christie. The busiest room in the house is the large den, appointed with a hooked rug over linoleum floors and a sofa and chairs in the Early American style and a huge television set outfitted with cable and, on the various thin faux-paneled walls, three stuffed and mounted deer and a wild turkey personally "harvested," as they say, by Peanut himself.

If Ferguson's Grocery is Little River's de facto city hall, then Peanut is its mayor and Sue the vice-mayor. After all of these years as the center of the community, a beacon in the night along that forlorn forty-mile stretch of road between Stockton and Uriah, the store is Little River's anchor. There are a couple of other places nearby selling alcohol and basic supplies, at a small BP station and at the County Line Package Store, but this is *home,* and it is Peanut and Sue who make it so. They are a couple in perfect rhythm. Both are short, slightly graying, even-tempered, and have no known enemies. They first-name everyone coming through the slapping screen doors. They know who's sick and who's recovering. They know when a job opens up, and who might need it. They know who's philandering, divorcing, faking disability, staying drunk, or cheating on income taxes, as well as knowing not to talk about such. They know names and ages and birthdays and anniversaries; of salary raises and new pickup trucks and grandchildren; of good cotton crops and eight-point bucks and record largemouth bass. Peanut's two healthy kids from the first marriage have finished college and found careers, and half of the time he has custody of the damaged daughter, who happily bags groceries and sweeps the floors and gamely tries to converse with customers at the store. The twins scamper about on the wide green lawn separating the store from the house, romping with the latest batch of unwanted puppies and kittens left in the yard overnight, swinging in the play set, chasing butterflies, riding their gas-powered go-cart, playing house in the cardboard boxes tossed out the back door. Peanut fishes and hunts when he can, while Sue busies herself with doings at her father's church. (Peanut, it seems, welcomes the chance to mind the store while she is at church.) They manage brief escapes now and then, for a movie or a restaurant meal or a Mobile BayBears baseball game or a one-week driving vacation with the twins, but mostly they share the seventeen-hour days at the store with the help of a couple of married white women who live nearby, Sharon Scott and Karen Boone. Now and then someone will show up drunk and rowdy, requiring a gentle nudge toward home, and for a while there were nighttime burglaries until Peanut installed a high-tech alarm system. But intrusions of that sort are a rarity, as though the regulars feel a vested interest in the place, *their* store.

"It's been in the family for about seventy years now," Peanut was saying on another summer's day in '97. He stood behind the counter, beneath a cigarette rack plastered on the customers' side with scores of Polaroid shots from over the years, of proud hunters and fishermen posing in the store's parking lot with racks of antlers and strings of fish. "I still wait on customers my daddy had, and they still talk about him. There's some who even did business with my grandfather. We've all helped many a family, colored or white, when times were

rough. Most of the colored had to go away to find lives for themselves, but they still drop by to see me when they come to visit their
folks." He paused to ring up a case of beer for a young white man,
obviously heading for the boat launch at Dixie Landing, and gooey-
looking popsicles for three barefooted black children clutching nick-
els and dimes and pennies. "But I figure we've about reached the end
of the line. Scott's got a good job with ADT Security in Birmingham, and Bridget will teach school when her babies grow up a little,
and I've got better plans for the twins than this. In 'seventy-nine,
when my first wife got a job at Cypress Gardens in Florida, I turned
over the store to somebody else while I went down there to manage
a service station in Winter Haven, but I just couldn't see giving up
the store, and so we came back home. It's been hard work, and I sure
haven't gotten rich, but it's been a life."

THREE

The Preacher

IN NORTHERN BALDWIN County, as throughout the rural South, a profusion of black churches sprouted like kudzu in the years following the Civil War. They were founded by freed slaves in the tumultuous period known as Reconstruction, and they were not so much religious institutions as they were social and familial and, later, political groupings of the damned. They were small but joyous, stuck back there in the less-desirable crannies where the newly freed had been granted land or had chosen to homestead, and of little interest to the dominant white classes who had their own more sedate mainstream Protestant churches. To blacks, the church was their one safe haven, inviolate, *home,* where they could huddle together and do as they pleased without any interference from the whites. It was, at once, a place where they could wrap themselves in God's bosom, to note and record their own tragic ancestry, to marry and baptize and console and bury their own.

There were, in the late 1990s, nearly twice as many black churches as white in the area defined as Little River. The white churches tended to be larger and better-appointed (Sue Ferguson's father, Joe Roberson's, Holiness, with a covered open-air seating area and even a block of apartments for its annual camp meetings; the imposing steepled Little River Baptist on a leafy knoll above the river bridge; tidy little Mamie's Chapel, named for Peanut's grandmother, surrounded by a well-kept cemetery off Highway 59; the beautifully restored white clapboard Montgomery Hill Baptist, circa 1854, near the caution light at Tensaw, its wooden pegs and "slave balcony" still intact from the days of antebellum plantations). The black churches were much smaller and anything but graceful and elegant. "One reason there are so many of 'em," says Fred Gray, the black lawyer best known for representing Rosa Parks in the wake of the Montgomery bus boycott of the fifties, "the black congregations kept getting mad at each other and splitting up into cliques, sometimes for reasons as simple as the choice of hymns, and they'd say, 'To hell with you, we'll start our own church.' The other reason, at least in the old days, was political. Each church had its own wish list, whether it was a paved road or a power line or a well, and they would form a bloc and hand over their votes to the white politician who would promise to give them those things. The whites would get mad at each other and split up, too, but they already had political clout simply from being white folks."

If you drove far enough down any of the sandy bulldozed roads spinning off of Highway 59 between Tensaw and Little River, back into the woods and toward the swamps, you would suddenly come across another primitive little black church. There was the All-Seeing Eyes Holiness, of course, with its hand-painted logo of unforgiving human eyes (a bunch known even to other blacks as "the shouters"), but most of them were either African Methodist Episcopal or Baptist affiliates: squat cinder-block affairs with a power line strung to a telephone pole, some prosperous enough to afford a little white hand-crafted steeple, a silver-painted propane gas tank to supply heat during the mild winters, maybe a single window air-conditioning unit to make summer Sundays bearable, a block of marble or granite carved with the date of the church's birth (TATE CREEK MISSIONARY BAPTIST CHURCH, FOUNDED 1867) and a list of charter deacons and stewards; most of them with a fenced graveyard on the grounds holding the remains of ancestors who had first glimpsed Alabama from the rancid hold of a slave ship out of Africa in the late eighteenth century.

One of the least prosperous of those was known as St. Joe Baptist. To reach it, you hung a left at Dixie Landing Road, the paved county road about two miles north of Peanut's grocery that beelines to the primary public boat launch serving upper Baldwin County on the

Alabama River. You then angle left, just beyond the turnoff for Sawmill Road, onto a rumpled dirt road indicated as Tommy John Earle Road, and go about half a mile before reaching the church. St. Joe was, in June of 1997, about as unpretentious a church as you might see: a scruffy unpainted forty-by-sixty-foot cinder-block building with crank-out windows, no steeple on a roof still creased from a pine that had blown over in a windstorm some years earlier, a single creosote pole holding a power line and a hooded outdoor light with its bulb perpetually busted out by vandals, and a propane tank rusting in a clump of weeds. Across the road, which itself was barely wide enough for two pickup trucks to pass, was an ugly eighty-acre field, clear-cut and devoid of all life except rattlesnakes and water moccasins and the field mice they sought. Now and then an egret or a hawk would hover overhead, take a peek, and then, finding nothing interesting, move on without touching down. Tommy John Earle Road continued past St. Joe for about three hundred yards until it opened up at a dusty cross-roads where there was another black church, Tate Chapel, a slightly larger and much tidier cinder-block affair with a white steeple and stained-glass windows; and took a right turn onto a paved access road leading to the only point of historical interest in Little River: an engraved marker noting the gravesites of Red Eagle and his mother, the princess Sehoy, with three sets of whitewashed concrete picnic tables and benches which are used less by tourists than by bored local white teenagers, who regard it as a great place for a party.

St. Joe had been founded in 1886 by freed slaves, and this current building had been erected in 1960. For more than a century it had served some of the poorest of the poor in Little River, descendants of slaves and sawmill workers and woodsmen and moonshiners, most of whom had settled in the squalor of what once had been known as Benjamintown, named for the predominant black family there during the early twentieth century. Now the area was referred to as "Sawmill," for Sawmill Road, the unpaved three-mile loop that connects Highway 59 and Dixie Landing Road. There were seventeen structures on Sawmill Road—eight trailers, four brick houses, four of wooden frame, and one wasted travel trailer—many of them with jerry-built wooden handicap ramps leading to the front door, housing more than seventy people in all. At either end of the road there were a few whites. All the rest were longtime black residents bearing surnames familiar to the old-timers: Benjamin, Porter, Dees, Montgomery, Williams, Brown. Located exactly halfway down Sawmill Road, in a beige doublewide trailer, there lived the Rev. Joe Lewis Dees, the latest pastor in the long history of St. Joe Baptist Church.

THE FERTILE DEES family had been living in Benjamintown for as long as anybody could remember, dating back at least to the founding of St. Joe Baptist after the Civil War. Jim Dees, the patriarch, had scrambled to make a living during the Depression, as had most men of both races—cutting and hauling timber, working in the sawmill operated by the big white landowner Cleveland Gantt that gave Sawmill Road its name, growing subsistence crops, even being licensed to sell beer and wine at one point—while his wife stayed at home to birth and raise thirteen children. They were, as the saying goes, "poor as dirt," but they endured, and a big part of what made life bearable was the little church in the woods. Joe was born in 1949, when times had improved substantially with the postwar demands for lumber, but it seemed as though he was fated to spend a life of hard labor in the forests, like most other men of his generation. Growing up during the fifties and sixties, he swam in the rivers and played sandlot basketball with the white kids, feeling he knew them almost as brothers, but all of his formal education would come at the woeful segregated schools in Stockton and Bay Minette. He got into some mischief once as a teenager when, aimlessly roaming the streets of the Mobile suburb of Prichard, he and four other black kids roughed up a man, leading to enough time in jail for him to ponder where his life might be headed.

His chance to break the chain, to get out of Little River, came when he joined the navy, a step ahead of the draft, after graduating from high school in 1968. He was dispatched to Orlando, Florida, for basic training, and after five months he was "doing okay" until he awoke one morning and thought, *Wait a minute, they're gonna send me to Vietnam and I won't come back.* He had a severe nervous breakdown and was hospitalized for three months, put on a heavy regimen of drugs, including the powerful antipsychotic Thorazine, and soon was given a medical discharge. So it was back home to Little River; back to the swamps and the dead-end jobs in the woods.

The chemical imbalances discovered by the Veterans Administration doctors laid a curse on him to the extent that he has never been able to fully follow through on any endeavor since. "I was drawing checks for my discharge, and I worked for a while in the woods, doing manual labor," he says. "I enrolled in electrical engineering at Tuskegee [Institute, east of Montgomery], but I dropped out after a year because it didn't feel like the right thing for me. Then I got married in 'seventy-two, started having kids and working odd jobs. In 'seventy-six I got a job driving the school bus and spent a quarter studying accounting at Faulkner [Community College, in Bay Minette], but when my regular GI benefits ran out, I had to start working full-time for the Scott Paper Company." He was doing all right—drawing a paycheck as a driver and troubleshooter for Scott, happily married to a beauty from down the road in Latham, raising five kids, who would turn out to be achievers, attending St. Joe Baptist—when disaster struck in 1982. He was driving home from an assignment for Scott in Knobtown, Mississippi, 120 miles to the west, and was less than ten miles from home when he wrapped a company pickup truck around a tree at Tensaw, at dusk, on Highway 59. He came out of it with a broken neck, five busted ribs, and a punctured lung. "I must've gone to sleep," he says, but surely there was more to it than that; for he was not only outfitted with a fanciful metal harness to protect his broken neck, he was also shipped off to a state mental institution for "medication and rest." He was only thirty-two, and that was "the end of my working career."

It was while he was laid up at Searcy Hospital, he says, that he "felt the call to preach." He had been a member of St. Joe since he could remember, trekking down Sawmill Road with his parents and siblings and cousins on the Sundays when the church met, and the days seemed numbered for the aging pastor there. By now Joe was drawing a full array of government disability checks, both mental and physical, and he made another attempt at college, this time studying theology at the University of South Alabama in Mobile, but that lasted no longer than the others. Finally, when his preacher died in his eighties in 1986, there was a meeting of the congregants—fewer than twenty, all of them Joe's blood relatives or in-laws, most of them living on Sawmill Road—and he was elected to be the new pastor of St. Joe Baptist. Now it was "Reverend Dees" (Little River's gaggle of rednecks, Klan sympathizers if not out-and-out members, began dismissing him as "Saint Joe" behind his back), and he was in charge of a poor little church without any visible means of support. An older brother of Joe's who had made good in the automobile business in Michigan sent regular checks, and "love offerings" would drift in now and then from black church groups in southwest Alabama, but that was about the extent of any financial support. The members ranged from people like his parents, too old and sickly to work, to little children, with hardly anyone gainfully employed. Congregants died, got sick, or moved away. The church building, a prime target for white teenaged vandals drinking beer and whooping and throwing rocks and firing guns as they rumbled through the back-road "niggertowns," began to deteriorate.

And Joe's troubles had mounted. In '84, just two years after his near-fatal wreck at Tensaw, he again lost control of a vehicle, this time taking on a building in downtown Mobile, resulting in another broken neck and another trip to Searcy Hospital, in Mount Vernon, Alabama—only fifteen miles across the waters and swamps from Little River the way the egret flies, but a fifty-mile drive due to the shortage of bridges over the Alabama and Tombigbee Rivers. That first wreck had cost him his job with Scott Paper, and now his errant driving was becoming legendary. Nearly everyone knew by now that it wasn't the drugs Joe might take, like alcohol or marijuana or cocaine (none of which he uses), but the ones he *failed* to take. It was a Catch-22 situation: "The doctors tell me I can't drive when I'm on my medication, but if I can't drive I can't do my work, so sometimes I take 'em and sometimes I don't." There would be another wreck, or Joe roaring away from Peanut's store in a storm of dust in his boxy black four-door Ford sedan, or the sight of Joe aimlessly walking up and down Highway 59 (once, while holding a squawking chicken under one arm and whipping it with a switch), before a neighbor or one of his sons would be loading him up for another haul to Searcy or one of the VA hospitals on the Gulf Coast.

Finally, in the most hurtful blow of all, Joe's wife Shirley, the mother of their five kids, couldn't take the mood swings any longer and left him soon after he had taken over the church. "She was afraid of him," says Peanut. "Joe's bright. He's a good man. But when he gets off his medication he becomes somebody else. When Shirley left, it about drove him crazy and here he went again. Everybody's learned to stay home when Joe gets out on the road, doing eighty miles an hour, back and forth, in that big car of his." Says Sharon Scott, one of the clerks at Peanut's: "Lord, Lord. I don't know what to do when Joe gets like that. One time he walked right into his buddy Fred Porter's house with an axe and reared back and split Fred's coffee table right in half. He'll come into the store, break into line, and then buy a twenty-seven-cent soft drink with a hundred-dollar bill. He'll write a check with some odd date in history, like 1813, the year of the Creek Massacre, or 1776, or 1492, or his mother's birthday, and wink and say, 'Bet you don't know what happened that year.' I know it's time for 'em to take him off to Searcy again when that stuff starts happening."

EXCEPT FOR AN unsightly tangle of lower teeth that causes him to mumble when he speaks, Joe Dees is a handsome man with an athlete's trim build—muscular, about five-ten and 175 pounds, with smooth chocolate skin and close-cropped hair, his widow's peak remindful of Harry Belafonte—and he appears ten years younger than his years, especially when dressed as he was on this summer morning, in a white Nike T-shirt and black jeans and dusty Reeboks *sans* socks. His new doublewide sat exactly halfway down Sawmill Road, and he had been living there alone since his five kids had grown and left. He had scraped out a tight little circular drive to the trailer, where the presence of his black Ford sedan announced that he was home. In the front yard were a Primestar cable television dish, a basketball hoop on a black metal pole, some wild palmetto bushes and gnarled pine seedlings. Cast aside were a cannibalized automobile and the rusted shell of a singlewide trailer that had been dragged away after being cleaved by a tree during a storm. This new trailer was neat and well-appointed—carpeted, air-conditioned, blond-paneled, not a dirty dish in sight, as under the care of a meticulous housewife—and propped in the wide front window were framed five-by-seven color photographs of his children and of his estranged wife, Shirley, for whom he still pined even though their separation was in its tenth year.

Remarkably, in light of the fractured marriage and the fact that he gets by on various government checks totalling $1,100 a month, the Deeses' children were managing splendidly. Tim, the oldest, was about to complete his fifth year in the army and was contemplating whether to re-up or to marry a girl he had met while serving at Fort Jackson in South Carolina. Michael, twenty-two, was now a senior majoring in psychology at USA in Mobile, thinking of a career as a prison counselor; Carlos, twenty, was a sophomore in pre-med at Auburn University, hoping to go into pediatrics; Christine, eighteen, was spending the summer working at a McDonald's at Gulf Shores before entering the School of Nursing at the University of Alabama–Birmingham in the fall. The fifth child, twenty-four-year-old Joe Jr., had been swept up in a drug bust five years earlier but had straightened out and now was fully employed on the production line at Standard Furniture in Bay Minette. "That's not bad," he said. "Eleven hundred dollars a month isn't much, but it'll go a long way in Little River. The kids have jobs and loans and scholarships. There's a lot of the whites who own land and have a lot more money than me, but I'm not sure any of 'em"—naming the Boones, Cumbies, Deans, Coxes—"have had a single child go to college. Maybe we [blacks] have to try harder." Shirley, who lives near Stockton, suffers from asthma and "nearly stopped breathing one time," he says, and not a day passes when he doesn't see her or talk to her on the phone.

VIOLENCE AND EARLY death were nothing new to the Dees family. Of his twelve siblings, three died in infancy and a fourth was killed by a local white man. Joe is still haunted by the shooting death of his brother Ralph Edward Dees, one year younger than he, in the spring of 1975. "Ralph was just twenty-four, trying to find himself, and there's two sides to what happened. Some say he was messing with marijuana, selling it for Raymond Cumbie, but I don't know. Raymond ran what's the County Line Package Store now, near the river, and one afternoon Ralph went into the store and got into an argument with Raymond. My brother had a pistol with him, and pretty soon both of 'em had their guns out and were shooting. Ralph stumbled out into the parking lot and died right there. My sister and some of the other family heard about it and drove over there and put Ralph's body in the car and brought it back to Sawmill. The case went to court, second-degree murder, but a white jury in Bay Minette said Cumbie was not guilty, and that was that."

And so Joe Dees and the rest of his family endure. His older sister (and the church's secretary), Margaret Dees Montgomery, lives just down Sawmill Road from Joe's trailer, with a gaggle of siblings and offspring and squalling barefoot grandchildren in a frame shotgun house with only a flapping scrap of canvas for a front door during the summer, its gray paint long ago flaked away. His brothers Larry and Eugene were arrested for distribution of crack cocaine in '92, in the same incident involving his son, Joe Jr.; and Eugene, nearly blind from diabetes, was now ensconced in a mental hospital in Mississippi. Another brother, lyrically named Lawyer Dees, works full-time at a sawmill in Mobile, making him the only member of St. Joe Baptist drawing a salary. The only one of Joe's siblings to become an unqualified success was the brother who had moved to Michigan many years ago and was doing well enough in the automobile business to be able to send regular checks to help keep the church afloat.

It would be different in a big city, where a degree of anonymity is possible, but few days pass when Joe Dees doesn't get at least a glimpse of the man who killed his brother all those years ago; Raymond Cumbie is now sixty-three but still strikes out from his house on Highway 59 to work union construction jobs all over the region, and could be back in Little River and show up at Peanut's grocery store or the post office at any time. It's a price one pays for living in a close community like Little River, but Dees, unlike most blacks of his generation who were born and raised there, has never thought of moving away.

"They need me here," he said. He was beginning to fidget now, after sitting and talking for nearly an hour, tapping his Reeboks on the carpet and flexing his arms and flicking looks out the window. "My parents live across the road there, and they're old and sick. The kids in college need a place to come home to. I'm trying to pastor my flock, you know, pay the bills and keep the little ones busy in Sunday school and all of that. We don't meet but every third Sunday, but there's always somebody who needs to talk to the Lord. The church sits so far back there in the woods that we're always having some kind of vandalism from white kids running up and down the road. The street light's always shot out and the windows get broken. For seven straight years, we've had our electric pump stolen. Had that tree fall on the roof one time during a storm, and all we could do was drag it off. There's not much money, and I don't know what we'd do if my brother didn't send checks when he can."

"Surely, you get scared," he was told.

He laughed. "Only when I can't pay the bills."

"No, the Klan. The Boones. Cumbie."

"I can't say so. God help 'em. 'Red and yellow, black and white, they are precious in his sight. . . .' [The racism] is probably worse now than it was before Martin Luther King came along. About all I can do, though, is keep my eyes open."

"There've been these church burnings in the South lately. *Black* churches."

"Same thing. Nothing I can do about it. Look here"—suddenly he was springing from the sofa, quick as a grasshopper—"I've got to run down and check on my folks and go see my wife. Maybe some other time . . ." Soon his black Ford, caked with dust like a powdered doughnut, was careening down Sawmill Road, rooster tails flying in its wake.

FOUR

A Hard Life

WHATEVER ONE'S STATION at birth—black or white, comfortable or poor, landed or not—life had always been hard in Little River. The primary business there, after all, was to wrench trees from the ground. A white oldtimer, born to a timber man: "They would go to the woods and cut these huge trees in August, when they were green, and in October or November, when the sap was gone, they'd begin floating 'em down the Little River to Dixie Landing. When they got 'em there, they'd start putting together rafts that were about fifty feet wide and two hundred feet long, held together with spiked chains. They'd use poles and homemade rudders and the current to float the 'rafts' downstream, stopping at the sawmills on the rivers, selling logs as they went. It would take 'em up to three months to reach Mobile. Then they'd sell what was left and walk back home and start all over again." A black man, recalling the same period: "I was the 'snake man,' had a way with 'em, like the canary they send into the mines to be sure the gas is gone. We'd get to the woods and the boss'd say, 'Okay, Henry, go get 'em.' I'd go in there with a big ol' bolo knife, long as a sword, and start chasin' 'em out. One time I found thirty-six rattlesnakes on a job down near where the Stockton Gas Company is now, one of 'em with twenty-three rattles on it. I went in there and killed 'em while everybody sat around, drinkin' coffee, and then the boss said it was safe to go to work."

As a result, hardly anyone in Little River had made it through life unscathed. You could sit on the rickety bench in the shadow of the eaves in front of Ferguson's Grocery for a while, watching the people come and go through the double screen doors, and see the toll life had taken. Here would come Reverend Joe Roberson, Sue Ferguson's father, pastor of the Little River Holiness Church, who had lost both legs in a car wreck. Here was one old black man who had lost the use of one leg in a chainsaw accident; and his brother-in-law, who was skulled by a swinging boom while working on the Mobile docks. There was always an endless procession of the crippled, the dismembered, the deaf, the near-blind, the half-crazed; ditchdiggers and steelworkers and longshoremen and loggers, retired before their time, broken men not all that proud to find themselves sitting beneath the trees at the post office next door, awaiting the arrival of the government checks on the first and third days of each month.

There was George Scott, whose wife, Sharon, works long days and nights at Peanut's to supplement his disability checks. George had been a college football prospect in his youth, a chunky offensive guard at Monroe Academy in Monroeville, who seemed headed for Auburn on a football scholarship until he smashed a knee in his senior year of high school. He settled on spending a life in construction work, on jobs as far away as California, before ruining his back while unloading steel at the age of thirty-three. "I loved to work," he was saying one day as he gassed up his pickup truck at Peanut's. "All I ever wanted to do was work an honest day and then sit back when I got too old." Twelve years later, his wife was having to bring in the money while he tried to manage the pain. He had already had three discs removed from his spine and was undergoing surgery regularly to relieve the pressure, often sleeping on the floor, on his back, over a bag of strategically arranged tennis balls; or floating in their small backyard swimming pool for therapy. There is little he can do but fish, drink beer, watch television, and read books checked out from the county's bookmobile during its fortnightly stops at Peanut's store ("My favorite is *The Grapes of Wrath,* sort of like our life down here"). But he's lucky. His father has been blind since his forties, when he was spraying a field with insecticide and the hose got loose; and his grandfather was killed when he came upon a whole *house* that was sitting on a blind curve in the middle of a back road one night, being hauled to a new location on a flatbed trailer, left there without flares or lighting or any other kind of warning while the men were gone to find a mechanic to repair the truck.

Everyone seemed to know the story about the big-time cotton farmer up in southern Monroe County, beyond Uriah, who found himself nearly a million dollars in debt during the late seventies when the economy went bad. His wife and his children had begun "living a little too high on the hog, buying big cars and clothes and furniture and stuff," one of his neighbors recalls, and there seemed to be no way out. But then, in despair, he checked his life insurance policy and found not a word dealing with suicide. And so one day he simply slipped into his barn and closed the doors and solved the problems with a bullet to the head. "The irony of it is," says the neighbor, "cotton and the economy turned around in the eighties, and now the wife and kids are doing great."

AND THE ROAD is always there, a gauntlet to be run no matter the time of day or night. The deer run freely in the spring and summer when the hunters have put away their rifles, bolting across the road as they please (hitting one is drolly referred to as "hunting out of season"), and they are as much a part of the traffic hazards as the logging trucks and hot pickups and lumbering combines and other farm machines; but few bother to install the simple five-dollar whistle that can be installed in the grille and emits a wind-induced scream audible only to deer.

One never knows where death might lurk. A fellow named Kenneth Lambert was out on the roads in his compact car one morning, off on his rounds for one of the timber companies. It was just past daybreak, at first light, the hour of yellow school buses bulging with kids. He was tooling along the roller-coaster roads when suddenly he came over a blind hill and saw that two log-truck drivers were running their empty rigs side by side—they appeared to be *drag-racing*, for God's sake—as their morning entertainment. Coming from the other direction was a school bus. The drivers slammed on their brakes and went airborne. By some miracle, the kids on the bus and both of the truckers survived, but Lambert wasn't so fortunate. He lost control of his car and was paralyzed, to spend the rest of his life as a helpless invalid.

Seat belts? Forget about it. This is a world where a man's pickup truck is his proudest possession, even more so than his house, and he will be damned if he will let some bow-tied liberal bureaucrat up in Washington tell him how to drive a vehicle that might have cost him $30,000. Hardly anybody uses seat belts, including even Peanut Ferguson when he has the twins rattling around in the back of his van during a trip into Mobile to watch the BayBears play baseball. Country kids in the farming states have always begun driving at a very early age, as young as twelve or thirteen, a tradition held over from the days when they were needed to handle farm machinery out in the fields. During one July, in the late nineties, seven teenagers were killed in automobile accidents on Baldwin County roads, not a single one of them wearing a seat belt; and, begging a different question, one was a sixteen-year-old boy, out on the roads at 5:27 on a Sunday morning.

And so the twisting country roads are lined with tiny white wooden crosses, decorated with a victim's name and date of death and a cluster of plastic flowers. And there are three blue-lined parking spaces reserved for the handicapped, on voting days, in the lot at Ferguson's Grocery. And if drivers don't have the good sense to use their seat belts, at least they know to drive with their headlights ablaze even at high noon on the brightest of days, not to see but to be seen. But still they come: the runaway logging trucks, raw pinepoles swaying behind on skeletal trailers, some with mesh Confederate flags covering their radiator grilles; the teenagers' souped-up pickups jacked up in the back like cats in heat, decorated with shiny chrome mufflers and squirrel or raccoon tails and fuzzy dice, a red-trimmed black number 3 for the Chevy drivers enamored of the hard-charging stock-car champion Dale Earnhardt, or a decal of a cartoon figure pissing on a Chevy logo for the Ford believers; the fishermen, jouncing along in old trucks, pulling their clattery aluminum johnboats; and, joining the mix on weekends, roaring caravans of men and couples out for a lark on their monstrous Harley-Davidson motorbikes.

The carnage never ends, it seems, whether wrought by men or their machines or the whims of fate. DON'T SHOOT THIS WAY, reads a legend on the detailed topographical maps used by utility workers and Realtors and timber buyers, denoting occupied houses out in the woods that might be in the line of fire during hunting season. There were the three white kids from Little River who had made a drug buy in Clausell, a poor black neighborhood of Monroeville, and after finding as they drove away that they had been sold soap powder rather than cocaine—*That motherfucker!*—spun around, returned, raised hell, and, when the dealer leaned inside the cab to deliver the right stuff, rolled up the window on his head and arms, gunned the engine, and nearly dragged him to his death. There was the night that a husband and a wife left a roadhouse called Frosty Acres after a night of boozing, got into an argument, and the next morning she was found dead in a ditch with tire tracks imprinted on her back. And there was the day that one of the Boone men spun off of Highway 59, onto the gravel parking lot of the family cafe, and took a tire iron to a local black simply because he felt that the man had been tailgating him.

It's a man's world, especially among the whites, with an overdose of testosterone that often leads to trouble. Young boys are taught at an early age the art of handling guns and killing animals, as though these were still pioneer days. The slightest umbrage can bring about violence, as when a white man ambushed and severely wounded a black man who had inadvertently backed over some bushes while doing some yard work (although first, truth be known, the black man had answered a tongue-lashing by beating him up with his fists). There is a lot of drinking and a lot of drug use in Little River, but the weekly meetings of Alcoholics Anonymous and Narcotics Anonymous, held on Saturday nights at the Little River Baptist Church, are sparsely attended if at all. Every man a king: the biggest arsenal of guns, the fanciest boots, the fastest boat, the heaviest pickup, the prettiest wife, the toughest kid, the thickest bearskin rug, the buck with the handsomest set of antlers. Life is a competition for many of the men in northern Baldwin County, a competition that too often over the decades has become deadly.

GIVEN THE INEQUALITY of segregated schools and the overbearing presence of the Ku Klux Klan, there was no doubt that being born white gave a man a leg up in Little River. But that didn't mean anybody got a free ride. "We were all in this together, black and white, everybody poor," recalls Joe Phillips, a white born in 1921 to a large family of farmers who had been among the first pioneers in the area. "We all got equal pay for equal work, *hard* work, whether it was chipping and dipping turpentine or cutting trees. Some blacks even had it better, in fact. When I was a kid, we got our milk from some black neighbors who had cows."

Like many men of both races in Little River, Phillips's life would broaden considerably during the Second World War. He had gotten interested in building things as a teenager, while working in Civilian Conservation Corps camps around the country, and he chose the navy's SeaBees when he went into the military. He wound up in the Pacific in 1943, helping lay airstrips and throw up buildings as the air forces got closer to bombing range of the Japanese mainland, and when he returned home at war's end he embarked on a career in construction work. The postwar building frenzy was on, all over the country, and he managed very well.

The point about Joe Phillips is that he is one of the very few men in Little River to have made it through a perilous life without suffering any unseemly incidents. Never was he seriously injured on the job. Never has he or anyone in his family been in trouble with the law. There was a divorce many years ago, but his three sons showed no scars. And there was more to the new life he found when he remarried: "I found the church, and that made a difference. You look at all the crime with the kids around here and in Mobile, I bet none of 'em goes to church and about ninety percent of 'em don't have a home to go to. A lot of 'em here, they've got four or five places they can spend the night, and their parents don't exactly set a good example." He even quit hunting. "I used to be with the Little River Hunt Club, but I quit when they started to let the liars and cheats in. They'd shoot toward your house, kill the wrong deer, hunt out of season, all of that. People just didn't used to act like that around here."

In spite of all the hardships, it's been a good life, well-lived, making Joe and Letitia Phillips one of only four or five white couples in Little River who can be called upstanding citizens, respected by all. To the heart-of-pine house on Highway 59 that he built by hand after the war, he has added a two-car garage and a large fireplace and carpeting and ceiling fans in every room, plus a deck on the rear overlooking a rolling pasture and a fishing pond and a vegetable garden that produces more than a thousand tomatoes every spring. It's been helpful, he says, to mind his own business. "My father liked to tell a story about a man who couldn't help looking through his kitchen window every week when the woman next door was hanging out her laundry," he says, apologizing for the down-home homily. "He couldn't figure it out: she'd wash the clothes and hang 'em out, but they always looked dirty. One day, after she'd done the laundry and left her house to run an errand, the clothes looking as dirty as ever, he decided to go check it out. What do you know? The laundry was clean as new. It was when he was walking back to his house that he found out that his own window was dirty, not the lady's laundry."

BUT THEN THERE is Couglan Swamp. To get there, you drive four miles south of Peanut's on Highway 59 and then turn right onto the western end of Tommy John Earle Road, a bulldozed road that takes a northwesterly loop of about ten miles through the marshy forests before passing the Red Eagle gravesite and Joe Dees's St. Joe Baptist, finally hooking up with Dixie Landing Road near the boat launch. Through the piney woods, past hummocks and thickets thrumming with mosquitoes and frogs and birds, the turtlebacked road descends deeper into the forest. There is a glimpse of another black church founded by freed slaves after the Civil War, Tate Creek Missionary Baptist Church, and now and then the flash of a deer or the *whoosh* of a startled wild turkey trying to go airborne or the feverish splash of a bass feeding in a pond. There is the sense that you are entering the very heart of Southern darkness.

A left onto Couglan Road after three miles takes you into Couglan Swamp, named for a British doctor, Malachy Couglan (*KOFF-lin*), who had come all the way from South Africa in the early 1800s, during the pioneer and slavery days, like a missionary bent on serving the neediest in a third-world country. Today it is a prime area for hunting, far enough away from the clamor of human civilization to attract deer, turkey, grouse, mallards, and doves, even an occasional alligator or black bear. The hunters, mostly white men from places like Mobile and Bay Minette and Montgomery, have established "hunt clubs" behind locked gates, where they maintain camouflaged deer stands and duck blinds, further helping their cause by baiting the fields with corn and millet. During the fall and winter, with all of that firepower out in the fields, the place can sound like a battlefield.

Don't shoot this way. A veer to the right off of Couglan Road leads to the hunt clubs and, ultimately, the Alabama River delta. But the main road, if one can call it that, empties into a boggy swale that contains the homes of three aging sisters and their disabled husbands, all of them direct descendants of people who first saw the New World from slave ships arriving at the port of Mobile, after the treacherous crossing of the Middle Passage from the Gold Coast of Africa, to be sold at auction. Black as coal, of pure African blood, they are Catherine and Henry Brown, Elizabeth and Edgar Lee Marshall, Estelle and Roger Jones. Having been born during the 1920s, at the time of the boll weevil and the formation of the Klan, survivors of the Depression and the Second World War, they have seen the worst that Little River has to offer. They have endured and, in their own manner, prevailed.

THE FIRST OF the three houses that squat in Couglan Swamp is a tin-roofed yellow frame shack belonging to Catherine and Henry Brown, backing up to the edge of a pine forest and facing a yard half the size of a football field. The yard is littered with beer cans and wrappers and bottles tossed from pickup trucks by passing hunters and mean-spirited white kids, and decaying stumps and limbs felled during storms, brightened only by indestructible palmetto shrubs here and there. There is a tumbledown frame garage beside the house, its paint long ago flaked away, its roof near collapse, used these days to stow two faded automobiles of early eighties vintage. The windows of the house are covered from the inside by organdy curtains. Rusty television antennae sprout from the roof like wild sprigs of hair on an urchin's head. An oft-patched screened porch, a must in the swamps, runs across the front of the house.

Seeing a strange car roll up, Henry Brown eased up from his porch swing and tentatively opened the screen door. A large brown mastiff that had been dozing beneath the porch sprang to life, jumped to the waist-high wire fence and foot-deep moat that encircle the house, and began barking. "Hush up, Jack, hush up," Henry said as he began to negotiate the rickety wooden steps. He wore a pair of faded bib overalls and black rubber wading boots and a mesh gimme baseball cap from a Stockton service station. Shushing the dog, he limped through the weeds and leaned against the fence for support. He straddled the moat, which he had dug to channel the runoff during heavy rains.

After attending the segregated elementary school at Stockton for only four years, Henry Brown went into the woods as a young boy and spent the next fifty years cutting trees and dragging them to awaiting trucks. He was the "snake man" who was dispatched into the woods to make it safe for the cutters. His working days ended at the age of sixty, on a job for a paper company in Mississippi, when a chain saw "got loose" and nearly amputated his right leg. "A lot of folks I knew have gone on ahead," he said, "but I turned seventy-nine on April Fools' Day. That ain't bad." The dog, Jack, was a survivor as well; all of Henry's others had been shot dead in the yard by passersby.

Oral history, and scribblings in old family Bibles, are all that the three black families in Couglan Swamp have to tell their story, and what a story it is. "There were these three sisters and a brother, back around eighteen-hundred," Henry said. "Just teenagers. Must've been the great-greats of my wife and Estelle and Elizabeth. Anyway, they'd just got off a boat from Africa and they went up on the block at the slave auction. The three girls, one of 'em named Emmaline, they went in a package deal for sixty-five cents. Worked in the big house on a cotton plantation up in Clarke County. The brother, William, he sold for a dollar and wound up spending his life as a mule, dragging a plow behind him. But they were lucky." He paused to freshen his chaw of tobacco and let this sink in. "That old boat wasn't no good no more after that trip from Africa, so they loaded it up with the folks that hadn't been sold and sailed it up Mobile Bay and onto the Tensaw River. Anchored it, left it, and starting shooting holes in it until it sank. Everybody left on the boat died. Folks go fishing there today. They call it Nigger Lake."

Henry Brown looks back at the Second World War as his most vivid memory. He landed at Omaha Beach on D-day plus three, with the U.S. Army's quartermaster corps. "You can imagine what we saw," he said. "Bodies everywhere. We were unloading supplies on the beach when we looked up, and here came this one German plane flying low, strafing, going up and turning around and coming back at us again. Surprised us, because most of 'em had been shot down or chased away. There was this colored boy from South Carolina with us down on the beach, and he got mad and picked up a machine gun and started shooting at him and I'll be . . . He shot him down! *Yeah! Shot the plane down with a machine gun!* We liked to smothered him, hugging him and all. One of *ours* done shot down that German plane." Only a few months before this retelling, more than half a century since D-day, Henry had been sitting in the house watching the news on television, when he shouted, "Cassie, come here." His wife came into the room to see what was going on. "You remember that colored boy from South Carolina, one that shot down that plane in France? They finally giving him a medal." The United States government has found itself doing a lot of that lately; making amends, often posthumously, to black men who had served the country heroically, only to return to the same old degradations of the Jim Crow era.

The days are long and slow in Couglan Swamp. Henry tends a

garden patch of tomatoes, peas, and okra, does some fishing for the table, checks in on his hundred-and-four-year-old mother ("She's been trying all her life to get her hair straightened at the beauty parlor," he says with a laugh, "but it'll never work"), and makes the run into Peanut's and the post office from time to time. He and Catherine never had children, and thus much of their energy is focused on the prim little Tate Creek Missionary Baptist Church on a knoll about a half-mile away overlooking dusty Tommy John Earle Road. It is one of the prettier churches around: whitewashed cinder block, red roof, bell tower, two white columns flanking steps covered with green indoor-outdoor carpeting, a pebble driveway encircling a huge spreading pin oak that could be a century old. Henry's name is carved into the marble cornerstone, denoting him as a deacon and trustee when the new building went up in 1982 to replace the one founded in 1867 by his ancestors. The church is his family.

THE YOUNGEST OF the three couples in Couglan Swamp are Elizabeth and Edgar Lee Marshall, who live in what the Browns and Joneses refer to as "the big house," a rambling brick ranch affair, a sure sign of prosperity, with four bedrooms and carpeting and air conditioning. It sits grandly between the homes of Elizabeth's two sisters on forty acres of land, and out back there is a tall steel shed that houses tractors and trucks used by Edgar Lee in his diminished capacity as a farmer. "I'm three-score-twelve, and my husband's three-score-eleven," Elizabeth says, in a voice that is at once animated and cultured. They are in these relatively palatial surroundings, and reign as one of the most respected black couples in Little River, because of the astonishing job they did in raising their twelve kids.

Except for a son who "got his mind messed up in Vietnam" and lives at home, the children have soared far beyond the sorry conditions back in Couglan Swamp. The oldest played football and graduated from Georgetown University in Washington, D.C., but now suffers from cancer of the kidney. Another also played football and graduated from college, at Howard University in D.C., and now is a cop in Fairfax County, Virginia. The first daughter graduated from Georgetown and is a social worker in Americus, Georgia, where she and her husband own a twenty-one-acre farm. Two sons went straight to Maryland, where they own a successful trucking firm. Another boy was a trucker, too, but he got hurt on the job and is now studying at the University of South Alabama in Mobile to become a television sportscaster. The youngest son had been driving a concrete mixer but is studying at USA to become a nurse. Three other daughters graduated from college and became nurses far from home. Another son, who survived seven years in Vietnam, now inspects and repairs coffee machines in Maryland.

They made it through hard work, discipline, and knowing that there is little future for blacks in Little River. Until he was nearly burned alive in an accident, Edgar Lee was a stout bull who demanded that his sons work as hard as he. A man who owns a truck in Little River can make a decent living, with all of the stuff that needs hauling, and so he trucked and farmed and raised hogs and cows during his prime. But on a cold day in January 1967 he grew impatient and tossed gasoline on the fire in the fireplace of Elizabeth's parents' house, where they were living at the time, and *kabloom!*—there was an explosion that burned the house to the ground and left him crippled at the age of forty. Elizabeth had to go to work then, at age forty-two, as an obstetrical nurse in Bay Minette, a course she followed for sixteen years until her knees gave out. "I loved my job," she says. "Today, people still come up to me with their child and say, 'This was your nanny,' and that makes me very happy."

It was after the fire, with Elizabeth bringing in a paycheck and Edgar Lee on disability and the first wave of kids beginning to earn money, that Elizabeth and Edgar Lee built the house where they still live. The kids felt they owed their parents for steering them the right way, and they began to send checks with regularity, something they continue to do. And they even help Elizabeth's sisters when it's necessary. "The boys took a look at that old trailer where Roger and Estelle were living, the one in the back that they use for storage now," says Elizabeth, "and they said, 'We can't have Auntie living like that,' so they bought a new one for them, the one they live in now, and fixed 'em a screen porch. It might not look like much, and it seems like about everything they own is on the porch, but they're happy. They don't owe anybody anything, and don't have to answer to anybody."

ON AROUND THE bend, Couglan Road ends at that jury-rigged double-wide trailer where Estelle and Roger Jones live with so many cats they can't count them. Estelle is the oldest of the three sisters, at eighty, now in the middle stages of Alzheimer's disease, barely able to walk even with a cane. Roger, five years younger than his wife, had labored in the woods and in a fish cannery until he was nearly killed when he was skulled by a huge hook while helping unload a shipment of hardwood from South America at the Mobile docks, at the age of forty. "The company wanted to operate on me right then, but a doctor said if they did that, I'd die," Roger says. "See, the company wanted to fix me up so I could work and they wouldn't have to pay me no checks for being hurt." He has been drawing full disability ever since.

Their place, like the others, faces a sprawling front yard the size of a small pasture and backs up to the woods. It is actually two single trailers, joined together to form what is technically a double-wide, the back one being more or less a storage shed, the newer addition being their living area. Across the entire front is the screened porch the Marshall boys built, where they while away most summer days in front of a giant clattering floor fan, with blue plastic tarps taken from a roofing job serving to cover the sofas and chairs and other belongings in case of rain. Beside the trailer is the wasted carcass of a yellow seventies Dodge sedan slowly being devoured by kudzu, and in the gravel drive is the pale blue 'eighty-nine Ford that had recently cost them $800 just to keep running. There was no alternative to getting around, not since the woman who once ran a taxi service for aging blacks in the deep woods had taken her business to Bay Minette after her husband drowned.

Every day of the week is the same for them. At midmorning a

shuttle bus arrives at the trailer to pick up Roger and deliver him to an old-folks community center in Stockton, where a crowd of mostly old black men plays bingo or checkers or dominoes until lunch is served. The cost is a dollar for the bus, seventy-five cents for the meal. At about the time Roger has left on the bus, a black "home nurse" enters the trailer to look after Estelle, bathing and dressing her, making lunch and feeding her, making sure she is taking her medication, talking or reading to her, being her friend. On many afternoons, when Roger has returned and the nurse has gone, they get into the precarious old Ford and chance a trip into "town," meaning Peanut's store.

This made the third day in a row for them to have made that trip: Monday had been the first day of the month ("check day"), Tuesday an election day, and Wednesday another check day. As usual, they had dressed up for the occasion: Estelle in a flowery brown print dress, her short gray hair in a net; Roger in a pale blue short-sleeved shirt and beige wash-and-wear slacks and suspenders and blue mesh loafers. Estelle is a sweet little old lady, loved by all ("Uncle Sam sent me another nice present today," she always says on check days, eyes shining, addled as she is), but Roger is an original piece of work who can drive people nuts. Toothless, with only a little fuzz left to cover the knot in his head where he was whacked by the hook that disabled him, he can be an irascible old fart, overbearing, loud, bombastic, argumentative.

"I swear I'm gonna go out and dance in the road when he dies, if he ever *does*," says Sharon Scott, trying not to smile. "He's aggravating. He cuts in front of twenty people just to pay for a candy bar. Since he quit drinking and got churched, whenever he sees somebody buy beer he follows 'em out into the parking lot, preaching about the evils of drinking. But what really gets to me is the way he treats Estelle. We'll cash their check, she'll count it out, and then he'll snatch it from her and count it again. We'll set her up in a chair when they come in, because you know he's gonna stay and argue for two hours. Lord. And then he gets into that car and drives twenty miles an hour no matter where he is—the parking lot, the highway, the dirt road."

They had left Peanut's around four o'clock on a steamy afternoon, after collecting their checks at the post office and hobbling next door to get them cashed and settle their bill and pick up a large box of lemon cookies special-ordered by Peanut (one of Roger's indulgences, cheaper by the carton) and going through their usual visit— Estelle sitting under the air conditioning in a dinette chair, nodding and mumbling, her hands firmly clasping the purse in her lap, while Roger raved on about a gallery of perceived enemies—and soon they were weaving along Highway 59 at glacial speeds. When Roger caught the frightful sight in his rear-view mirror of a Peterbilt logging truck bearing down on him, belching, pulling a full load, hitting the air horn and blinking its lights, he eased off onto the shoulder to let it pass. In due time he was turning off the road, onto Tommy John Earle, slithering and slinging dust in a desperate attempt not to end up in the ditch and go asking for a tow again, which had happened more than once. His bony hands clenching the steering wheel in a death grip, he looked like a black Dale Earnhardt taking the first turn at Daytona.

Finally home at the trailer, nestled into fraying overstuffed chairs on the screened porch, the floor fan roaring like a helicopter, a half-dozen black kittens fighting for lap space, they rested. Roger has curious speech patterns, partly from the isolated life he has led but largely a result of having not a tooth left in his head, and a stranger can have a difficult time following him. He had been looking back over his life, about the jobs he had held before his disablement, and spoke of once working in what sounded like a canary mill in Bimini. His *can-AIR-ee* turned out to be a cannery, his *Bee-men-AY* meant Bay Minette.

When asked if he attends Tate Creek Missionary Baptist, the beautiful little church where Henry Brown is a steward and deacon, Roger was on his feet, off and running. "Go to *church*?" he shouted, shooting a look of disbelief at Estelle. "I been *sanctified*. Washed in the blood of the lamb! Wrapped in the arms of the Lord! Saved from the devil! They savin' me a place up yonder for the day He says I'm done down here! 'Go to church'? Hah! He that believeth not—"

The phone rang. Roger reached for his cane and limped inside the trailer to hear Elizabeth Marshall deliver some bad news. That was a distant cousin of theirs, she told him, Tony Williams, who had mysteriously died over the weekend in the Mobile Metro jail. It was in that morning's Mobile paper. He was thirty-nine and had been arrested for possessing drug paraphernalia. "Williams," Roger said. "Tony. I don't know. Got all these kin. Hunh. Dead in jail. Happens a lot . . ."

While her husband was on the phone, Estelle had started a story from her childhood, a time when she had been orphaned. "I was being passed around, was with these mean people, got pushed off a porch one time—"

"*Who!?*" Roger shouted when he came back, in mid-story. "Who pushed you off a porch?"

She shrank from him. "I was just a baby."

"Who? Ain't nobody pushed you off no porch."

This time she smiled sheepishly, letting it go.

"Mean folks everywhere," Roger said. "I remember when the Klans killed that boy and hung him from a tree in Mobile [a famous case in 1987, wherein the Southern Poverty Law Center bankrupted the Klan]. Them Klans just a bunch of fools. Don't worry me none, long as I got this." He stuck his hand in the right front pocket of his beige slacks, revealing the outline of a pistol he has been carrying for twenty years. The only time it isn't in his pocket is when he goes to church and leaves it in the glove compartment of his car. "Go down there to *Bee-men-AY* every May the first to pay my twenty-dollar license. This time the license man said, 'Well, Mister Jones, here you are again.' Said, 'You're not doing anything you're not supposed to do with that gun, are you?' Told him, 'If I do, you'll be the second person to hear about it.' Hah! Klans don't scare me none at all."

FIVE

Trouble

———

MEN WHO HAD FOUGHT in Vietnam characterized the nature of that particular war as "hours of boredom interrupted by brief moments of stark terror." Life in Little River was much the same, except that the hours usually stretched into days and weeks and even months. "Hell," said one of the disabled white oldtimers, "boredom's the number one cause of death around here." Not counting the minor accidents and pitfalls that were regarded as inescapable—car wrecks, fistfights, drug busts, divorces—it had been a good while since real trouble had visited the little hamlet. But then, in the first six months of 1997, there came a double dose of violence that, in retrospect, seemed to set the tone for a coming storm.

It all began in the fall of '96, actually, when Joe Dees got a call from his twenty-four-year-old son, Tim, saying he had been drummed out of the army and was coming home. Although three of his children were in college and another was gainfully employed after beating a drug habit, Joe was no less proud of Tim. The boy had gone directly into the army after his graduation from high school in Bay Minette, had served in the Desert Storm campaign, and was pondering a twenty-year hitch. "They say he looked just like me," Joe would say later, and indeed he did: a handsome, virile lad with the same chocolate features and hairline as his father. But now Tim had been caught using marijuana at Fort Jackson in Columbia, South

Carolina, and abruptly received an honorary discharge for "misconduct" after five years of service.

Joe was devastated by the news, of course, but he welcomed his son home. Tim moved into the doublewide trailer with his father and began commuting to USA to study accounting while he tried to sort out his life. Any plans had become complicated by his having fallen in love with a comely black student at the University of South Carolina, during his stint in Columbia, and he wanted to marry her even though she had revealed that she was pregnant by another man. ("He didn't believe in abortion, and he loved her anyway," said Joe.) And so, during the Christmas holidays of '96, Tim made the round-trip to Columbia in order to bring the girl home and introduce her to his family. Three weeks later, he would be dead, leaving Joe to forever wonder why: "Something went wrong. I could tell that when he got back from Columbia. Maybe they had an argument, or she didn't like what she saw here, or they called it off, I just don't know."

At any rate, on a cold night in the middle of January Tim had "said he felt the presence of the Lord and could we go down to the church for a while. We bundled up and drove down there, I turned on the lights, and we talked and prayed for a couple of hours. It got to be about ten o'clock, and when I said we ought to go, he said he'd like to be alone for a while, that he'd walk back. I gave him my leather jacket and drove on home and went to bed. About one o'clock in the morning there was this banging on the door and when I opened it there were two deputies. One of them held up a Polaroid picture and said, 'Joe, is this your son?' There was blood everywhere. His chest had been blown away. It was my boy."

The way it was reconstructed, Tim Dees had turned out the lights and locked the church and then begun to walk the two miles back to the trailer. On his way, he inexplicably began shedding his clothes (unknown to Joe, at the time, the boy had done the same thing a week earlier and been sent home by deputies), and he was completely nude by the time he strolled into the warren of two shabby trailers and a discarded Airstream that formed a sort of gypsy compound, a caravansary, at the intersection of Sawmill and Dixie Landing roads. It was home to a family of white newcomers to the area, Jerry and Audrey Maddox and their three grown children, who seemed to spend their days sitting on sprung lawn chairs, amid oil cans and garbage and broken furniture and cannibalized cars, drinking beer and shooting menacing looks at people passing by on the dusty road. "They pop up here and there, and not a one in the bunch has a steady job," said Peanut. Tim Dees banged on the door, stark naked, and when he tried to barge into the trailer he ran straight into a shotgun blast from Jerry Maddox, fell backward, and died in the yard.

The killing was worth a mention in the Baldwin insert of the Mobile *Register* and in the weekly Baldwin County *Times*, but there was no public outcry, no filing of charges, and that was about it. The boy was, after all, "a Dees," and naked to boot, the thinking went in the white community, and what was a man supposed to do, anyhow, when somebody tried to storm his home like that? The story died and went away just as surely and as suddenly as the Reverend Joe Dees had lost his son.

THEN, SIX MONTHS later, on a morning in mid-June, Peanut Ferguson was jumped by a wandering ex-convict and nearly beaten to death with a ball peen hammer. Given the store's isolation, on a lonely two-lane state road where it can take up to twenty minutes for the law or medics to respond to an emergency, it was amazing that nothing like this had happened in the thirty-three years that Peanut had been running the place. "We'd had break-ins at night," Peanut says, "and sometimes there'd be a stranger just sort of hanging around or maybe a shoving match between some party boys [Peanut's euphemism for drinkers] out in the parking lot, but we'd been pretty lucky over the years. When I found out that the guy had done time at Holman Prison [Alabama's 'big house,' site of its death row, near Atmore], I figured he'd heard about this little store out on the highway from prisoners who'd worked on road gangs when they were widening the road or mowing the weeds."

At a few minutes before eight o'clock that morning, during the rare lull between the early rush of fishermen and commuters and the daily procession of the housewives and disabled and other stay-at-homes, Peanut was out back cleaning the minnow vats when Sue came to the screen door and asked if he would tend the counter while she went to the house to look for the rubber stamp used to endorse checks. There was a customer at the pumps, she said, who had paid seventy-five cents for some gas and needed water for his radiator. Peanut had no reason to think anything of it as he washed his hands and went behind the counter, to see a large black man in his thirties coming through the front screen doors. There was no one else in the store, nobody lolling around outside that he could see. The man's car was at the pumps: a beat-up aqua Chevy Cavalier with a busted rear window, its hood raised.

The man seemed nervous as he looked around the store. When Peanut reminded him that he had pumped a dollar's worth of gas, not seventy-five cents, the man asked Peanut if he would pour some water for the radiator while he went outside to fetch another quarter for the gas. When he returned, he had a large dirty towel over one hand. Peanut was bent over the sink basin toward the back of the store, between the meat counter and the soft-drink cooler, filling a jug with tap water, when he heard the man say, almost calmly, "This is a robbery." Peanut barely had time to raise his head and turn around and protest—"Aw, man, you don't want to do this!"—before he saw the flash of a hammer, which had been concealed beneath the towel, and felt the first blows to his head. Blood splattered everywhere as the two men began to grapple. When a customer innocently opened the door and took a step inside and saw the scuffle in progress, Peanut's attacker shouted to him, "Get yo' black ass out of here!" sending him bolting for help, and continued pounding Peanut's head with the sick thuds of someone thumping a watermelon. Peanut went into a clinch to give his attacker less leverage, like he had seen the fighters do during the weekly boxing matches he loves to watch on television.

Sue had found the rubber stamp and checked in on the twins, unaware of the attack on her husband, and when she reentered the store she came upon Peanut moaning and lying nearly unconscious in a pool of blood. As it turned out, the man had dropped the hammer, grabbed an armful of cigarette cartons when he was unable to open the cash register, and roared away in his car, northbound toward the county line, with the hood still up. As many as half a dozen people soon had dialed 911 for the medics and the cops—the customer who had come upon the beating in progress, the postmistress next door, a couple of Boones who were having coffee at the family restaurant on the road, even the folks just opening the County Line Package Store—and the chase was on. Within thirty minutes, Peanut was being sped to the hospital in Mobile by paramedics, and his attacker, having abandoned the car on Dixie Landing Road, had been arrested by Monroe County deputies as he walked aimlessly toward the Little River bridge. When they brought him back to Ferguson's Grocery, to turn him over to Lt. Huey ("Hoss") Mack and the other Baldwin County deputies who had arrived, a crowd of locals, both black and white, had gathered and were rumbling like a lynch mob. "You're damned lucky they [deputies] got to you first, buddy-boy," one of them yelled, "or we'd o' torn yo' ass to pieces."

When Peanut was delivered to the University of South Alabama Medical Center (he had been conscious enough to insist he be taken there rather than to the closer but much smaller county hospital in Bay Minette), his face a bloody unrecognizable pulp that looked like a bruised prune, he was put under for three hours of delicate surgery. He came out of it with a turban of gauze wrapped around his shaved head, a steel plate in his skull, black eyes and purple bruises, blurred vision and wooziness, and a blood clot in one leg that would require surgery in the future. "I thought he'd been shot when I found him, there was so much blood," said Sue, "but this might've been worse than that. He's lucky to be alive."

The attacker was Ronald Hines, a thirty-two-year-old from Mobile who had spent half of his life incarcerated for violent offenses, the latest stretch being for ten years at Holman for armed robbery and assault with a deadly weapon, and now he was locked up in the Baldwin County jail for what would turn out to be a very long stay. David Whetstone, the feisty district attorney who can breathe fire when riled, was trying to find a way to put Hines away for life. "To the folks in Little River," he said, "doing this to Peanut amounts to trying to assassinate the president. Good thing we *did* get to the guy first. We might've had some sure-'nuff trouble on our hands if the crowd had gotten their hands on him."

What was this all about? From Roger Jones down in woeful Couglan Swamp, a black man toting a pistol in his pocket out of remembrances of the past, to the white Joe Phillips with another fine crop of tomatoes growing in his patch behind a brick house on the highway, the people of Little River could only hope that these two events were aberrations. Few could blame the Maddoxes, whoever they were, for protecting themselves from a naked man trying to burst into their home at midnight. And they could only marvel that no violence had ever come before to Peanut and his store, stuck out there as it is on the dark, lonesome road. Consuming the sparse reports in the media about Tim Dees's killing and Peanut Ferguson's beating, listening to the gossip at the store and the churches and the cafes, they presumed that life would go on as before.

LIKE HANK WILLIAMS's "midnight train whining low," fading mournfully into the distance, farm life in America had been slipping away since the men went off to fight in the Second World War. Another popular tune, left over from the war that was supposed to have ended them all—"How you gonna keep 'em down on the farm, after they've seen Par-ee?"—expressed only one small reason for the decline in one of the most enduring fantasies about the United States: the family farm, that holy entity, a self-sufficient endeavor that happened to be blessed from above. Daddy in the fields with the boys, Mama in the kitchen with the girls, all for one and one for all, the family and the Lord pitted against nature and its critters. Southern music and literature throbs with morality tales about the dangers to be found beyond the farm, but there was hardly any home to go back to anymore, once the war had ended. The land was being gobbled up by huge corporations, or by developers of sprawling suburban housing tracts, their bulldozers coming like swarms of locusts to sweep away nearly two centuries' worth of family histories. One man against nature had been a heroic story, but one man against a corporation was ugly.

Entire towns brimming with migrants from the southern Applachians sprouted in the industrial Midwest, especially in Ohio and Indiana, where there were plenty of low-paying factory jobs. One of them was East Dayton, Ohio, where the visiting Southern workers were sneered at and called "Briarhoppers." A body of mean-spirited jokes followed them. The answer to the riddle, "What's the first thing Neil Armstrong saw when he set foot on the moon?" was, "Six Briarhoppers in a forty-six Ford, looking for the Frigidaire plant." Most of them never bothered to change their permanent address, working four ten-hour days so they could go back home for long weekends, prompting another joke: that the reason there was a split-level bridge over the Ohio River at Cincinnati, the one on top southbound, was so "the Briars headed home for the weekend can drop their shoes to the ones going back to work." In fact, a sheriff from a county on the Tennessee-Kentucky line won reelection in the sixties when he wisely took his campaign to the seedy streets of East Dayton, shaking the hands and kissing the babies of people who had never changed their voter registration.

Blacks had left in the 1930s, well ahead of the poor whites, looking for places in the big Northern and Eastern cities to escape from their de facto slavery, and whites had followed them out of economic necessity. Forty acres and a mule wouldn't cut it anymore if you wanted to keep up with rising prices in the ascending postwar economy. You needed more land and modern machinery to work it if you hoped to compete against the big outfits in what now was called agribusiness, and you could either hock the farm or go into debt or take a salaried job in town to keep up. It had always taken a large family to keep the homestead afloat—the more sons, the merrier—but now those sons had been exposed to a larger world and wanted more. They had seen Paris, had learned new skills, had been offered a chance to improve themselves through the GI Bill, didn't relish returning to a sunup-to-sundown regimen of milking cows and killing hogs and plowing fields, and so they were the first generation to go off to college. They would become engineers and scientists and agronomists and pilots and teachers, never to return to the land of their childhood.

It left Mom and Pop at home, alone, selling off pieces of the farm as the need for cash arose, even becoming clerks in town in their desperate attempts to hold on to the only sacred piece of earth they could call their own. By the end of the twentieth century, a puzzling new age of computers and mechanization and cold statistics, they had become quaint relics of the nation's past, like the Norman Rockwell illustrations that celebrated them and decorated their kitchen walls. Even the little crossroads towns that had served them on weekends when they drove in for their needs—sugar and coffee, seed and feed, haircuts, fuel, banking, an outing—had been boarded up now, the cozy family cafes and hardware stores and gas stations and groceries having been bought out or replaced by big national chains, requiring them to drive another hour to "retail trading centers" located, more often than not, in strip shopping centers beside the interstate highway.

Now they could only look forward to the weekends and the holidays, when their children and grandchildren came to visit. New automobiles bearing out-of-state tags filled the driveways and lawns during these reunions, at Christmas and Thanksgiving and Easter and in the summer, and for brief golden moments the farmhouses resonated with echoes from the past. For the children, now middle-aged, there might be some sour memories to be overcome—gathering eggs at dawn, plowing at dusk, chopping wood, reading by kerosene lamp, nailed to the land while the town kids played—but to *their* children, city-bred grandchildren who had never heard a rooster crow, this was a fantasyland: cows, chickens, hogs, geese, rabbits, deer, turkeys; creeks to swim, trees to climb, horses to ride, fish to be caught. Stories around a fireplace not used since the last visit. Songs not sung since radio came. Jigsaw puzzles not solved since television.

Canned preserves not seen since the first supermarket opened. Fried chicken, sawmill gravy, scratch biscuits, tomatoes and peas from the garden, sweet tea and homemade ice cream and watermelon. Another world, long gone.

As the people in Little River were about to be reminded of, during a summer of 1997 that would turn out to be turbulent, country life had lost its appeal to the young. The teenagers, and even their parents, simply didn't remember the good times. About all they knew was that it sounded like a hell of a lot of work for very little profit. Only the grandparents and the great-grandparents knew the simple joys of small-scale farming, of turning the soil, sowing the seeds, nurturing the plants, praying for rain, and overseeing the miracle of growth; of building one's own house and raising one's own barn and digging one's own pond; of being one's own boss, caring for one's own people, growing one's own food, in the grand tradition of American steadfastness; of being able to say, as they might on a Sunday morning in church, *Look what me and the Lord did this week.* No; no one born after, say, 1930 would know anything about any of that.

So while this new world swirled around them, the old-timers in places like southwest Alabama could only fall back on their fond memories of the past when farming was a noble calling. There were some younger ones, vigorous men in their forties and fifties, who were still doing very well with huge spreads—Danny Harrison, from up above Uriah, was expecting to gross $480,000 from the cotton he had planted on six hundred leased acres—but most of them kept a few chickens and hogs, nurtured some corn and tomatoes and the like for the kitchen, and might have a stand of pines that represented more of a legacy to the kids and grandkids than a steady source of income.

Semiretired now, the old ones have learned to stretch out the languorous days by making a morning's work from an hour's errand: helping a neighbor with a fence, weeding tomatoes, burning leaves or tree stumps, cleaning algae from the pond, washing the truck, visiting with Peanut down at the store. Six days a week there is a gathering for lunch at the Country Kitchen, just off of what used to pass as the town square at Uriah, now battened except for a feed-and-seed store and a gas station and a teenagers' burger-and-shake drive-in, and at the Kitchen there is always a group of farmers, old and middle-aged, their tawny arms spread on Formica tabletops as they talk of the weather and crops and old times. ("With two cafes and five beauty shops," an old nester in a McCullough Cotton Gin gimme cap was opining on one of those broiling days in July, "ain't no excuse for nobody in Uriah being hungry or ugly.") Such a bunch in New York City, say, would be watching the pigeons and the cabs go by; here, in Uriah, Alabama, they observe the buzzards and the pickup trucks. You work with what you've got.

AND FINALLY, AS the sun slips below the tree line, there are the sweet evenings. On a Saturday in late August, a good week's work behind him even if he is semiretired, the old boy can relax now. The trees he planted are out there growing without the help of anybody but God, and the first snowy cotton bolls have burst forward in the modest cotton patch, and the winter's firewood has been neatly stacked beside the house. Barefoot, shirtless, down to his jeans now, he flops back in a tattered aluminum-and-web lawn chair, out in the middle of the yard, and clasps both hands behind his neck to enjoy the show. Cicadas chatter back and forth from the road. Bullfrogs boom up from the pond. Bats dive for insects. Crows yawk in the pines. When the orange ball of sun finally falls away, the horizon suddenly explodes into a majestic magenta glow announcing sunset. Through the cirrus clouds, cleaved now and then by the contrails of jet planes climbing toward Atlanta and God-knows-where-else, stars twinkle like Christmas tree lights and a new moon rises with a cockeyed smile. Let the young-'uns cavort at Frosty Acres, their parents drive into Mobile for a movie, but this is the place to be.

Fried chicken and biscuits tonight, with corn and okra and tomatoes and peas from the patch, plenty of time for it to settle before the

Opry comes on. He was a toddler when the Grand Ole Opry was born, in 1925, the boll weevil gone and the Depression on its way, and the Opry had been created just for him and his generation: a Saturday-night extravanganza of fiddling and buck-dancing and sad songs and corn-pone humor, live from Nashville, Tennessee, over WSM radio, 650 on the AM dial, "your fifty-thousand-watt clear-channel voice direct from Music City U.S.A." At nine o'clock, when the airwaves have been cleared of all the tinny little local daylight stations, he hears the familiar words of Judge George D. Hay, the man who started it all, preserved for all time—"Let 'er go, boys!"—and here it comes, wavering in and out over the radio in the living room, from four hundred miles away. There's a story about an old fellow, just like this one, who finally made it to Nashville for a live performance of the Opry, and when he got back home and was asked how it went, he said he was surprised to find "there wadn't no static." But it wouldn't be the Opry without the static. The fleas come with the dog.

Like nearly everything else in his world, country music as he knows it has changed and fallen out of favor. Demographers have done their polls and surveys, checked record sales, and found that nobody with disposable income wants to spend it on the kind of music that was country, the stuff that made the Opry: Hank Williams's cries from an anguished heart, twangy steel guitars and howling fiddles, heartfelt recitations about faithful old dogs and unrequited love, cornball reports on the latest doings from mythical Grinder's Switch by Minnie Pearl ("How-dee! I'm jest so proud to be hyar!"). Everybody's left the country and gone to the cities now, leaving few people behind who might need a new tractor or flour for making biscuits from scratch or, God knows, a 78-rpm album of Ernest Tubb's greatest hits, and now on the eve of its seventy-fifth anniversary, there is serious talk that the Opry might soon be closed down forever. Several of the longtime stars of the show literally approach the mike on canes and walkers these days, croaking songs they recorded in the forties and fifties, when "country music" meant just that. The new audience, it has been discovered through market research, are exiles to the city who want to hear music that is deemed "country" only if it has a steel guitar or the faintest trace of a "y'all" or an "ain't" in it somewhere.

From week to week, the Opry is always the same—the only place left where you can still hear the survivors of the last good time America's small farmers can remember—and that is its charm. Roy Acuff is dead now, rest his soul, but you can count on somebody singing "Wabash Cannonball" every Saturday night. Jeannie Pruitt is always going to be there, singing her one big tune ("Satin Sheets"), and George Hamilton IV doing "Abilene," and Jim Ed Brown with "Jimmy Brown the Newsboy," and Little Jimmie Dickens with "Take an Old Cold Tater and Wait." They were all there on a particular Saturday night in the spring of 1997, doing their thing as usual, when Porter Wagoner brought down the house with a story he had been telling for forty years: "I was born ugly. Mama had me on a bus one time when this drunk got on and sat next to her and started saying her baby looked like a monkey. She got mad and said, 'You're just a no-good drunk,' and he said, 'Yeah, but I'll be sober in the morning, lady, and that baby's still gonna look like a monkey.' She grabbed me and went up to the driver and asked him to throw the drunk off the bus. The driver said, 'We're out the middle of nowhere, lady. I can't do that. Tell you what, though, there's a rest stop coming up. How 'bout we all go inside and talk it over? I'll buy some coffee for the drunk and some peanuts for your monkey.'"

THE OLD BOY has heard it many times before, of course, but that's the appeal: the ritual, the dependable, the assurance that some things, at least, will never change. Not for him are the newfangled gadgets, the programmed obsolescence, change for the sake of profits. What in the world is this Cuisinart, anyway? Computers, calculators, answering machines, digital clocks, E-mail; unnecessary toys, for him, "progress" only for the hucksters who sell them. He will continue to write letters and awaken to the rooster's call and dead-reckon arithmetic in his head, thank you, and if he isn't there to answer the phone they can just keep calling until he gets home. He has just seen something on television—he broke down and bought a TV set, yeah, but not cable—about a deal called Dial-a-Steak, where you call a number and they start cooking it like you want it while they're driving to your house to deliver it, and thought it was about the laziest thing he'd ever heard of.

Black or white, it's the same for both races of that generation. Black folks don't have an Opry to look forward to on Saturday nights, that being poor white folks' music, but they have their blues crackling up from WWL in New Orleans and gospel music all over the radio dial. What the two cultures share are the old-fashioned verities, found right there in the Bible, the Ten Commandments being their guide: Do your work, mind your own business, love your family, get along with your neighbors, praise the Lord. All of the old folks in and around Little River seem to have a variation on Joe Phillips's parable about the man who kept looking through his kitchen window, sure that the woman next door was hanging dirty clothes on her line, only to discover that it was his own window that needed washing.

And so, after one of those sweet evenings in the country, they might be able to look forward to a visit the next day from the kids who had left to find what they wanted in the towns or the cities. Breakfast, church, then Sunday dinner with the kids and the grandchildren; that can top off just about a perfect weekend. One of the most difficult things the wise ones can remember having to do was to convince their children that there was no future for their generation on the farm—*Go away, get an education, come see us when you can*—but it can seem to have been worthwhile on those blessed weekends when they see the kids roll up in their new cars and hear the yelping of "young-'uns" as they gallop toward Grandma and Grandpa with arms spread like angels.

THE PROBLEM WAS, those were anything but angels that the old-timers were seeing out there on the road these days. To this new generation of teenagers in Little River, listening to the Opry and chopping trees and watching the crops grow were the least of their passions. As far as they were concerned, in fact, that was all a bunch of crap. They had missed out on the basic verities that had held their grandparents together in a harder and simpler time—love of the land, faith in the church, patience above all—and they wanted immediate gratifications to appease their restlessness.

There was a gaggle of about two dozen of them out there on the twenty-mile stretch of road between Little River and Uriah: white kids who were about to graduate from high school, sons and daughters of dysfunctional families, kids with few hopes and dreams beyond finding some menial job or marrying within the clan, kids who had not even been given a road map about how to live a noble life, a whole generation with no idea of how to comport themselves in a grownup world. They were rejecting the antiquated life of their forefathers, but at the same time they lacked the skills to face this new world they had chosen. The sins of their fathers, and their mothers, were soon to become evident.

The first sign that "this bunch," as they were known, would become troublesome came in the late spring, on the eve of graduation ceremonies at J. U. Blacksher High in Uriah. Everybody at Peanut's knew of the car that had been abandoned on the road, but few thought anything about it because it happens all the time in Little River: an old heap dies, there's no money to revive it, the owner walks. It had sat there for a while, maybe a month, unattended but with no note saying that the owner would come back to take care of things, and then the inevitable news reached the store. The car had been vandalized—tires punctured, windows smashed, seats slashed, the whole thing finally torched in a frenzy that passed for entertainment—and the people at Peanut's sensed that there might be more trouble ahead.

"You think they're crazy now, wait 'til the summer," said Sharon Scott. The older ones knew of the restless kids, knew them by name, knew where they came from—children of divorce, teenagers with little hope, unread kids with throbbing libidos, just *babies* with enough money to keep their cars running and buy beer and cheap drugs—and they held their breath as the long hot summer set in. The combination of bored kids and stultifying weather and a world without purpose added up to a brushfire waiting to happen. All it would take was a match.

PART TWO

A World on Fire

SIX

Disturbing the Peace

—————

ONE MORNING IN LATE June of 1997, when the temperatures had begun to drive entire families to a favored swimming hole beneath the bridge where Highway 59 crosses the Little River at the county line, some Klan graffiti was found sprayed in black paint on the concrete abutment. There were drawings of a hooded Klansman bearing the initials AWK, the logo for the Alabama White Knights of the Ku Klux Klan, known by the Baldwin County prosecutor David Whetstone and the Southern Poverty Law Center in Montgomery as a new splinter group operating from a post office box in Semmes, a crossroads northwest of Mobile near the Mississippi state line. It amused no one, not even the closet racists, except, obviously, the person who had put it there.

Although nearly anyone with any good sense was ridiculing the once-feared Klansmen these days—seeing them as a pathetic remnant of white-trash losers still living in the twenties, when the Klan was at its peak and even substantial whites such as the Birmingham lawyer and future Supreme Court Justice Hugo Black felt it necessary to join in order to continue doing business—the very word "Klan" still brought a chill to the hearts of both blacks and whites in the darkest corners of Alabama and Mississippi. Alabama remains as the only one of the United States with a constitutional ban against interracial marriage, although the law is ignored, and that is only one of the legacies of the Klan. The last time anyone could remember a full-dress Klan rally in these parts, replete with a cross-burning, had been in the mid seventies. And most felt they had heard the last of it in 1987 when Morris Dees of the SPLC got a $7 million judgment against the United Klans of America for the cold-blooded murder of a black teenager in Mobile.

The victim in that one was Michael Donald, a nineteen-year-old who worked in the mailroom of the Mobile newspaper while studying at a technical school in Mobile. Angry over the impending dismissal of a black-on-white murder case, some members of the UKA had gathered guns and knives and a thick rope for a noose, and piled into a car to go looking for a black person, any black person, to lynch. They saw Michael Donald walking the streets of a deserted area one Friday night, on his way home after buying a pack of cigarettes, and simply snatched him, flung him into the car, and drove away. They headed straight for the dark marshes of northern Baldwin County, where they commenced to torture the terrified young man for more than an hour, thrashing him with tree limbs, kicking him, and finally slashing his throat until he was dead. They loaded up the body and drove back to Mobile, where they looped a rope over a tree limb and tied a noose around the neck, and that was what people saw as they reported to work the next morning: a "lynching" right there in downtown Mobile.

With their group bankrupt and officially dead after the $7 million judgment, the members of the United Klans of America had simply split up and formed small local klaverns like the Alabama White Knights in Semmes, Alabama. Now and then, Klan literature would show up overnight on lawns throughout Baldwin County, spewing diatribes about Jews and "niggers" and "Julios" (Latinos) and international conspiracies threatening the "purity" of "European-American" blood. There were phone numbers for a Klan hotline, even a racial joke line one could call in Michigan. (A caller had to sit through a five-minute pitch, in a humorless Midwestern voice, for "Hitler Was Right" bumper stickers, biographies of such Klan heroes as the "American Nazi" George Lincoln Rockwell, videos and compact discs "about you-know-who" that "you and your kids can sit around and enjoy forever," before getting to the jokes: "What do you get when you cross a groundhog with a Negroid? Six more weeks of basketball." And, "What's mass confusion in Harlem? Father's Day.") The Klan had been forced to go underground more than ever before. Besides, blatant racism had gone underground, not only in the South but all over the country, had been preempted by the Republican Party's response to Lyndon Johnson's Great Society and the huge strides made in civil rights during the sixties. In order to regain the South from the Democratic Party, whose populism had appealed to Southerners for most of the twentieth century, the GOP developed what it called a Southern strategy. That "strategy" was little more than a way to say "nigger" in codes.

SINCE MOST OF what they regard as news is confined to local gossip, not a larger picture, the majority of folks in Little River were only vaguely aware of the rash of black church-burnings that had been sweeping through the rural South like an outbreak of measles during the past year. There had been more than a hundred already, fourteen in both Mississippi and Louisiana, a dozen in Alabama, and about a fourth of them had been traced to the Klan. "They're about equal parts Klan-inspired, mischief, accidental, and insurance fraud," said Richard Cohen of the SPLC in Montgomery. They had brought about the creation of a federal task force to investigate the arsons, and a new hate-crime law that would bring a ten-year federal sentence without parole to anyone found guilty of "conspiracy to intentionally deface, damage and destroy religious real property by use of fire." There seemed to be more awareness of the world beyond Little River among its blacks, since most of the employed whites were more concerned with buying a better bass boat or a bigger pickup truck, but even the blacks, with the possible exception of the preachers like Joe Dees, figured it wouldn't happen here.

But Peanut Ferguson's antennae had gone up. Never one to rush to judgment, he nevertheless had been keeping his eye on a somewhat secretive newcomer to the area, a man named Phil Smith, who had moved into a farmhouse on five acres along Highway 59, between the mainly black communities of Tensaw and Blacksher, about nine miles south of the store, and was living behind a locked gate guarded by large and menacing German shepherds. Smith was in his late thirties, about Peanut's size, with the beginnings of a beard, given to wearing cheap white cotton socks yanked up to his knees and flowery Hawaiian shorts and running shoes whenever he came into the store or checked his rental box at the post office. Generally noncommunicative, Smith had told Peanut that he had been disabled on a construction job—had to run up to Birmingham every month, in fact, for therapy on his back at the hospitals there—and once had lifted his shirt to show Peanut the scars from his surgery, saying that the insurance settlement had enabled him to buy this property where he now lived with his wife and two little girls. "She was pleasant and pretty, *real* pretty, and I couldn't believe it when I read the paper," Peanut said.

What he had read in the Mobile paper, back in mid-April of '97, was of the conviction of a "thirty-three-year-old Tensaw woman" on two counts of selling drugs in a raunchy strip club in southern Baldwin County, Jerry's Cabaret, which had been shut down by Whetstone for everything from violating obscenity laws to padding customers' credit-card accounts with unauthorized charges. Her name was Susan Rena (pronounced *Ree-NAY*) Clark Smith, best known to the boys leering from the front tables as "Wild Child," one of the club's headliners. She was already on probation for the same crime, and now the daughters were being fostered out while Mom went off to jail. It was Phil Smith's wife, all right, and now word came to Peanut that the postal box Smith came to check out at the little post office next door to the store was rented in the name of the Alabama White Knights of the Ku Klux Klan.

Toward the end of June, out of the hospital so briefly that his hair had barely begun to grow back from the surgery, Peanut saw Phil Smith come into the store with a big smile on his face and a load of handbills in his arms.

"Well, ol' buddy," he said, "I'm about to throw some business your way."

"I can use every bit I can get."

"I mean some *big* business."

"The bigger the better."

Smith, glancing to see that there were no blacks in the store, said, "There's gon' be a Klan rally at my place Saturday night. Lots of people gon' be wanting cold drinks, candy, cigarettes, gas, you name it. I'm gon' tell 'em all to come to Peanut's."

"Well, I appreciate it"—*Good God!*—"but I . . ."

"Wonder if I could leave some posters with you?"

Peanut was mortified. Hell, he was in business. White *and* black. What if a Klansman tried to hand out some literature or got into a conversation with a black? Visions of shouting matches and fistfights between old white guys in sheets and outraged young black men, right out there in the parking lot, swirled in his head and made him dizzy all over again. He rejected the idea of putting up any of the Klan posters and tried to explain his position to Smith, who mumbled that he understood and then went on his way. "No hard feelings. See you this weekend, buddy."

PEANUT HAD PLANNED to break away and go fishing that Saturday, as is his wont, but that was out of the question now. *This thing could get out of hand real quick,* he thought, aware that this generation of blacks lacked the fear of the Klan that many of the older ones still harbored. It would be another of those steaming languorous nights in the Alabama boondocks, the last Saturday night of June, with nothing to do for entertainment but eat catfish at the Dixie Landing Cafe or go drinking and dancing to a live band some twenty-five miles away at Frosty Acres, the blue framed roadhouse plopped on a huge gravel lot near the railroad crossing and the lumberyard at Huxford. Peanut decided to stand guard at the store, all the way through to the ten-thirty closing that night, and could only hope for rain.

None of the other businessmen up and down the highway were willing to allow Phil Smith's posters to be tacked up on their property, but the Klan's private postal system—careful to avoid using the U.S.

mail for circulating what was officially regarded as "hate" literature, they left bundles of literature in yards overnight—ensured that the word got out. The rally was to begin around four o'clock in the afternoon, at Phil Smith's field, with speakers at six and a cross-burning at dusk. "No Drugs/No Firearms/No Alcohol/No News Media," read the advisory, printed on a copier. "Open to the white public. . . . Bring lawn chairs for your comfort. . . . T-shirts and souvenirs will be available. . . . Segregation yesterday, today, tomorrow, forever. . . . White Power! ! !"

So Peanut stuck around the store, dreading the worst. There was no rain, just the same stultifying humidity that had been threatening the corn and cotton crops in northern Baldwin County, but neither were there any sheeted Klansmen. Instead, there were emboldened young blacks, at home for the weekend from their daily labors in the factories of Bay Minette and Atmore and Monroeville, buying beer or ice cream or hoop cheese or steaks from Peanut, and whooping with bravado: "Hey, bro, you see them *clowns* down the road? Look like the Barnum and Bailey come to town . . . *Boo! Gotcha!* . . . That sheet *smell,* man, whyntcha get the ol' lady to wash 'at motha?" The gates at Smith's place nine miles south had been swung open now, bedecked with a giant brightly colored Confederate flag, one Klansman in a hideous purple satiny hooded outfit peering into the old sedans and new pickups idling in line to enter, quick flashes of the Nazi salute from the guards, a half-dozen young skinheads wearing camouflaged military fatigues and brandishing plywood shields and carbines of Second World War vintage, the whole scene eerily silent. David Whetstone had dispatched his deputies there to observe from a distance, cruise up and down the road, maintain presence, *let 'em know we're there.* One of four old black women, watching the show from rocking chairs on a front porch a couple of miles away, preparing supper: "If they ain't got nothin' better to do, they could come up here and help us snap these beans." All was quiet on the southern front of upper Baldwin.

Fewer than a hundred people attended the rally, and when they were passed through the gates they were directed through a stand of scraggly pines to a swale where there was a makeshift podium and, dramatically, a wooden cross that had already been thoroughly soaked with kerosene. License tags revealed that they had come from all over the immediate area, not only from Baldwin County but from Mobile County and Mississippi and Florida as well, and they were a mixed bag of skinheads in fatigues and perky young girls in shorts, leathery old guys in gimme caps and work boots, only about two dozen of them signifying Klan membership by wearing their hooded getups. Among the inflamed speakers, in his Klan costume, was a "Brother Phil." No microphones were necessary, for their shrieking voices sounded like Hitler and his clones off on a rant, echoing through the trees and up into the steamy mists of the Southern gloaming, as they ran through the litany of Klan enemies—"*Julios! Niggers! Hebes*"— and harangued the crowd to chant after them. *White Power! Today! Tomorrow! Forever!* It was chilling, but, as the Texas columnist Molly Ivins once said of a particularly nasty speech by the rabble-rousing Pat Buchanan at a Republican convention, it was "much more effective in the original German." Take away the virulent subject matter, it was a hootenanny, a rock concert, a pep rally, a feverish tent revival, followed by a bonfire. By ten o'clock a roar went up as the cross burst into flames, black smoke spiraling into the high sky, a full moon rising, chants of *White Power* sailing with it, and soon there was the firing of engines and the honking of horns and the mad dash to the gates so those who could afford the pay-per-view cable television fee might make it home in time to watch two black men pummel each other for the world's heavyweight championship. They would be rooting for Evander Holyfield, whom they could claim as a local hero on the basis of his having spent the first two years of his life in a weathered shack thirty miles away in Atmore.

IT APPEARED THAT the rally had come and gone without incident. Peanut, a big fan of the fights, was able to lock up the store at the regular hour on Saturday night in time to walk the path to his house and catch the fight. This was the one that would become infamous when

Mike Tyson bit off a chunk of Holyfield's ear, out of desperation or rage or mere madness, and that was what most of Peanut's customers were talking about on Sunday as they drifted into the store after church. There was little mention of the Klan rally. The two or three locals who admitted they had attended were laughing it off as a little harmless Saturday-night entertainment, surreal as it might have been, before moving on to speak of the weather and where the fish were biting.

Straight ahead lay the insufferable days of summer in the swamps, the crazy time, when the main piece of business was finding ways to escape weather that sometimes seemed like something right out of the Old Testament. In the spring there are the tornadoes, preceded by hellacious storms of hail tattooing tin roofs with the manic ferocity of the jazz drummer Gene Krupa on a roll, and in the early autumn there are the hurricanes swirling in from the Gulf with the power to shred roofing and uproot trees and drown what cotton hasn't already been harvested. The mild winters are the best time of all, with their toasty family-oriented holidays and homecomings that find scores of cars with out-of-state tags, chariots belonging to the young who had to emigrate to find work, crowding around the lonely trailers and shacks and modest houses strung out in the dark woods and the swamps or along the highway.

The summers meant scorching fifteen-hour days, two-week droughts under a merciless orange sun followed by torrents of rain making the mostly bulldozed roads virtually impassable, the incursion of bomber-size mosquitoes and no-see-'um chiggers and flying roaches and 'possums and armadillos ("'possum on the half shell") and alligator sightings in the marshes. The men who work the woods go out at daybreak and knock off around three o'clock in the afternoon to avoid the heat, and the itinerant construction workers have angled for summer jobs as far away from this hell as they can get. For the poor of both races there are huge whirring fans, rather than air conditioners, to stir the suffocating heat, and lots of time fishing or swimming in the streams and rivers under lush green canopies of water oaks and willows and sweet gum trees. But the main enemy during these stretches of days without end is boredom. The men have their work, if they haven't yet been chewed up by a chain saw or maimed by a timber rattler or crippled by a piece of machinery, but it is no place for women or for teenagers. You can watch only so many soap operas, catch only so many fish, swim for so many hours, drink so many beers, make so many trips to the scorching beaches of the Redneck Riviera. Where to go? What to do?

SEVEN

Wild in the Woods

—————

ON TUESDAY MORNING, the first day of July, the Klan rally now gone and more or less forgotten, Peanut arose early to open the store and make sure everything was in order so he could get away for his weekly shopping expedition. His routine was to buy most of his seafood at a wholesale market in Pensacola, Florida, and then his fresh meat and vegetables in Mobile, a journey requiring most of a day. Less than three weeks had passed since his beating and the long, delicate surgery that had saved his life, and he wasn't feeling so chipper—numbness in his arms and legs, dizzy spells, headaches, double vision, sleepless nights—but duty called. His route would cover about two hundred miles, in that heat and on hairy country roads fraught with logging trucks. By eight o'clock he had cranked his pickup and was on his way toward the bleak Florida Panhandle, "L.A.," and the Gulf Coast.

Soon after Peanut had left, a black man named Murray January was hitching his boat trailer to his reliable old black Ford pickup in hopes of a day on the water. A tall, slouching, deliberate man, Murray had recently gone into semiretirement as a sheriff's deputy for Baldwin County after sixteen years on the force. He still put in nineteen weeks every year at the Baldwin County courthouse, when court was in session, available for such duties as minding the metal detector at the door and directing traffic in the hallways, but his real value, to the solicitor David Whetstone, had always been as "our eyes and ears, an ombudsman for the folks" in Little River, that most distant corner of the county. He and his wife, Cora, had raised six remarkable daughters in their cramped little frame house in the woods a mile south of Ferguson Grocery, five of them now enjoying success in careers far from home, and he figured he had earned the right, at the age of sixty-three, to fish whenever he damned well felt like it.

Murray had pulled up out of the bulldozed clearing where his house and that of his seventy-two-year-old brother, Jesse, a retired sawyer, stand side by side beneath a grove of oaks and pines in sort of a country cul-de-sac, bumped onto Highway 59, stopped for some gasoline and live bait at Peanut's, continued up the highway and finally turned left at the Little River Cafe onto the paved Dixie Landing Road that would take him to the boat launch. He had just passed the turnoffs for Sawmill and Tommy John Earle Roads, less than a half-mile from the banks of the Alabama River, and was admiring the bucolic scene of Percy and Edith Cox's cattle munching in a pasture, when he did a double take. *Wait a minute, somethin' ain't right here.* Peering toward the stand of scraggly pines beyond the Coxes' pasture, he couldn't see the roof of St. Joe Baptist Church. The fish could wait.

Turning his rig around, Murray doubled back to Tommy John Earle Road and sloshed through the mud puddles left by a recent gully-washer. On the left was the stark clear-cut eighty-acre field fit for nothing but rats and snakes, and he expected to see Joe Dees's solitary little church coming up soon at a bend to the right. But when he reached the site of St. Joe, his heart leapt. The cinder-block walls were charred, the roof and its timbers and some cushions still smoldering, the whole thing apparently a total loss. At first he wondered if it had been struck by a bolt of lightning, which had zapped many an old farm shed back in the woods over the years, but couldn't remember if there had been a thunderstorm during the night. He continued up the bumpy road another three hundred yards to Tate Chapel AME, the neat little church where the one of his daughters who had chosen to stay in Little River served as secretary, and what he saw there told him that this had been no act of God. The double doors of the church were cocked haphazardly, sprung from their hinges, obviously kicked open. He got out of his truck and went inside for a closer look, and found that there had been clumsy attempts to set fire to this church, too, and that someone had even defaced the framed photos in the rear corridor that ran behind the choir box; a sort of African-American Wall of Fame, with images of a dozen black icons ranging from Booker T. Washington to Bill Cosby.

Back in his truck now, adrenaline pumping, Murray rumbled down the dirt road that runs beside Tate Chapel, Pat Haywood Road, named for an early black landowner. The road dead-ends after half a mile, at the weathered gray frame shack belonging to George Thomas, a seventy-three-year-old steward and trustee of the church. Bald and sinewy, Thomas was sitting in the dark of his cluttered screen porch, pulling on his boots, as it turned out, in preparation for moseying up to the church to mow the lawn that very morning. The bombastic old church deacon was aghast when he heard what Murray January was saying, said that he had noticed no unusual sounds during the night, simply could not believe what he was hearing. Murray slid into the cab of his pickup, got on his cell phone, and called it in to the Baldwin County sheriff's department. He was told to seal off both churches with yellow police-scene tape, which he always carried in the bed of his truck, and once he had done that, he and George Thomas sat amid the ruins and waited for the world to discover Little River, Alabama.

BY ELEVEN O'CLOCK in the morning, Highway 59 looked like a drag strip. About the only time the media ever wandered up the road as far as Little River, this last outpost in Baldwin County, was to update the tourist board's latest attempts to make something of the scant remains at Fort Mims or to produce features about the men and boys from the cities swarming to the woods for the opening of the various hunting seasons. This part of the county had always been a black hole as far as the media was concerned. But now the residents of that stretch of Highway 59 between I-65 and the Monroe County line were startled by the calamitous rush of a screaming caravan of fire trucks and police cruisers and television-station vans and carloads of reporters and photographers from the Mobile *Register* racing northward, past the rotting old barns and dilapidated trailers and tidy chapels and rolling meadows and deep forests, hell-bent for Little River. Most of the media were seeing the place for the first time.

When Murray January drove back to Peanut's to buy some jugs of Gatorade for the law enforcement people who had arrived and set up a field headquarters under the grove of trees at the Red Eagle gravesite—fire marshals, sheriff's deputies, FBI and ATF agents, Lt. Hoss Mack and David Whetstone, a representative of the National Church Arson Task Force—he found the warped old asphalt parking lot teeming with locals, both black and white, who had drifted in to see what in the world was going on. The killing of Tim Dees and the beating of Peanut Ferguson had been nothing like this. This being the first day of the month, "check day," some of the disabled and retired people from the distant swamps had blindly stumbled upon the scene as they rolled up in their belching old patched-up cars to await the arrival of the mail truck. Peanut, the "mayor," was still away, so now everyone was yelling questions at Murray that he couldn't or wouldn't answer. "Lightnin' get it, or what, Murray?" . . . "Joe have any insurance on that ol' place?" . . . "Wadn't nobody sleepin' in there, was they?" . . . "Who th' hell woulda done somethin' like that, anyways?" His truck loaded with drinks and snacks for the investigators, Murray implored them not to go to the scene, but they cranked their cars and trucks and followed him anyway, like vultures smelling roadkill.

Inside the yellow tapes, the investigators were at work: measuring, bagging, photographing every square inch of the two churches and their grounds. Fresh tire tracks were all over the place, up and down the dirt road connecting the two churches, and they found some odd ones that might be telling a story; evidence that one of the suspected three vehicles was a light pickup truck outfitted with one of those undersized temporary "donut" spares on its left front wheel. Sifting through the ashes inside the blackened hull of St. Joe Baptist—sofas and pews, Bibles and hymnals, ceiling fans and oscillating fans, the melted remains of a battery-operated wall clock bearing a depiction of the Last Supper—they soon determined that gasoline had been used to set fire to the curtains and a sofa, that at some point, curiously, someone had tried to quell the fire by tossing cushions outside and beating out the flames; that, without a doubt, it had been an arson. At Tate Chapel, farther down the road, there had been an unsuccessful attempt to set fire to the building, first to the inflammable drywall in the foyer and then to the frayed rope dangling from the steeple bell, after the doors had been knocked in. Hunkered over the white-washed concrete tables under the trees at Red Eagle's grave, grim marshals and deputies and agents were saving evidence in plastic bags and calmly speaking on cell phones to their offices back in Mobile and Bay Minette and even in Washington, D.C. Meanwhile, all around them, egrets and hawks, bulls and heifers, rattlers and moc-casins and alligators were going about their business on just another day of ungodly heat in the swamps and streams and pastures of dark-est south Alabama.

Joe Dees had driven into Bay Minette to do some shopping early that morning, before Murray had come upon the disaster at St. Joe, and found out about it around eleven-thirty when he happened to call his estranged wife, Shirley, from a pay phone inside the Kmart on the northern edge of the town. "I felt some anger," he would later say. "I felt some hurt. I felt some frustration. It was loud and busy where I was calling from, so I hung up and went into my secret closet with the Lord [tapping a finger on his heart]. And then I drove back as fast as I could, straight to the church, and there were all of the peo-ple: ATF, FBI, sheriff's deputies, reporters, television cameras. They had thousands of questions, and I didn't have any answers. I just didn't know what to say. I had to think it out." Dees hated this sort of thing, being in the public eye, due in part to the fact that he could never be certain whether his medication was working properly, whether he was stable or drifting toward another manic fit, but he knew he had to say *something*. The church was not insured, he told them, and it might take, oh, about eighty thousand dollars to rebuild it. In the meantime, he said, his congregants would probably crowd into his trailer on Sawmill Road until they could find another place to hold their Sunday services. Although he acknowledged that the killing of his son and the beating of Peanut Ferguson had "gotten people stirred up," he, like nearly everyone else, was pointing directly at the Klan rally as the triggering event. Then he tossed in some Christian boilerplate to satisfy the press: "The Lord wants me to be at St. Joe Baptist. . . . Whoever burned the building didn't get our church, because the church is in our hearts. . . . Satan is loose in this world. He's an evil being and he works on the hearts of people, but love is stronger than hate."

Peanut got back home around four o'clock in the afternoon, having been so out of pocket that he was completely unaware of the day's events, and ran smack into the roiling crowd in the parking lot of his own store. Typical of him, he cautiously drawled platitudes about how the folks in Little River were "just up here being poor together," how the races had always seemed to get along, that he had no idea who might have done it, and that he didn't know much either way about whether the Klan rally might have affected things. For the rest of that day, and into the next, the people of Little River, responding to an urban media corps that seemed to treat them like lost tribesmen discovered in a rain forest, expressed shock, dismay, and outrage. "It's bad enough to set fire to a trailer, but to set fire to a place that belongs to God and where people go to worship, now," began Herman Jarrell, a retired white man who had spent his entire life there, "well, whoever did it ought to be set on fire just like they did the church." James Eason, a twenty-nine-year-old member of St. Joe Baptist, reached into his 'sixty-nine Ford pickup and produced a baseball bat: "I see an arsonist, I'll use this on him." Another young black native, Ronald Brown, who commuted to his janitorial job at one of the schools in Bay Minette (and soon would take over as the driver of the infamous yellow school bus) so he could raise his two young daughters in the tranquillity of Little River, said the mood had changed since the Klan rally. "I used to drive down to Tensaw at night, when it's cooler, to see my mama, but now I'm scared about what might happen if I had a flat tire. The other night my wife and I drove up to the creek [at the Little River bridge], where somebody sprayed that Klan stuff, same place we all used to go swimming, and a bunch of white kids in a truck drove up in front of us and cut us off. I'm not fixin' to run, I'm just worried."

OVER THE NEXT few days, for the first time in history, the developments from Little River blared on the front page of the Mobile *Register* and led the nightly reports on television and radio stations up and down the Gulf Coast. Not many people up there had ever subscribed to any newspaper at all, using television and radio for their mindless entertainments and background music, but now they were scrambling to find a *Register* and gathering in front of their television sets and radios to learn the latest findings by all of these "outsiders," the investigators and reporters, who were spending their days roaming the backroads and hanging out at Peanut's store to interview anyone who came into their sights. Peanut and Joe Dees and Murray January and David Whetstone and Hoss Mack, plus a host of federal agents, were becoming familiar faces on the evening news. "Lookie there, ain't that Jeremy, Debbie and John's boy?" And, "When they gon' talk to the Klan? Bet they're behind it." Said Hannis Cumbie, in her eighties, living with her retired steelworker husband, Bill, in a comfortable old tin-roofed house just across the river: "That's just about the horriblest thing that's ever happened around here. I'm sure the Klan rally started it." Said Davida Hastie, seventy-three, northern Baldwin's historian, from her airy, decaying, story-and-a-half 1903 house in Stockton: "If they wanted to pick a church to burn down, they got the right one. That one [St. Joe Baptist] doesn't do much."

One of the more persistent of the reporters on the scene was Roy Hoffman, the *Register*'s "writer-in-residence," who had come across three white teenagers during his perambulations in Little River. On Wednesday, the day after the news broke, he talked to a red-haired teenager, Brandy Boone, who was waiting tables at the Dixie Landing Cafe. "They've [her customers] just been talking about the rally.

Somebody said [the Klan] did it. Somebody else said Joe Dees did it so he could get a new place. It's [the church] been there forever, and suddenly it's gone." In the parking lot at Peanut's, he found a group of kids. "I feel that whoever did it had to burn a church," said Kenneth Cumbie, no relation to Raymond or Bill and Hannis Cumbie, telling Hoffman that he had already been questioned by the agents. "If it was a bunch of teenagers who got drunk, they should come on out and say it."

And then Hoffman approached a lanky teenager named Alan Odom, pumping gas into his pickup, his arms decorated with home-made tattoos of scorpions and the like. He had heard that it had been a bunch of white kids, drinking or high on drugs, Odom said, but, "I don't know who done it, 'cause I don't really hang around with people like that." He said he had just graduated from high school in Uriah, was commuting to a construction job in Mobile, hadn't attended the Klan rally but knew many who had ("not the old ones, but the mid-twenties and thirties"), and that he thought the rally had "put the black-white in 'em."

Hoffman's tape recorder was running as he asked, "You won't go to your friends [then] and say, 'There's this guy who wants to talk to you'?"

"No chance," he kid said. "Think of what could happen."

"Why are you willing to talk to me?"

"I have nothing to hide. I'd like to see them find out what happened."

"Anything like this happen in the past?"

Odom said, "Just little minor stuff, like tearing mailboxes down, knocking windows out."

"Of the blacks?"

"Yeah."

"What on earth do drugs have to do with all of this?"

"They get high, or they get drunk, and they just go crazy," said Odom. "That's what causes it all, 'cause you already got it in your mind about doing it, but they won't do it until they get messed up. 'cause then they don't care."

"This could get even more involved?"

"That's what I'm thinking. That's what I'm thinking."

"With the Fourth of July coming up . . ."

"Right, right."

"Why Little River, though?"

"People don't care around here. The white people don't care what goes on. Most people through here are on drugs. The kids from here, to the bridge, everybody on the side of the road, on drugs. Everybody. It's just ridiculous. Cocaine, crank . . ."

"Crank?"

"Methamphetamine."

"It's like in a pill?"

"No, you snort it, like cocaine. It's like speed. It just wires you real, real bad."

"Where do people get the money?"

"I don't know."

INVESTIGATORS COULD HAVE "started making arrests the night of the first day," Tuesday, said David Whetstone, the D.A., a man of fierce political ambitions, "but we wanted to give 'em more time to squirm." The perpetrators had done a poor job of, well, covering their tracks, for it was the discovery of the singular tracks left by the donut spare tire on one of the vehicles that broke the case open. That truck, a white Nissan Z-71 pickup, belonged to Alan Odom— the same truck he had been gassing up at Peanut's while he was telling the *Register*'s Roy Hoffman that he didn't "hang out with people like that"—and the arrests came easily once they had picked up Odom at the home of his father, who was gone most of the time, working on dredge boats in the forbidding Louisiana marshes. Agents read him his Miranda rights, drove him to the courthouse in Bay Minette, gave him a lie-detector test, took a written statement, and by six-thirty in the afternoon of July 3 were charging him with helping set the fire at St. Joe and vandalizing Tate Chapel. Once they had gotten Odom to talking, under the threat of the new hate-crime law, the rest came easily. The others began blabbing like the frightened children they were.

The news hit Little River like a thunderclap on Sunday. Spread below the masthead on the front page of that morning's *Register* was a banner headline, POLICE LINK ARSON, KLAN RALLY, with mug photos of five white kids from Little River and Uriah: Jeremy and Brandy Boone, Alan Odom (all cousins, of the two sprawling but diverse Boone families in Little River), Kenneth Cumbie, and Michael Woods. Except for Jeremy Boone, whose parents' marriage had been famously off-and-on for most of his nineteen years, all of them were products of homes broken by divorce. Except for Kenneth Cumbie, who was twenty-one and had held a steady job at the Vanity Fair textile mill in Monroeville for three years, and Michael Woods, a ninth-grade dropout, all had graduated in May from J. U. Blacksher High School in Uriah. None seemed to have any concrete plans for the future, just vague hopes of finding a mate and some sort of manual labor. Three of them, Brandy and Jeremy Boone and Michael Woods, had attended the Klan rally. The picture that emerged in the paper that day was one of a daylong drinking party that had turned into a rural wilding on the night of a full moon, Brandy Boone allegedly shouting, "Hey, I know what, let's go burn the nigger church!" in the flurry, resulting in the destruction of St. Joe Baptist and the vandalism at Tate Chapel.

"Let's see how cool they are after a night in jail," Whetstone had said. They spent the night of Friday, the Fourth of July, in the Mobile Metro jail, among mostly hardened black adult criminals from the inner-city ghettos, and the arrangement had turned nasty. Two other products of J. U. Blacksher High, white boys of their acquaintance, happened to be locked up there on burglary charges, and when they commiserated with the "Little River Five," loudly proclaiming that their romp had not been racial, the remarks enraged seven black prisoners who were not strangers to jail cells. The blacks began to hassle the whites, even spitting on their food, and soon a brawl erupted. It was a rude welcome to the underside of a relatively big city that most Little River kids never dared visit except in emboldened groups, even if to see a movie. On Saturday morning, exactly one week following the Klan rally, the five were arraigned in Mobile's federal district court, wearing orange prison jumpsuits, handcuffed and crying, before being put into a van and driven to the Baldwin County jail in Bay Minette for their own safety.

The five were trucked back to Mobile on Monday morning for a bond hearing, and now they had their families with them. This had not been a simple achievement. The adoptive parents of Michael Woods had been visiting with relatives in Jacksonville, Florida, all week, leaving him and Alan Odom alone at the house of Odom's absent father, and they didn't hear about Michael's arrest until they got a call from him, from Mobile Metro, on Friday night. Odom's father, at work on the water in Louisiana, was reachable only by way of a marine phone number, a number that Odom's twice-divorced mother had not been given. Brandy Boone's mother, *thrice* divorced, already the victim of two heart attacks at the age of thirty-seven, seemed incapable of making decisions about anything in her current brittle state; and her father, a logger named "Doll" Boone, had never been much of a part of her life since her infancy. Jeremy Boone's bond would have to be posted by his maternal grandfather, Raymond Cumbie, the one who had shot and killed Joe Dees's brother years earlier, since the boy's father, John Boone, simply had no money. Kenneth Cumbie's estranged father had to be tracked down in Evergreen, sixty miles from Little River, where he was a high school teacher.

The adults, once assembled, seemed most concerned about the notion that the crimes had been racially motivated. "If that's so, what're you gonna do about Michael's sister-in-law?" said David Woods, Michael's stepfather, a strapping truck driver for one of the timber companies, pointing to the young black woman who had married into the family. His wife, Mary, said that her new little (black) grandson was "as much a part of our family as anybody." All strove mightily to make a point that their kids played with black friends all the time, admired the black prizefighter Evander Holyfield, and were, in fact, watching a video starring a black actor (Eddie

Murphy in *The Nutty Professor*) at one point during the fateful night. Kenneth Cumbie's father said that his son's bedroom, at the boy's grandparents' house in Uriah, was wallpapered with photos of basketball players, "not a one of 'em white." It was not a moot question. They had good reason to worry, because punishment under the new hate-crime law carried an enhanced federal sentence of ten years without parole.

For the time being, they were being charged with "conspiracy to intentionally deface, damage and destroy religious property by use of fire." No one as yet had been sentenced under the new law, in spite of the spate of recent church burnings, because in every case the arsonists, Klansmen all, had escaped the maximum penalty, on the advice of counsel, by pleading guilty and turning state's evidence. A conviction in court would mean up to twenty years in prison and fines of $250,000 and, most likely, restitution to Joe Dees's St. Joe Baptist Church. So they fully understood the gravity of their situation on that Monday morning when they were released on $25,000 signature bonds apiece, and given strict rules to follow while they went home and awaited a trial by jury sometime in the fall: parental custody, curfews of seven o'clock at night until six in the morning, and stay away from drugs, alcohol, guns, the two churches, and each other.

THE FEDS WOULD get first crack at the case in court, probably in October, and maybe the kids were fortunate on that count. The county's district attorney, David Whetstone, was savvy and aggressive, the sort of man who causes other attorneys to play hookey just to watch him perform in court, and he was licking his chops on this case and hoped, at the very least, to have a shot at it in the winter or spring if any questions remained unanswered. A native of south Alabama, graduate of the University of Alabama's law school, he had built a strong liberal reputation in his three decades at law; especially as a young aide to then-Lieutenant Governor Bill Baxley, who had driven Governor George Wallace to distraction for years. He had been Baldwin County's D.A. since 1984, and time seemed to be running out for him to pursue his dream of becoming the state's attorney general. Short, balding, bespectacled, a clone of the actor Robert Duvall when angered, he wanted the Klan.

It was a few days after the kids had posted bond and gone home, moving into the thick of summer now, and Whetstone was rocking back and forth in a swivel chair in his office. Throughout the courthouse, clerks were hunched over computers, filing records, making phone calls. One of them, coincidentally, happened to be Debbie Boone, mother of Jeremy Boone, one of the few women in Little River with a decent job.

"They're just kids," somebody said. "Kids aren't buying the Klan these days, are they?"

"Tell that to the folks in Boligee and Greene County," he said, referring to two of the other places in Alabama where Klansmen had admitted burning black churches.

"Maybe they were just bored and drunk."

"They've been bored and drunk before, but they never burned a church."

"So it's the Klan."

"Alcohol and testosterone is an unholy mixture as it is," he said, getting warmed up. "That's the gasoline. Who do you think was the match? We've got a total of eleven suspects now, in all, and we think eight of 'em were at the rally. Eleven kids met at a house and drank about a hundred beers before they went out and burned a church to the ground. *Whose* house? *Whose* beer? These are poor kids from up in the boonies. Think about it."

"What about the parents?"

"Good question. They could be Klan, they could be sympathizers. We don't know, and it's beside the point." The phone rang. More trouble between the feuding families in Rabun and Perdido. "Look," he said, "I think both sides want to blame the Klan. The 'Evil Empire,' you know. It helps the kids, the parents, *everybody,* to say the Klan put 'em up to it. Otherwise, you've just got a bunch of kids on the loose, running wild, with nobody looking out for 'em, no sense of what's right. I hate to think it's come to that up there."

EIGHT

Five Kids

––––––––

WHAT MOST PEOPLE were wondering was whether the Klan rally
had inspired the kids to go on their rampage, exactly forty-eight
hours after the cross burning; a question leading to catchy headlines
in the Mobile *Register* and breathless teasers on the television stations
up and down the Gulf Coast and fodder for spirited debates at
Peanut's and the County Line Package Store and Dixie Landing Cafe
and all of the other places where people congregate in Little River
and its environs. Opinions seemed to be hotly divided, and not nec-
essarily along racial lines. Peanut couldn't say for sure, either way, but
he worried that Phil Smith, the Klansman, would be "asking for real
trouble if he keeps this up." His cashier at the store, Sharon Scott, was
adamantly certain that the rally was at the root of the wilding; period,
no ifs, no question mark. Most of Little River's blacks, quietly smoldering with disgust, felt it was a moot point, the same old crap, sins of
the fathers, further proof of what the white folks *really* thought of
them. The parents of the five, of course, had gone into deep denial
that racism had anything to do with it at all, and some were calling
Joe Dees not with apologies or commiserations but with persistent
attempts to get him to say publicly that this hadn't been racist. And it
seemed a given that federal prosecutors, armed with the new hate-
crime law, intended to make that connection.

But there was one philosophical point that the more substantial
old-timers of the community, people like Peanut and Murray January

and Joe Phillips, agreed upon: that this generation of kids had grown up in an atmosphere vastly different from the one they had known. "We thought we were really something if we sneaked off to the woods and smoked a cigarette and had a beer," Peanut was saying one day. Then, remembering one of the first trips he had ever made to big bad Mobile as a teenager: "A friend said he was going to show me the *real* city one night. We saw all these good-looking women hanging around on a corner and I said, 'Man, that blonde's really something, isn't she?' and he said, 'Her name's *Frank.*' Then we went into a bar with some rooms upstairs, and when the lady that ran it saw I was drinking Cokes and wasn't buying any drinks for the girls, she came over and said, 'What's your *problem,* sonny?' I told her there didn't seem to be anybody my age and she said, 'Look, kid, I ain't runnin' no damned kindergarten here,' and kicked me out." They were country boys, so many Huck Finns and Tom Sawyers, raised by parents who held a switch in one hand and a Bible in the other, and their pleasures were simple. The fathers worked while the mothers stayed at home to keep a tight leash on the kids as they fished, hunted, frolicked in the river, and shot baskets in the driveway. Even if they were lucky enough to have a car, their options were few.

But "this bunch," as the older ones called them, with some disgust, had been thrust into a meaner new world before they could handle it. The white kids saw this universe they were inheriting as a candy store, a carnival of previously forbidden delights: people fornicating (or appearing to) right there on X-rated cable television, whiskey and beer everywhere, cheap drugs less than an hour's drive away. There were no stay-at-home mothers anymore, since both parents not only in Little River but all across America now had to work to pay the bills; nor, in such an isolated hamlet, a library or a YMCA or a community center of any sort; nor kindly resident academics or doctors or preachers to patiently guide them; not even friends who had somehow overcome all of this to succeed in school, peers whom they could emulate. So they were stuck and in danger of entering a cycle: boredom and despair leads to drugs and alcohol leads to crime leads to jail leads back to the beginning, the cycle repeating itself.

The only way they could see to get out of it was to turn sixteen, get a driver's license, finagle a set of wheels, thus presuming adulthood, and ride away from it all.

It wasn't the same with the black kids, because black parents in Little River had been working with a different agenda for a long time. *You've already got two strikes on you when you're born black in Alabama,* was the black parents' mantra, by way of explaining the remarkable number of black kids who continue to stream off to college from their unpromising roots on Sawmill Road and in Couglan Swamp. They had to try harder, and they and their parents knew it. Most of the white parents, meanwhile, had been making a critical mistake; they assumed that everything would work out fine in their favor, just like it always had, simply because of the color of their skin. It was as though they thought it was still the time of their own youth, the pre–civil rights day, when George Wallace was king and the Confederate flag waved o'er their domain and an honest day's labor brought a good day's pay. All of that was gone now—white supremacy, untethered race-baiting, an economy tilted their way—but they had missed the news. In contrast to all of the black kids from Little River who had gone to college over the years, only one member of the two white Boone families had been educated beyond high school in the last three generations; and he, while a cop in Bay Minette, had gotten himself one of those night-school law degrees.

And the more the responsible people of the community chewed on it, took a longer view of the lives those five kids had lived, the closer they came to realizing that something like this had been bound to happen, sooner or later. "Each divorce is like the death of a small civilization," the novelist Pat Conroy once wrote, and the Little River landscape was littered with fractured marriages. Brandy's mother, Susan, couldn't stay married, and her father, Doll, had hardly given her the time of day as he went through two more wives. Jeremy's parents had clung to their messy marriage for twenty years, saying it was for the boy's sake, but they had been estranged for what seemed like half of that time. Michael Woods, virtually an orphan at birth, had never known his blood parents. Kenneth Cumbie's parents had broken up when he was little more than a tyke, and he had never approved of his parents' succession of new spouses over the years any more than he liked living with his aging paternal grandparents. Alan Odom's father had spent almost all of his time working in far-off Louisiana since the divorce, and the boy and his two siblings were latchkey kids, their father two states away, their mother working long hours at two jobs while engaged in an ongoing search for the right man. In short, not a single one of the five kids had experienced a normal childhood under the close watch of caring birth parents. Now, in their late teens, they seemed to feel they had only each other. In the spring, Kenneth and Jeremy had gotten drunk with two others on a spree in Bay Minette and, returning home in broad daylight, had torched the car that had been abandoned on the highway near Tensaw simply because it was there; and that was what their lives had come to. Come to think of it, the sages at Peanut's were saying now, Brandy was just the type to get all worked up, just trying to be one of the boys, and blurt something like, "I know what, let's go burn the nigger church." Come to think of it, since school let out they'd been running together like a pack of wolves. Come to think of it, those kids never had much of a chance.

IN THE CASE of Michael Woods, the boy was cursed from the very beginning of his life. He was born in April 1979 to Lauren Watson, father unknown, but at eight months was adopted by Lauren's sister Patricia and her husband, David Woods. The baby was bruised and badly undernourished, and Lauren (*law-RAIN*) "was still single and didn't want a baby around," says Woods. Soon after, Lauren shot and killed her black boyfriend when he tried to climb through her bedroom window during one of their spats and was sent off to serve two years at the Julia Tutwiler state prison for women near Montgomery.

But Michael was too young to know about all of that. His adoptive parents, his aunt Patricia and her husband, David Woods, gave him some stability in the early years of his life. Woods was a strapping, swarthy man, three-fourths Choctaw-Creek, a native of Uriah, whose father had spent his working life in the dye plant of Vanity Fair's textile mill in Monroeville. David had learned to work on diesel trucks at a trade school in Mobile, after graduating from J. U. Blacksher High, and would spend nearly eighteen years as a mechanic and truck driver ("I'll drive anything they've got") for the Scott and Kimberly-Clark paper companies. He and Patricia gave birth to two daughters of their own, Nicole and Jessica, and it was "a pretty normal family for the first four or five years. The kids was good and we had no problems." But then, when Michael was about eight years old, Patricia announced that "we were in her way, she had missed her teenage years and wanted to go back and find 'em, so we busted up and I got the kids."

The freedom Patricia had sought didn't turn out as she had planned. She married and soon divorced a man named Williams, keeping his surname as she then moved in with a construction worker in Little River, David Gentry, and began to drink ("If you catch her sober these days, you're doing good," says Woods). But it appeared that the boy, Michael, might finally be finding some love and comfort when his adoptive father married a divorcee from Jacksonville, Florida, Mary Shepherd Sturdivant, two years after Patricia's departure from the marriage. Mary brought two young sons to the marriage, Jason and Joey, and now David Woods was wrapping his strong arms around a covey of five kids. They lived out in the country, just beyond Uriah in a hamlet known as Goodway, where Woods was putting the finishing touches on a big new house across the road from his aging parents. He was a man's man, a good-natured giant who thrived on work, and Mary was a sweet, quiet woman who loved her man and doted on her children. "For the first couple of years there was some resentment [over his remarriage], but now they think more of Mary than they do me. Michael and Mary have always been close."

There was something missing, though, with young Michael Woods. Maybe it's true, that the course of our lives is fixed by the time we are about four years old. There had been too much calamity in his formative years, long before he had started school, and David could see trouble when his adopted son entered Blacksher High. "He hated school and had a hard time fitting in." Michael, like many of the boys, had a thing for the perky redhead, Brandy Boone, and she spent many hours trying to tutor him in basic English and math. He was a woefully thin redhead, not strong enough for competitive sports, often coming home bruised from playground fights. He dropped out of high school after one year and began working odd construction jobs with his uncles, and helping his adoptive father build the new house. He would work at dull labor all day, while all of his old friends were involved in the teen rituals of high school life, the social clubs and courtship, the pep rallies and football games, and when they got home every afternoon he was ready to party. The fun in his life, what little there was of it, was centered some twenty-five miles away in Little River. Among these friends he could be forgiven for being barely literate; in his scrawled affidavit to the agents following his arrest, there were seventy-two misspellings in the six-hundred-word document: "a statmint witch concist of 4 pages . . . I wasn't in my wright mind . . . the chirch curtins . . . compleated 8 yeas of school and can read and right . . ."

MICHAEL'S BEST BUDDY down there was Alan Odom, another lanky kid just six months older, who had also gone through some trauma of his own at home. His father was Ted Odom, a hardworking man like David Woods, but the problem there was that Ted's work had always kept him far from Little River, mostly in the marshes of Louisiana, where he labored in virtual isolation on dredge boats that were constantly clearing the waterways for shipping traffic. Alan was left at home with his mother, Darlene, one of the two spirited daughters of Ray and Kathryn Boone, a brassy redhead programmed to take no crap from anybody. Alan was thirteen, about to enter high school, when his parents divorced and Darlene promptly married Greg Middleton, who worked for the area's power company. Darlene moved in with Middleton, up toward Uriah in southern Monroe County, hoping to take her three Odom kids with her—Alan, Wendy, and Tommy—but none took too kindly to Mom's new husband.

"Alan flat didn't like Greg," says Darlene, who ended that marriage three years later, "and he changed a lot then. He wound up blaming me for the divorce from Ted because I never took up for myself. He listened to things he shouldn't have listened to. I never said, 'Alan, this is why me and your daddy's not married.' I thought he was too young to understand. For years, then, he thought it was all Mama's fault, because that's what Daddy said. He was sixteen when he finally asked, and I told him, but he's still not over it." By the time of the Klan rally and the subsequent night of wilding, Darlene was living in a trailer on a ridge some eight miles north of Peanut's store, with Wendy and Tommy. But Alan, still on the outs with his mother, was spending his nights either with his paternal grandparents, four miles down the same county road from Darlene, or next door to them, alone, in the house his mostly absent father had built on stilts.

Unlike his best friend, Michael Woods, Alan was competitive and athletic. He had played basketball for a while with a team sponsored by the Little River Baptist Church, and in his senior year at J. U. Blacksher High, so small a school that it competed in the state of Alabama's lowest classification, he went out for football and was startled to find that he loved it. "He was tall and skinny, you know, and they made him a pass-catcher and he turned out to be real good at it," says Darlene. "He told me, after he'd graduated, that he wished he'd played football all the way through school." He "could have been a straight-A student if he'd applied himself," but what he wanted to do was "get a truck, find a job, maybe go to work with his daddy or end up on construction work with my two brothers [Danny and Roger Boone]," who spend months at a time on jobs all over the country.

Darlene, herself, is a piece of work. Hefty, freckled, with the flaming red hair of that strain of Boones who had migrated to Little River two generations earlier, from a town in neighboring Escambia County called Booneville, she and her sister Susan (Brandy Boone's mother) had learned to fend for themselves as little girls. Their father,

Ray Boone, a hard man with a close-cropped gray marine corps buzz cut, once served time for making moonshine and described himself these days as a "disabled construction worker." Never holding a full-time salaried job, he had raised the girls in a masculine world of two brothers and a passel of uncles. Darlene worked where she could find it, most recently as a cook in the Boone-owned Little River Cafe and as a clerk at the County Line Package Store, and since her second divorce she had been busy, as the country song goes, looking for love in all the wrong places. On the night of the Klan rally, she had taken along her niece Brandy while she went "looking for a friend," and having no luck, left Brandy behind with all of those fire-breathing yahoos at the rally to continue her search at the Frosty Acres road-house ("Live Band Fri–Sat Nites") some thirty miles away in Escambia County. "I'm the only one in Little River not married or living common-law with somebody," she said. "It's not easy, being single around here. I don't have a life."

AS THE ONLY girl in the bunch, and the one whose alleged call to "burn the nigger church" had lit the torch, as it were, Brandy Nicole Boone was getting the most attention from the media and the local gossips. Given her need for action, to be at the center of whatever was going on, she probably liked it like that. She was another of the redheaded Boones, born in December 1978 to young parents whose own fathers were fourth cousins: Doll, now forty-one, and Susan, now thirty-seven. Brandy had been known as a quiet and pretty girl until she got a driver's license and a little blue Toyota halfway through high school, at which time she "turned wild," as the folks down at Peanut's put it. "I do funny things when I drink too much beer," she told one of the agents during her interrogation, and that had been happening a lot lately. She had become one of the more popular girls at J. U. Blacksher High, where she was a decent student and worked on the school newspaper, and she had so many boyfriends that the name of her latest at any given time kept the grapevine humming. She laughed, she partied, she had her own car, and she was ready for anything; everybody's girl, in the middle of the spontaneous parties that might begin after school at the burger-and-shakes hangout in Uriah and end late at night under the trees at Red Eagle's grave in Little River.

But there was another side to Brandy, usually seen when the party was over or when she had been rejected by another boyfriend, and it had taken a toll. Here she was, eighteen and just graduated from high school, and behind her back there were people clucking about how she "used to be so pretty." With no marketable talents or plans for a career, she worked as a waitress at the few fish-and-hamburger eateries in the area, the Country Kitchen in Uriah, Dixie Landing Cafe, and the Boones' family cafe in Little River. Her permanent bedroom was in her mother's house on the paved Gantt Road, next door to her grandparents, Ray and Kathryn Boone, but that house wasn't much of a home. Her mother, Susan, had already suffered two heart attacks and gone through three divorces, given birth to two more girls by two different husbands, held a part-time job looking after Kenneth Lambert, the one paralyzed when he came upon the two logging trucks running side-by-side that foggy morning at the school-bus hour, and was going through a series of boyfriends herself. ("Susan's house is looking great," one of the old nesters said. "It's like she'll have a screen-porch man for a while, then a fireplace guy, and then a fellow good at flooring.") Now they were saying the same thing about Susan that they had been saying of her daughter: *and she used to be so pretty.*

Brandy's desperate need to be loved, to have a boyfriend she could hold on to, surely could be traced to the sense of rejection she shared with her mother. Like mother, like daughter. Brandy's father, Clayton "Doll" Boone, Jr., now lived with his third wife in a fine new house near the intersection of Highway 59 and Dixie Landing Road, in full view of anyone passing on Little River's two busiest roads, but it was a place she never visited. Said Peanut: "I can't imagine how she must feel, passing her father's house every day but never talking to him." Doll cuts a fancy figure when he isn't in the woods with his father and his five brothers: graying neatly cropped hair and beard, ruddy face, small but powerful frame, starched jeans, pair of resplendent gray snakeskin cowboy boots. But he had left before she had a chance to know him, to be replaced by all of those men sniffing around after her mother, and the lesson she must have learned from all of that is clear. Men leave.

And so there were sightings only now and then of the two, mother and daughter, in the summer and on into the fall, as the date of the trial in Mobile of the Little River Five approached. Susan, alone again for the most part, donning sunglasses and hustling her two younger daughters into a silver van with darkly tinted windows, to drive across the highway and spend the day looking after a man in a wheelchair while the girls splashed in his pool. Brandy, under house arrest from sundown to sunup, spending her days waiting tables at the hole-in-a-wall Country Kitchen in Uriah, tending to the needs of the cotton farmers and cattlemen and loggers who crowded the Formica tables for long storytelling lunches, with plenty of time to ponder the latest boyfriend who had ditched her: Jason Sturdivant, Michael Woods's twenty-one-year-old stepbrother, who had dated Brandy for two years before marrying a young black girl who had already given birth to another man's child.

ALTHOUGH HE WAS an only child, Brandy's cousin Jeremy Boone had every reason to feel his family was in shambles, even though his parents had never divorced. "I remember seeing him at Peanut's one day when he was about twelve," says Joe Witherington, "and when I asked him, 'How's it going, Jeremy?' he just dropped his head and said, 'Aw, my parents are separated again.'" His mother, the luscious Deborah Cumbie, had quit school and left home at the age of six-teen, ostensibly to marry a fellow named Jack Odom but in fact to be with John Boone. Debbie's father, Raymond Cumbie, the one who had killed Joe Dees's brother, had forbidden his beautiful young blonde daughter to marry John on the grounds that "they were kin, and I don't believe in that. When she left to marry Odom, it was just a tool to see John." John Boone, an uncle to Doll, was a strapping broad-chested galoot who worked when he ran out of money, but he fell deeply in love with one of the prettiest women Little River has ever seen. "Debbie could have married a lawyer, anybody, but she chose John," says Joe Witherington, "and getting her to marry him was probably the greatest moment in John's life."

All of these women, looking for love. There was Michael Woods's adoptive mother, Patricia Williams, bailing out of a marriage because she had "missed my teenage years"; and Alan Odom's mother, Darlene, going to look for a boyfriend at a Klan rally; and Susan Boone, having three children by three men, but still in the hunt. Debbie had sat by, as a young girl, and learned from one of the best. Her mother, Carol Cumbie, said Raymond, was a "runaround woman who liked to honky-tonk and be with different men." She had scores of them in her time, to hear Raymond tell it, causing many ruptures in their marriage (and many lustful thoughts in the minds of young boys who used to go to a store where she worked in hopes she would bend over, with her silicone-enhanced 38-DD breasts, to scoop some ice cream). Carol divorced Raymond a second and final time in 1984, to marry a man the same age as her daughter Debbie, then twenty-six, and met her end one night soon after; they had a spat after leaving Frosty Acres, she got out of the truck on a lonely backcountry road, and her body was found the next morning with tire tracks up one side and down the other. It was ruled an unsolved hit-and-run, but don't tell that to the Cumbies.

And don't try to tell Raymond Cumbie that his daughter's one-week disappearance in 1972, when she was fourteen, was anything but an abduction. "Carol and me and Debbie was staying in a motel in Colorado while I was working out there, and there was a hippie with one of those vans painted with flowers and all staying at the same place. One day she just disappeared, and a week later she got away from the guy in Tampa long enough to call some relatives there. The guy had kidnapped her, raped her, drove her all the way to Florida. I mean, that's the Mann Act, taking a minor across state lines for sex, but the law didn't do nothing about it. See, anybody who's had dealings with the law like I have knows it's rotten from top to bottom. . . ." It would be two years later that Debbie would drop out of high school to marry just to get out of the house, then divorce and marry John Boone, and give birth to Jeremy. Soon, to her credit, she was earning a GED high school diploma, learning secretarial skills at a community college, then landing a job as a clerk at the Baldwin County courthouse that gave her independence and leverage in her tempestuous marriage to John Boone. "They'd go dancing at clubs," said Joe Witherington, "and she'd drive John nuts dancing with other guys. She had him by the tail."

Jeremy had grown up amidst this upheaval, being dragged all over the country, from Richmond to Oklahoma City, while his father and his grandfather worked at jobs ranging from heavy construction to landscaping. John "would work awhile, complain he'd hurt his back, draw workmen's compensation for two or three years while he sat back and smoked dope," says Raymond, "and he finally got a settlement for forty thousand dollars." For much of that period the three were living with Raymond and Carol, in their house near Peanut's on Highway 59 in Little River, and if Jeremy had a father figure it was his grandfather, Raymond, who not only had killed a man but also served time for his part in a botched marijuana sale. "John didn't spend any money on Jeremy because he and Debbie spent it all," says Raymond. "I bought him a car when he was in the eleventh grade, and a computer when he was planning to study at Faulkner Community College and working the second shift at Southern Aluminum. I bought him one of those jet-ski boats, paid for his lawyer in this mess, even gave a little money to St. Joe and Tate Chapel to show it wasn't a racist crime. I know I've spoiled the boy, but he and Debbie are about all I've got left."

RAYMOND HAD ALSO come up with the cash to bail out Kenneth Cumbie, the twenty-one-year-old from Uriah, who was but a faint relation to his side of the family. "I'd gotten to know him a little bit lately. He was one of the boys who used to shoot baskets right here in my driveway, both black and white, nothing racist about any of 'em, and I didn't know much about him but I kinda felt sorry for him." Most of the people in Little River felt that way about Cumbie. He was the one of the five whose involvement had come as a surprise, even though they knew he had joined Jeremy and two others in the random torching of the abandoned car near Tensaw around the time of the Klan rally. "I'd seen him over the years, but not much," said Sue Ferguson. "But then he started running with Jeremy and I remember one day he showed up with this [skinhead] haircut and I wondered what was going on. I mean, he was older and quieter than the others and he'd had a regular job for a long time."

These Cumbies were rooted up the road in Uriah, and the one thing that Kenneth shared with the four others arrested in the St. Joe arson was his coming from an unhappy home. He was barely of school age when his parents divorced, and for most of his life he had been faced with three options about where he might call home: with either parent, or with his paternal grandparents in Uriah. The boy wasn't particularly happy at any of those places. "I remarried and had two children," said his father, Robert Cumbie, a high school teacher in Evergreen, about sixty miles from Little River. "Kenneth didn't especially approve of my second wife, but mostly he felt I cared more for my new kids than I did him. His mother [now living in St. Petersburg, Florida] has married four more times, and he couldn't get along with any of her husbands. About the best he could do was live with his grandparents in Uriah, but his grandfather was a retired military man who was very strict on him, probably too strict, so he wasn't happy there either, until his grandfather died."

To a father who had graduated from Troy State University and devoted his life to teaching, it hurt when Kenneth showed no desire to attend college. "His grades were good, but it just didn't appeal to him." Instead, he took a job in the dye plant at Vanity Fair in Monroeville, moved in with his grandparents, bought a Ford Ranger pickup, and found girlfriends; all in all, a pretty dull life for someone who had just turned twenty-one. The best times he had ever known, in fact, might have been when he was a basketball player for the J. U. Blacksher High Bulldogs. "He loved it and he was good," said his father. Robert Cumbie would argue that the arson couldn't have been racially inspired because his son's bedroom walls were covered with pictures of black basketball players, but the argument seemed troubling when he expanded on Kenneth's passion for basketball. "I tried to make as many games as I could, but he started playing what you might call 'black' basketball. You know, all of that flamboyant stuff with the high-fives and dunks and celebrations. I came over for a game one time and told him beforehand that if he kept it up I'd quit coming to the games. Well, he pulled the same stuff that night, maybe just to test me, so I never went to see him play again."

An intense, serious man who could be characterized as a control freak—tightly wound, precise, well-groomed in the manner of the eternally young rock 'n' roll entrepreneur Dick Clark—Robert Cumbie seemed to be more puzzled than any of the other parents about the turn of events. "Kenneth was raised as a Christian," he said. "I think it really was a case of being at the wrong place at the wrong time. It's strange, isn't it, how timing can play such a part? He was with his girlfriend earlier that night of the party and the church burning. Usually, she would start complaining whenever he said he had to leave her to go somewhere. She'd throw a fit. But some of her friends had recently told her to back off, give him some room, and this night she did. That's how he wound up at the party, and finally at St. Joe Baptist."

TRACKING DOWN THE kids and arresting them, in such a small community, had been a cakewalk for the various lawmen who had come rushing to Little River. The key clue, of course, had been the donut tire tracks left by Alan Odom's pickup. The agents had already heard from one Mickey Pumphrey, an employee of the power company, who had loaned Alan his tools and helped put on the spare that night when the tire went flat on the dirt road in front of his house. Pumphrey had gone to the Little River Cafe, where Darlene was cooking, to apprise her that they were looking for her son. "That was Thursday, July the third," she said, "and when I got off work and was driving home I passed his daddy's house, and the ATF was all in the yard and Alan and Michael [Woods] was out there with 'em. I turned and went back and I asked one of 'em, 'What's the problem?' and he says, 'We'll have 'em back in a little while.' And Alan says, 'Mama, it ain't nothing to worry about. They're just gonna take us down there [to Bay Minette] and talk to us for a while and they're gonna bring us back.' And I said, 'Aw-right,' tried not to panic. 'If you need me for anything, call me at Kenneth's [Lambert], 'cause I'm fixin' to take Wendy and Tommy to the pool.' Alan just never came back home."

Brandy's arrest was a bit more traumatic. The ATF and others had spoken to her briefly on that same day, but on Friday, the Fourth of July, four ATF agents in a black car came looking for her. Finding no one at her mother's house on Gantt Road, the address on the warrant for her arrest, they tried her grandparents' home next door. Ray Boone, the bullish patriarch, answered the door and said Brandy and her mother were at Kenneth Lambert's and it would be easier if he led them there. They found the mother and her daughters swimming and laughing, the makings for a July Fourth barbecue already sizzling on the grill, and one of the agents told Brandy that she hadn't been "entirely truthful with us." Sopping wet, wrapped in a towel, she was hustled into the car for "a little ride," squeezed between two menacing agents, a hulking white man in wraparound sunglasses and a persistent black female, who claimed that Brandy had admitted to making the "nigger church" remark. Her family didn't hear from her again until around nine-thirty that night.

Meanwhile, on that same afternoon of the Fourth, three carloads of ATF agents rolled up and blocked the driveway of the house Raymond Cumbie had bought for Debbie and John Boone, a few hundred yards down Highway 59 from his own home. John and Debbie were hosting a family cookout attended by Raymond ("I'd invited a couple of girlfriends, but neither one of 'em knew I was seeing the other one"), his sister Betty and her common-law husband, Leroy Boone, and some friends. "I couldn't believe it," said Raymond. "There was about seven or eight of 'em [agents] and they were walking around the house and yard, checking it out, before they banged on the door. John had fried some fish and we'd already finished eating. The agents said they wanted to talk to Jeremy. He'd spent the night on the river with some buddies, so John had to go get in a boat and bring him back. Jeremy acted surprised about everything and I told him, 'Don't tell 'em nothing.' They carried him to Bay Minette, and then they cuffed him and chained him and took him to Mobile." The agents found Kenneth Cumbie at his grandmother's house in Uriah, where they manacled him in the front yard, to complete their roundup before the sun had fallen on the Fourth of July. "I know how they work," said Raymond Cumbie. "When they had Kenneth in the car, they asked him if he knew his 'granddaddy' had once killed a man. Hell, they knew we was hardly related. They just wanted to get those kids shook up."

NINE

Cleanup

KIMBERLY-CLARK, THE last of the big paper corporations to still be harvesting trees in northern Baldwin County, made it a company policy to help out in times of need by cleaning up debris left in the wake of such calamities as tornadoes or hurricanes or fires. It was pro bono work, a little public relations gig "for the good of the community." As soon as the investigators were finished combing through the remains of St. Joe Baptist Church and had removed the yellow police-line tapes, the company ordered a crew to run over to Tommy John Earle Road and clean up the mess left by the arson. One of the men assigned to the job was David Woods, the adoptive father of Michael Woods, and he recognized the irony as he drove up in a company dump truck. "It was a mess, all right," he said, trying to visualize his son setting fire to the curtains with a cigarette lighter on that night. The crew made quick work of it, and when Woods had hauled off the last load of charred cinder block and burnt furniture piled into his truck by a bulldozer, little evidence remained that there had ever been a building on the site. Soon, nature reclaimed the little piece of land: weeds sprouted, snakes and field mice returned, bright green needles grew high in the pines where they had been scorched. The only signs that there once had been human traffic there were the forlorn creosoted pole holding the perpetually busted street light, and the rusted propane gas tank. St. Joe Baptist was gone from the face of the earth, with hardly a trace.

Also gone, just as suddenly and mysteriously as it had appeared, was the Alabama White Knights graffiti that had been sprayed on the bridge over the Little River in advance of the Klan rally. Phil Smith, the Klansman, was checking his mail after dark, lying low, as were most of the other people of a hamlet whose serenity had been so rudely interrupted. Reporters got nowhere when they came around to record reactions, getting a "Go-to-hell!" as they asked for comments through closed doors where the five kids were sequestered under house arrest. The only visitors to Little River these days were lawyers representing the two sides as they prepared for the trial at the federal courthouse in Mobile, scheduled for late October.

There had been a flurry of interest in the arson and vandalism from well-meaning outsiders. A professor of sociology at USA in Mobile had opened a St. Joe rebuilding fund with $1,000. A general fund had been set up at a bank in Bay Minette to receive donations, that one seeded by a check of $5,000 from the Alabama Baptist Convention in Montgomery. The Stockton Presbyterian Church had sent a gift certificate worth $3,000 toward building materials from Swift Lumber Company in Atmore. Another church in Stockton had donated several rows of old pews found in storage, depositing them in the weeds behind Dees's trailer, where they lay exposed to the weather. A grant of $30,000 might be available from the nonprofit National Council of Churches, based in New York, if Joe Dees could file papers showing he and his church could handle it. ("I don't know about that," said Peanut. "His sister Margaret is church secretary, and she's about the only one of my customers I have to pester about paying their bill at the store.") An architect from Mobile, Jackie McCracken, was offering to design a new church and waive the $9,000 fee. But from the whites of Little River, there was mostly silence.

That was in keeping with an essay that appeared on the Op-Ed page of the *New York Times* on July 14, two weeks after the attacks on Tate Chapel and St. Joe. It was written by Mary Frances Berry, chairman of the United States Commission on Civil Rights, who had gone to Alabama, Mississippi, and Louisiana with the National

Church Arson Task Force to conduct forums in towns where some of the more than one hundred black churches had been burned. "[We] found that though there was a wave of outside support for rebuilding, the already poor race relations in many communities failed to improve," she wrote, adding that, conversely, there had been racial polarization. "The only whites who came to the public forums were one or two politicians whose votes depend on blacks, a reporter or two, and the transcriber." She quoted a seventy-three-year-old black preacher in Boligee, Alabama, a three-hour drive north of Little River on country roads, whose church had been torched along with two others there: "Remarking on the lack of interest among local whites in helping, he said that in his town blacks and whites 'were taught to be against each other' from childhood."

Peanut had immediately told Dees that the store was available if he wanted to put on an auction or any other sort of fund-raising event, a kind offer that went unused for the simple fact that Little River's blacks hardly owned anything worth auctioning, and that was the extent of interest from Little River's whites until Joe got a call one day in July from Raymond Cumbie. Raymond said that he and John Boone wanted to hold a community meeting at the Little River Holiness Church, a fund-raiser and show of support for the two black churches, and he would like for him to come and speak. "I thanked him and I might've said maybe, but there was no way I was going to go," Dees said later. "Raymond Cumbie killed my brother, you know. And if he and John Boone were suddenly churchgoers, it was news to me." The event was held on a Saturday in mid-July, and about the only people who came were Raymond and John, the grandfather and father of Jeremy Boone. "I wrote a seven-hundred-dollar check to Joe, and three hundred for Tate Chapel," Raymond said, "just trying to show it wasn't racist." He was similarly rebuffed when he called someone at Tate Chapel, offering to pay the bill for all repairs, "but he just said, 'Naw, we don't want to do it that way.' Didn't hardly even thank me. Hell, all I wanted to do was help out."

THE MEN OF Tate Chapel had learned long before to be self-sufficient, to give the white man a wide berth, and it was with some satisfaction that they chose to slap Raymond Cumbie's hand. These
were the same people, after all, who had erected this building, in
1990, replacing the one founded by freed slaves in 1870, with their
own sweat and their own money. "Not anybody had anything to talk
about," said George Thomas, the steward and trustee who had
learned of the vandalism from Murray January just as he was headed
off to mow the church lawn that morning after. "But we were gonna
build that church ourselves. The men paid two hundred dollars a
month and the women a hundred until we had enough." The damage to the building had been slight, and it didn't take long for the
stewards to right the double doors and patch the two-by-four-foot
section of wallboard and the bell rope where the kids had tried to
start a fire and to get new prints of the African-American heroes for
the Wall of Fame in the back hallway. They never missed a meeting
or a church service. "It's the only church I ever belonged to," said
Thomas, "and it's a lot like taking care of your mama. You don't let
nobody hurt your mama."

Joe Dees was still stunned. First he had lost his son, and now his
church. "They didn't get the church, 'cause the church is in our
hearts," he would begin, when asked how things were going, but he
knew that wouldn't do. The Bibles, the hymnals, the folding chairs,
the robes—*everything* was gone. It was all he could do to remember
his medication and keep himself together as he telephoned around
the country and drove to Bay Minette and other points in lower
Baldwin County to talk with bankers and personal friends and black
churchmen who might be able to help rebuild the church. Unlike
the relatively younger and more vibrant members of Tate Chapel, the
aging congregants of St. Joe Baptist had virtually no personal assets
or income other than their pitiful household belongings and their
monthly government checks, so they would have to rely on outsiders.
They tried meeting in Joe's double-wide trailer on Sawmill Road a
few times, for Sunday school and informal services, but that didn't
work. By late summer they were meeting at the old tumbledown

frame chapel that was the black Mt. Triumph Baptist Church, on a narrow dirt road just north of Ferguson's Grocery, and Peanut observed them in their diaspora every third Sunday morning: a gaggle of a dozen St. Joe members, ranging from spry little girls in dreadlocks and ribbons to barely ambulatory octogenarians, being met by Joe in his Sunday suit and tie and tasseled loafers, to buy ice cream or coffee or soft drinks before queuing up for the short walk along Highway 59 to the church.

"I've been talking to the Lord about it a lot lately," Dees was saying one day in August, "but I still can't figure out for sure why it happened. Was it the Klan rally or not? I just don't know. I guess we might find out some things when they have to testify under oath at the trial." He was leaning toward the belief that it had been inevitable, due to a mix of latent racism, bored kids and alcohol, and a history of meanness toward the black people along Sawmill Road and in Couglan Swamp. "I'm aware of the Klan, don't know who belongs, but they're watching, they keep track, and you have to watch what you say. They preach hatred, and it goes back a long way. Little kids aren't born saying 'nigger.' They learn it from their parents." He reached over and straightened the array of frames holding photos of his living children and the deceased son, Tim, propped up in the wide front window of his trailer. "The Boones, the Gantts, the Coxes, the Phillipses, the Deans, all of those folks, they had land and opportunities. Sometimes I think about Doll [Boone] and Brandy. Our daughters are the same age. *Mine's* at UAB, studying to be a nurse. Where's *his*?"

BRANDY'S FATHER MIGHT have been asking the same question these days, for there were some fascinating reports now of a "new" Doll Boone. He had been pretty much of a rounder for much of his life, a drinker and brawler of some local renown, and since he worked in the family tree business for his father he was free of the restraints he would have felt if he had been on salary for a big company with government-ordained rules regarding, say, equal employment opportunities. His first marriage, to Susan, had been brief and chaotic, and he left it soon after Brandy's birth. Then he married a woman named Donna who worked for one of the timber companies, but that union ended not long after he and some pals ganged up during a company picnic and beat the hell out of a guy who had been frolicking with her. Another time, he bought a new boat, got drunk to celebrate, and promptly got stopped by a warden for "boating under the influence." (A week later the same warden discovered the tires had been slashed on the boat trailer he had left parked at Dixie Landing, though no one ever connected it to Doll.) But now, at forty-one, Doll was married to a woman of some substance, Teresa, who had arrived with a teenaged daughter from the east Alabama town of Tallassee and was working full days sewing together surgical gowns at a plant up the road in Frisco City. They had gone through a period of honky-tonking together as newlyweds, but she soon tired of it and now— *lookie here*—Doll had given up drinking, even tossed out his cigarettes, and joined the church.

This was the stuff of legend in a tiny place like Little River. *Doll's been saved!* The grapevine tingled with the news, rumbled and pumped like a generator, as the word spread from Peanut's to the Dixie Landing Cafe and all the way to Frosty Acres and back. The love of a good woman! "That one [Teresa] comes from good stock," said Percy Cox, ever the cattleman. "Doll and Teresa come to Mamie's Chapel about every Sunday, with her daughter," said his wife, Edith, the postmistress, "and at least once Brandy was with them. It seems I even saw Susan with them one time." Everybody was buzzing over this new development, putting it into a fuller context by rehashing some of the "old" Doll's greatest moments—the boating-under-the-influence story was, hands-down, the favorite— and noting that, come to think of it, there were no more of those weekend parties amid the heavy machinery littering Clayton Sr.'s yard, in front of God and everybody at the corner of Highway 59 and Dixie Landing Road, orgies of yowling at the moon and using beer cans for target practice and pushing and shoving and lighting the night sky with fireworks and bonfires. The Boone brothers' leader had gone and defected.

It was a major step for Doll Boone. He had seldom come around to Peanut's, even for groceries, preferring to restrict his movements to what amounted to the family compound surrounding his father's place (all six sons lived within a mile of the house where they were born), and he wasn't about to start now. "You know what it's all about," Peanut said. "It's Brandy. For all of those years, he didn't pay much attention to her, and now she's in big trouble. He's got to be feeling pretty bad about that. And I'd say Teresa helped him along in his thinking. He feels guilty." There was some evidence that he hadn't changed completely—he groused about how the media attention to the arson was "just stirring up the folks on Sawmill," and explained that a For Sale sign that had attracted a black couple from Mobile to an old house directly across the road from his had disappeared the very next morning when "a storm blowed it away," and would have some choice invective for Joe Dees at a chance meeting during the day of the kids' sentencing in Mobile—but he was keeping his own counsel. No interviews, for nobody, never. One day at a time.

WITH THE TRIAL now scheduled for late October in Mobile, the media had retreated and left the people of Little River to ponder the meaning of what had happened. Whether the kids' actions had been inspired by the Klan rally meant, at once, nothing and everything, depending on who was talking. "I ain't much of a churchgoer, and St. Joe wasn't much of a church, but they shouldn't have burned *any* church," said George Boone, Doll's disabled fifty-six-year-old uncle. Elizabeth Marshall, the black mother who had sent two of her twelve kids all the way from Couglan Swamp to Georgetown University, had her own ideas about punishment and restitution in case the five should be found guilty: "Making prisoners out of 'em would probably make 'em *worse*. Jail ain't where they belong. They oughta make 'em clean up the mess they made, rebuild the church brick by brick until it's fixed, then forget about it and go on with their lives. This *hate!* God won't allow no hate in heaven. The Bible says *all* of his children. Don't say nothing about color. . . ."

Nobody was immune to the troubles, even those of whom it might be said, in the rustic Southern vernacular, "ain't got no dog in that fight." Bill and Hannis Cumbie fit that description. They were in their eighties now, retired, their children from earlier marriages reaching retirement age themselves, and they were living out their long lives peaceably in a fine little dark-stained frame house, with a tin roof and a screened porch beneath a grove of ancient cedars, right on the highway beyond the Little River bridge. They were a threat to no one, and yet vandals had stolen some $9,000 worth of boats and motors from their shed in recent years, and Klan literature regularly appeared in their yard on dewy mornings. It was Hannis who had called the church-burning "the most horriblest thing that's ever happened around here," and was fully blaming the Klan. Bill, another of the Cumbies who had gotten a union card and worked on steel construction jobs all over the country after learning the trade in Burma and India during the Second World War, laid it on parents who "were too busy doing other things instead of working. The boys never worked a day in their lives, but here they are driving new cars." As for black people, he had "no beef against any of 'em. Our neighbors are black. He's a disabled logger and she drives eighty-three miles each way every day to clean houses at Gulf Shores, and they've got a bunch of kids. They're good people, and we've never had any problems. I don't throw off on nobody. A lot's made about how everybody's always talking to each other at Peanut's, both races, a big happy family and all, but now I don't know for sure about that."

Meanwhile, Joe Dees found himself in the awkward position of defending himself in the aftermath of the destruction of his own church. He had taken great umbrage when he got a call from John Boone, asking if he would write a letter to the judge who would sit at the trial, saying what a great kid Jeremy Boone was. "He's asking me to endorse a sacrilege!" Joe said, in disbelief, "the burning of a *church!*" Parents and relatives of the five were turning up the heat now, passing petitions in behalf of their kids and speaking disparagingly of Dees and his church. Said David Woods, Michael's adoptive father: "Me and the wife was just talking about how Joe was spending that money on his church, but if the church is his trailer, then he's spending the money on his own trailer." Dees was even hearing that some of his longtime black friends and neighbors were questioning the disposition of checks and cash that might have bypassed the St. Joe Baptist Rebuilding Fund at the bank in Bay Minette and gone straight into Joe's hands. That one hurt the most of all, and it would continue and lead to ugliness within the black community for more than a year.

Except for those rumblings from Sawmill Road and Couglan Swamp, which could only be explained as loose talk among poor black men with too much time on their hands, the charges that Dees was misusing funds targeted for rebuilding the church were simply the centerpiece of an unspoken campaign by hostile whites to denigrate Dees himself. The big money, the "official" St. Joe Rebuilding Fund, was tied up in escrow at the bank. There had been many offers, not of cash but of professional services and building supplies, if and when the rebuilding began, so there was nothing to be "stolen" there. Whatever no-strings-attached funds that came Dees's way, in the form of cash or checks, something that the big-time television evangelists prefer to call "love offerings," was free of any restrictions. "I can't even keep my car running," Dees said, vehemently denying any wrongdoing. The rumors appeared to be nothing more than a smokescreen to deflect from the fact that a black church had been burned to the ground.

The five kids were in limbo. Some had listlessly returned to their jobs—Brandy at the Country Kitchen in Uriah, Kenneth at the Vanity Fair plant in Monroeville—but others, suspecting that soon they might not need any money for quite a while, simply moped around and considered a future that looked anything but promising. Jeremy, afforded a new car and a computer and even a jet-ski boat by his grandfather, was spending his time not at Faulkner Community College but messing around in the fenced backyard of his mother's house with a pet deer he had caught in the woods during the weekend between the Klan rally and the church-burning, "Chester" by name. Now the insufferable heat of summer had passed, making way for fall, the best time of the year with its crisp weather and hunting seasons and high school football games, but life was going on without them. Poor Nicole Woods, the sister of Michael and the steady girlfriend of Alan Odom, and a majorette for the J. U. Blacksher High School marching band as well, gamely tried to smile as she strutted out onto the dimly lit field at Uriah for the halftime show during the Bulldogs' first home football game of the season.

TEN

Country Goes to Town

————

THE TRIAL WOULD BE held at the federal district court in Mobile during the last week of October, likely ending on Halloween night. Except for war times, when many of the men had been employed at the state docks, Mobile was seldom a destination for the people of Little River and Uriah, who felt much more comfortable in Monroeville and Atmore and Bay Minette or at play on the Redneck Riviera. Mobile predates New Orleans by a few years, but it was quickly outstripped by its sprawling neighbor to the west at the mouth of the Mississippi: the "Big Easy," birthplace of Dixieland jazz, home of Creole cooking and the bawdy French Quarter, the Mardi Gras and the Superdome. Mobile, the "Little Easy," never quite made it to prime time. The city hosted the annual Senior Bowl football game for graduating college stars, and the America's Junior Miss Pageant for teen queens, and a second-rate Mardi Gras of its own. The state's second-largest city, next to Birmingham, it had been the birthplace of many legendary athletes, most notably the home run champion Hank Aaron. But mostly it is a smelly old port town, marked by seedy bars and skeletal cranes that look out over the docks like praying mantises, interrupted here and there by new skyscrapers on the edge of a hapless downtown area that measures only about twenty-five square blocks.

In the houses and the trailers of northern Baldwin and southern Monroe counties, on that last Monday of October, alarm clocks began ringing well before daybreak, ahead of the roosters and cows and the first horn-blattings of the logging trucks. It was the day of reckoning for the five kids and their friends and extended families. For these people, country folk at the lower end of the social and economic ladders, little good had ever come from a visit to the big city. Awaiting them, amidst all of that cold concrete and clamor, would be a wall of dark forces—deputies, jailers, lawyers, prosecutors, a judge in a black robe, twelve jurors with no names, the media they had come to despise—people who knew nothing of the easy familiarities of their homes in God's country, and couldn't care less. *Did you do it? Yes, or no?* There would be no time for philosophical discussions about bloodlines and parenting and the joys and sorrows of living in such isolation. Just the facts, please.

Piling into their pickup trucks or old sedans, some bringing sack lunches, they eased onto Highway 59 to begin the hour-and-a-half drive through the familiar and into the void. They could have been Okies headed for California—parents, grandparents, siblings, cousins, aunts, uncles, friends, the accused—as they left the interstate and followed the Hank Aaron Loop to the narrow downtown streets; circling Bienville Square, gawking at the drunks asleep on park benches, not stopping until they had found uncovered parking lots that charged only two dollars for a whole day. The temperature was in the fifties, up-country, but down here on the Gulf it was below forty with the windchill factor. Wrapped in thin sweaters and windbreakers, their polyester skirts and trousers whipping in the nippy breeze, they walked as one in search of the fierce granite federal government building on St. Joseph's Street, no one seeming to notice the irony in the name, and then ran smack into nearly two dozen representatives of the media. "Brandy, over here!" "Mister Woods, could we have a word?" "The preacher coming through the back door, you think?" Alan Odom snickered and pointed when a photographer, backpedaling, stumbled on a curb and broke his camera.

ANY JOCULARITY THEY might have felt, however forced, disappeared the moment they got off the clattery old elevators on the second floor and walked into the courtroom. This was a long way from Peanut's store and Dixie Landing Cafe and Mamie's Chapel; rather more like a cathedral, with its twenty-foot ceilings and muted brown paneled walls and soft aqua carpeting. Pale blue velvety drapes covered the windows along one entire wall behind a jury box holding a dozen stark black leather swivel chairs. The jurors would be able to look to their right, against another wall, and see the judge's bench and, beside it, the witness's chair; straight ahead to the well of the courtroom, holding two long rectangular tables for the defendants and their lawyers and the prosecutors, a podium with a microphone, a television monitor, and an easel holding a rough sketch of the Little River area; and, to their left, five long rows of shellacked maple pews for spectators and the media. From somewhere came the sounds of seagulls and waves lapping a shore, generic Muzak, a tape that would be played whenever there was a sidebar, in order to drown out the private consultations between the judge and the lawyers.

Clearing their throats, the people from northern Baldwin County all turned right as they entered through the massive oak doors and instinctively headed for the spectators' pews in the rear. Brandy Boone and Alan Odom and Kenneth Cumbie had gone ahead of them and now were seated at the long table reserved for the accused and their lawyers, now and then peeking across the room to the team of prosecutors in their dark suits or behind them to their siblings and parents and other relatives. Jeremy Boone wouldn't be needed until later in the week, when the Tate Chapel vandalism would be tried separately. Known to only a few at that time, the fifth of the accused, Michael Woods, was in the judge's chambers, pleading guilty to the St. Joe arson in order to escape the mandatory ten years without parole that a conviction under the new hate-crime statute would bring.

And so they sat and waited: Brandy in a thin floor-length dark print dress and black flats and a white knit cardigan, a double chin and baby fat and too much eye liner, scribbling notes on a yellow legal pad, smiling brightly when she glimpsed her birth parents sitting together for one of the few times in her memory. Odom with a white dress shirt over a visible T-shirt, a clip-on tie, khaki trousers, tan buck loafers, auburn hair closely cropped, a kid with a perpetual smirk on his face; and Kenneth Cumbie, at twenty-one the only adult defendant, dressed more tastefully than the others in a waffled white cotton long-sleeved shirt and cuffed brown wool slacks and soft black shoes, pensive and frowning. And in the pews: Doll Boone in creased jeans and a pearl-buttoned cowboy shirt and his amazing gray snake-skin boots; Susan Boone, gaunt and crying softly as if in mourning, a tragic figure, a wilted rose, old before her time; David Woods, the hulking trucker, wearing jeans and only a T-shirt, his brawny arms folded, looking straight ahead; flame-haired Darlene Boone Odom Middleton; Cumbie's prim-looking schoolteacher father in a loud red wool crewneck sweater; Patricia Williams (Michael Woods's aunt and first adoptive mother) in a bright red turtleneck pulled over her Sunday coif; and a dozen stern uncles and grandfathers with graying crewcuts and scuffed work boots and faded flannel shirts, their mesh feed-store gimme caps now rolled up and stuffed in the hip pockets of their jeans. It was country comes to town.

THE TRIAL WAS to have begun at nine o'clock sharp, but there was a delay due to Michael Woods's guilty plea and to some more mischief from the Klan. Their couriers had been at it again over the weekend, tossing plastic bags of Alabama White Knights literature on lawns in six towns and communities throughout Baldwin County, the closest one to Little River being Stockton. The AWK wasn't claiming responsibility for the church crimes in Little River, and it had broken no law by passing out the literature except, perhaps, Hoss Mack said with a shrug, "criminal littering," but the timing was certainly sus-pect. That was only one of the matters on the mind of the judge when he made his entrance at 9:31 and summoned the half-dozen lawyers to the bench.

The judge was Richard W. Vollmer, Jr., a dour veteran of decades on the bench, and he let it be known in his instructions that he was less than eager to tie the Klan rally to the events that had occurred two nights later, although he did intend to poll the jurors on whether they had seen the Klan literature distributed over the weekend. Then he asked the three federal prosecutors, "Does the government have evidence that a conspiracy was formed [by the time of the Klan rally]?" and when the response was no he told them to strike the phrase "overt acts" in parts one and two of the five-count indictment. Murmurs and tight smiles passed among the crowd from Little River, their number now grown to forty, as they wriggled into the pews and settled in for the first day of what promised to be a very long week.

They had more reason to smile when the jurors were called. As the fourteen, including two alternates, entered the hall and moved to the black swivel chairs in the jury box, the Little River people liked what they saw: nine whites, three blacks, two white alternates, not a ponytail or dreadlocks among them. None had seen the Klan literature over the weekend, they told Vollmer, who then laid out the ground rules. They would be "semi-sequestered," to avoid chance meetings with "interested parties," he said, gathering at 8:45 every morning in an undisclosed location already determined, and he would try to break off at four o'clock each afternoon so they could beat the traffic and be home before dark. Finding that the only black male juror was faced with a 148-mile drive each way, from his home to the federal building, Vollmer advised him that he was entitled to free housing in a motel but the man said he would rather "be home in my own bed every night." Then, patiently, the judge walked the jurors through the basics: what is evidence, what is not; the court's definition of "reasonable doubt"; the differences between a civil case and this, a criminal case. He read and explained the five counts and told them that the St. Joe Baptist arson would be tried first, the Tate Chapel vandalism later in the week.

SQUARED OFF AGAINST each other, at the two opposing tables, were three federal prosecutors and three Mobile lawyers representing Brandy Boone, Alan Odom, and Kenneth Cumbie. The prosecution was led by a federal attorney named J. Don Foster, a grimly officious man, compact, with short steely hair, amiably referred to later by an assistant as "our CEO." His top aide was a lanky U.S. attorney named Greg Bordenkircher, thirtyish, with a wispy blond mane, who would do most of the talking. The third brought chills to the Little River crowd: Cynthia Tompkins, representing the National Church Arson Task Force in Washington, D.C., a woman with clout, very large and very black. Representing Brandy was a tall, handsome, articulate lawyer by the name of Richard Yelverton. Cumbie's attorney was Dennis Knizely, a short man with the pugnacious manner of a club fighter. For Odom, it was James Harper, his copious brown hair swept up in a pompadour, who would turn out to seem much less sure of himself in a courtroom than the more experienced Yelverton and Knizely.

Showtime. Foster stepped to the microphone in the center of the room, the nearby easel holding a rough map of Little River, to deliver the prosecution's opening statement. "It's about the burning of a church first organized by freed slaves in eighteen-eighty-six," he began, "where baptisms, weddings, and funerals have been held, where twenty-one black citizens pray and worship, a place with pews and Bibles and hymnals and other religious materials. . . . On June the thirtieth, about midnight, in Little River, Alabama, that church was burned to the ground. Destroyed. You can expect the evidence to show that Brandy Boone [pointing at her] said during that night, 'Let's go burn the nigger church,' and that she egged on Michael Woods and Alan Odom to do just that." *Let's go burn the nigger church.* That phrase was the engine driving the prosecution's case, the one volatile line to be left hanging in the air, and Foster would deliver it with a particular panache no less than five times before he sat. *Let's-go-burn-the-nigger-church.*

When he moved to the easel to outline the events of that night, the Little River crowd turned rapt as though they might learn something. Most of the parents had confessed to friends that their kids had been less than forthcoming about what had actually happened that night, either out of denial or a code of silence, and so they leaned forward now as the prosecutor took a baton in hand and reconstructed the kids' movements. In broad strokes, he outlined the night of destruction. There had been a "drinking party" at the home of a construction worker named David Gentry, on the gravel Buck Phillips Road, he said, showing the house's location just up from Peanut's store off Highway 59. There was talk of setting fire to a car that had been abandoned along Dixie Landing Road, and nine of the eleven at the party left in three cars to do just that. There was a stop at Peanut's, closed at that hour, to siphon a few ounces of gasoline from the pumps into a small glass vial. When they couldn't find the abandoned car and had rendezvoused at Dixie Landing, Brandy allegedly yelped her call—"I know what, let's go burn the nigger church!"—and off they went to Tommy John Earle Road. At St. Joe Baptist, he said, Woods and Odom kicked in the rear door and set the sofa on fire. One member of the party, Patrick Redditt ("the one hero that night"), made Woods and Odom put out the fire, saying he wasn't going to "go to jail for something like this." Woods and Odom pretended to be heading back to the Gentry house to continue the party, but they doubled back to St. Joe instead, and this time set the curtains on fire to complete the job. Foster said, "There were other things to burn, but no, ladies and gentlemen, 'Let's go burn the nigger church.' We will have a witness—let's call her 'Jessica, of Ohio'— who will testify that Brandy was at the Klan rally and that it was Brandy who said, when they were all together two nights later, 'Let's go burn the nigger church.'" He paused. "'Let's go burn the nigger church.'"

The defense attorneys were scribbling notes now, waiting their turns, ready to have at it. First up was Dennis Knizely, who first entered a plea of "not guilty" for Kenneth Cumbie and then proceeded along the line that all of them would try to pound home: that it was just a bunch of bored kids in a lonely place who got very drunk and made some childish mistakes. "There's no McDonald's in Little River, not even a Dairy Queen in Little River, just meeting up at Dixie Landing or Red Eagle's grave to drink and party and have some fun to beat the boredom." Knizely wasn't about to admit that his client had made any mistakes other than being at the wrong place at the wrong time. "Kenneth Cumbie has worked for three years at the Vanity Fair in Monroeville. Kenneth Cumbie didn't go to the Klan rally. In fact, Kenneth Cumbie put the first fire *out*. Then he went back to the Gentrys' by himself, wound up taking a friend who'd gotten scared to her house in Frisco City, and then went home himself. Kenneth Cumbie didn't start the fire, ladies and gentlemen, he put it *out*."

Alan Odom, said his attorney, James Harper, "never had any racial problems in Little River or anywhere else he ever went. He was just an eighteen-year-old doing what an eighteen-year-old boy does in Little River: drinking beer, watching movies, chasing girls. There's nothing else to do in Little River, Alabama. It's the kind of place where you don't even have to use your turn signal because everybody knows where and when and why you're going to make a turn." Harper became the first to identify the prosecution's mystery witness, "Jessica, from Ohio." She was Jessica Perry, a pert young woman who had met one of the Gentry boys in Dayton, Ohio, where he had been working a construction job, and moved in with him at Little River during the spring and early summer. He would argue that it was she, not Brandy, who had egged the boys on. "Those kids had been passing that church for fourteen years but they thought it was abandoned. They'd never seen any cars there, or any lights turned on. They couldn't find the car they wanted to burn, and they still had the gas they'd siphoned, and now Jessica Perry was calling them 'wusses' and 'chickens' because they wouldn't burn the church. There were more than a hundred beers consumed that night. It wasn't a conspiracy, folks, it was teenagers and beer and somebody goading 'em on. Alan Odom was *re*acting, not acting, that night. . . ."

Now came Richard Yelverton, Brandy's attorney, whose client was going to need all the help she could get. As the only female of the five, and the one identified in the media as the instigator with her alleged cry to burn the church, she stood out from the others. Yelverton began, naturally, by painting a picture of his client as a sweet kid: on the rolls of the Poarch Indians, thanks to her grandmother, "a proud high school graduate in May. It was summertime and she had a job in a cafe. Yes, she *did* go to the [Klan] rally, with her aunt, but she was scared more than anything. She's a big fan of Evander Holyfield and she wanted to see the Tyson fight that night. *Two black men.* The only reason they went to that rally was out of curiosity, to see a horse with two heads. Murray January will tell you what life is like between the races in Little River. They were even watching *The Nutty Professor,* a movie starring Eddie Murphy, *a black actor,* that night [of the arson]." He cut to the day of her arrest. "It was the Fourth of July, and she planned to swim and eat barbecue like every other kid in America, but here came a car with three federal agents who wanted to 'have a few words' with her. Here she was, a frightened teenaged girl in a wet bathing suit covered by nothing but a T-shirt and a pair of shorts and a towel, being thrown into a car and driven to the jail in Bay Minette, where there was air conditioning and no windows. Picture that. It took them four hours to get a statement from her, and it was way after dark before she was even allowed to call her folks and tell them where she was. Ladies and gentlemen, Brandy Boone *never even got out of the car* that night at St. Joe Baptist Church."

THE PROSECUTION HAD some pieces of business to get out of the way, and after a break for lunch they called a half-dozen witnesses to establish the undisputed facts. There was Hoss Mack, the affable Baldwin County deputy sheriff, narrating a videotape of the smouldering fire and the odd tire treads left at the scene; an ATF agent showing a total of forty-two slides he had made to show that the fire had been started "maliciously"; a nervous Joe Dees, wearing his black double-breasted Sunday suit and white shirt and black-and-gold tie, telling of the church's history and his pastorate, then reading from a list of the contents that had been destroyed; a preacher from Daphne testifying that St. Joe Baptist was, indeed, a dues-paying member of a national association of black churches; Laura Ann Porter, the one daughter of Murray January who had chosen to stay in Little River, a striking young mother who served as secretary for Tate Chapel, offering a brief history of the two churches and their importance to the black community in Little River. Finally, as the shadows grew long on the streets of Mobile, the prosecution called a black female ATF agent named Sybil Hall-NcNeil.

She looked and acted the part of an agent—curt, pedantic, grim, just-the-facts—and Yelverton, from the looks of him as she took the stand, couldn't wait to get at her. Hall-McNeil had been one of the three ATF agents who followed Brandy's grandfather to the home of Kenneth Lambert on the Fourth of July, where Brandy and her mother were lolling around the pool, in order to talk further with her. Al Hardman, one of the other agents, had arrested her, Hall-McNiel said, because they "felt that she had not been entirely honest with us in our first talk with her. We read her her rights. She wasn't shackled. It was about two o'clock when we put her into the car for the drive to Bay Minette. It's eighty-three miles from Little River to Bay Minette, you know, a two-hour drive"—there were muffled chuckles in the rear pews, from people who knew the actual distance is thirty-seven miles—"and we questioned Brandy on the way, and then we got a signed voluntary statement from her at the jail." Brandy had freely admitted attending the Klan rally and "told me some of the things said there about 'niggers' and 'Julios' and 'mongrels.' She told me that around ten-thirty the night of June thirtieth she said, 'Let's go burn the nigger church,' randomly and out loud. She then told me that she wished they hadn't burned the church."

Yelverton, convinced that the confession had been frightened out of Brandy, was all over Hall-McNeil. Having gotten her to say that she had testified in similar situations at least forty times in her career, he said, "Your job, then, is to prepare testimony." "My job," she snapped back, "is to be honest." It sounded good at the time, but over the next two days Yelverton, given a long leash by the judge, was able to leave the impression with the jury that the ATF agents had been overly zealous in getting a "confession" from Brandy.

"'Randomly'?" he sneered. "A little country girl with a high school education said 'randomly'?"

"It's in her statement."

"Some things are in there, and some aren't, right?"

"Well, sure . . ."

"I don't see anything in the statement that says Al Hardman is a big man, bald, wearing dark wraparound aviator glasses, and he had her scared and crying."

"We can't put *everything* in there."

"I should say so. You didn't put in that she got so flustered that she finally said, 'All right, if you say I said "nigger church," I guess I must've said it.' Did you, now?"

"But she said she said it. In so many words."

He let it hover, like a foul odor. "And do you mean to tell us it took three hours to get only six pages out of her?"

"We wanted her to get it right."

"Oh, I see," Yelverton said, turning toward the jurors, rolling his eyes, and smirking. "So that would explain the thirty-seven places where we see her initials."

"Correct. Where she okayed changes."

"I see. *Changes.* In her 'voluntary' statement."

The judge broke in to say that was enough for one day, and instructed the members of the jury as they prepared to drive home for the night not to discuss the case or read about it or watch the news on television. Out front, on the broad steps where they had shivered through many smoke breaks during the long day, the Little River contingent was trying to shove past the photographers and the reporters hustling for snippets. This was big news for the Gulf Coast, being covered by the Cable News Network and National Public Radio and the Associated Press in addition to the local newspapers and television stations, and leading the news would be the allegations of Brandy's "burn the nigger church" statement and Michael Woods's plea of guilty. But around the nation this was a minor footnote. In Denver there was the trial in the bombing of the federal building in Oklahoma City that had taken 168 lives, while in Boston there was the juicy story of the teenage British au pair who had seen an infant die on her watch. This was small stuff to people in the rest of the country, just some more redneck foolishness down in that god-forsaken place, Alabama.

ON THE SECOND day of the trial, a fuller story began to emerge of exactly what had gone on during the Klan rally and the night of destruction at the two churches. With the exception of Brandy's heartsick mother, so distraught that she couldn't take it anymore and would never return, the full complement of friends and family from the Little River–Uriah corridor once again crowded the spectators' pews. One would have thought there had been a work stoppage among the whites of northern Baldwin County, this being the biggest story of their lifetimes. Richard Yelverton began the morning by finishing his pestering of Sybil Hall-McNeil, and a couple of other young men who had been running with the pack that night but were not being charged with anything filled in some of the blanks, but the day promised the two most dramatic moments of the entire trial: the testimony from Michael Woods, who had pled guilty in order to escape the hate-crime sentence; and the appearance of Jessica Perry, the mysterious woman from Ohio, who had been granted immunity by the prosecutors in their hopes that she would nail Brandy, once and for all, with the call to "burn the nigger church."

Nothing in Woods's appearance and demeanor belied the sad facts of his life. Wearing a bright purple shirt and a clip-on tie and ill-fitting khakis and off-brand black-and-white basketball shoes, his red hair in an odd bowl cut that sprigged out on the sides like Dagwood Bumstead's, a ninth-grade dropout whose entire working career had consisted of being a carpenter's helper for his adoptive father and uncle, he stared straight ahead and mumbled in a monotone during his hour and twenty minutes on the stand. He had admitted his central role in the burning of St. Joe from the very first, and his attorney had wisely counseled him to follow his adoptive father's advice: "Just tell the truth, son, and pay the consequences."

First things first. He had attended the Klan rally on that last Saturday night in June, he said, as had the cousins Jeremy and Brandy

Boone. "I wasn't excited, I just wanted to see the cross burn. Brandy seemed pretty scared and was talking about watching the [Holyfield-Tyson] fight more than anything else, and her and Jeremy left kinda early." But Daniel Gentry and Jessica Perry stayed throughout and she seemed especially enthusiastic, shouting "white power and all of that." Then came the following Monday, a full day of drinking and carousing that had begun for some at noon, climaxed by the torching of St. Joe Baptist and the vandalism at Tate Chapel, and there was some coughing and even gasping from the pews in the rear of the courtroom as the adults began to grasp the enormity of it all: the amount of beer consumed, the building anxiety to go out and *do* something, *anything,* the sheer spontaneity of it all.

Earlier in the day, Woods said, he had knocked down a six-pack of beer while sitting beneath the Little River bridge, in view of the Klan's sprayed graffiti. He ran into Daniel Gentry and Jessica Perry there, doing the same, and they invited him to the Gentry house that night for some "drinking games." (That house was owned by Daniel's father, Dave Gentry, who now had as a roommate and bride-to-be Michael's aunt and adoptive mother, Patricia Williams, but they happened to be out of town that week.) Word had spread about the party, and kids began to stream in from all over, bringing beer— Woods counted a total of 126 beers for eleven people, and figured that he, a skinny 150-pounder, consumed "fifteen or twenty" more at the house on top of his six-pack—before nine of them set out to filch gas from Peanut's pumps and look for the abandoned car. When they didn't find it, they regrouped at Dixie Landing, still pumped and buzzing from the alcohol, not ready for the night to end, and decided to move the party to Red Eagle's gravesite. It was then, as they turned onto Tommy John Earle Road, that Woods heard somebody shout, "I know what, let's go burn the nigger church!" but he couldn't say whether it was a male or female voice. "That's the first time I thought about doing it," he said.

The three vehicles—Odom's white Nissan pickup, Brandy's blue Toyota compact, Cumbie's black Ford Ranger pickup—followed the dirt road and skidded to a stop at the forlorn little cinder-block building crouched in a grove of stunted pines. Woods and Odom promptly kicked the back door from its hinges (as a measure of the spontaneity of the entire affair, they were barefooted throughout the evening), splashed some gasoline on a sofa, and began passing Odom's cigarette lighter back and forth to set it on fire. No sooner had the blaze begun than Patrick Redditt, an older man from Uriah (and Brandy's latest boyfriend), came upon the scene and made them put out the fire. They did that, and, with Jessica Perry with them in Odom's pickup (her boyfriend, Daniel Gentry, was back home, passed out from the beer), they pretended to drive on down the road toward the Red Eagle grave, past Tate Chapel, but doubled back to St. Joe when everybody else had left and this time set the curtains on fire. "I wouldn't have done it if Redditt hadn't made us put the first fire out," said Woods. "That made me mad. And Jessica kept saying we were a 'bunch of wusses' for putting it out. When we left that first time, I'd made up my mind I was gonna go back and set it on fire again." He said that Jessica was shouting *"Sieg heil!"* and "White Power!" as the church became engulfed in flames. The three of them then drove back to the Gentry house and joined the others, who now were watching the movie *The Nutty Professor,* fetched when Brandy sent a couple of the boys to get it from her mother's house. It wasn't until the next night, while they were all together again at the same house, watching the news on television, that Woods began to understand the seriousness of what they had done and "got worried." They found the glass vial and tried to burn it on the barbecue pit, tossing it under the house, and then huddled to begin putting together an alibi.

FROM ALL THEY had heard so far during the trial, and from what little the five kids had told them, the folks from Little River were more than a little interested to hear what this Jessica from Ohio had to say. After Michael Woods's testimony, in fact, they were wondering why she had been subpoenaed by the prosecution and thus granted immunity in the first place. Back in Little River, Peanut Ferguson was still saying that Brandy was just the impetuous sort to have shouted "burn the nigger church" to keep a party going, and that Jessica Perry had been so new to the area that it was unlikely she would have known that the building was a church of *any* kind, especially on a calamitous night with all of that drinking going on. But the parents and friends weren't seeing it like that. The thinking was that another one of these "outside agitators" had come along, just like during the civil rights days of the sixties, and now she was repaying the prosecutors for a favor by blaming it all on one of theirs. Who was she, anyway?

She was pretty, for one thing, a right fetching prize for some old boy to be bringing back home to a dirt road in Little River, Alabama: about thirty years old, with a button nose and a cupid mouth and handsome cheekbones and blond hair tied back in a bun; a tasteful package dressed in high heels and a white blazer with padded shoulders draped over a powder blue skirt. And she was cool. She had met Daniel Gentry during the spring, in Dayton, Ohio, she said—"*Oh-HYE-oh*," not the Southerner's "*O-HI-uh*"—and followed him down to Little River, to get a taste of life in rural Alabama. "I went to the Klan rally that Saturday night just to see what they were like," she said. "They don't have that sort of thing in Ohio, you know." Judge Vollmer had to gavel the Little River crowd to order when they began laughing out loud. She continued: "I went with Daniel and Michael Woods, and we stayed through the cross burning. They [Klansmen] were asking everybody to shout 'White Power' if we agreed with what they were saying, and there were some things they were saying about the government that I agreed with, so I shouted 'White Power!' We all did, including Brandy, who had come there with her aunt. Brandy rode back with us, and we watched the fight at the house."

Her account of the daylong drinking binge and the night of carousing varied little from what had been admitted by Woods and the others, with one glaring exception. Unlike the others, she was swearing that Brandy had been the one who shouted, "Let's go burn the nigger church!" She admitted to serving as a lookout while Woods and Odom torched St. Joe Baptist, but nothing more, trying to leave the impression that she was an innocent abroad, a mere observer of these curious Southern rituals. "The next day," she said, "we were at Kenneth Lambert's pool and when I told Brandy that the law was in Little River, asking questions, she said she couldn't believe it, that when she'd said 'burn the nigger church' they'd actually *do* it."

Here came Yelverton, licking his lips and rolling his eyes heavenward. He would save the heavy stuff for his closing statement the next day, with a resounding lament over Alabama's having to endure the blame for the racial atrocities of the sixties in places like Birmingham and Selma and Montgomery, but for now he would settle for picking at this impertinent Northerner.

"You say you went to the Klan rally out of curiosity?" he said.

"Yes, sir."

"Because they don't"—he flipped a page on his yellow legal page—"here it is. Because they don't 'have that sort of thing' in Ohio."

"Not that I know of. No, sir."

"And so you joined right in with 'White Power' and so forth."

"When I agreed with some of the things they—"

"Well, Miz Perry, is burning cars something else they don't do in Ohio?" Hoots erupted from the rear pews, bringing out the judge's gavel again, and a threat to clear the courtroom of all spectators.

She wouldn't crack. All that Yelverton and the two other defense lawyers would manage to accomplish was to put it on the record that Perry had admitted to being "coached on what to write" by the federal agents, that they had taken a statement of only two pages from her without even questioning her about the Klan rally, and that she had hired a lawyer in Dayton to represent her. "I wonder why," Yelverton said of that before letting her go. It was her word against everybody else's. Jessica Perry was on the next plane back to Ohio.

The state was more or less resting its case on Michael Woods's confession and Perry's avowal that Brandy had said "burn the nigger church." For the rest of that day and all of the next, the defense would call a string of witnesses to say wonderful things about Brandy, to show that Kenneth Cumbie had actually helped put out the first fire at St. Joe Baptist, and to demonstrate that the kids weren't racists.

Those two days didn't pass without their lighter moments for a jury and an audience that was showing signs of flagging. When the judge and the lawyers curtly dismissed Brandy's crotchety grandfather, Ray Boone, just as he was trying to "explain" some things, he snarled and stomped off the witness stand, muttering under his breath—"damned judges and lawyers"—nearly getting a lecture from Judge Vollmer until the jurist, who had reached for his gavel, apparently decided that the old backwoods codger wasn't worth it. When Brandy's aunt and Alan's mother, Darlene Middleton, said she had gone to the Klan rally "looking for a friend," there were snickers from the knot of reporters in the rear: *Cruising for a date, at a Klan rally?* And Brandy's former high school English teacher brought levity to the show when she corrected Yelverton's grammer in mid-sentence: "It's *whom,* not *who.* I'm sorry, but I just can't help myself."

THE CLOSING ARGUMENTS were presented on Thursday morning. Greg Bordenkircher, the lanky blond who had done most of the talking for the prosecution throughout the trial, clearly wanted the hate-crime penalty and thought he would get it if he could convince the jury that Brandy had made the crucial remark. It had become a conspiracy at that moment, he argued, because she had dared them to do it, and both Woods and Odom had complied. He spelled it out for the jury: "Count One, then, is the conspiracy. Count Two, to 'destroy religious property,' there's no doubt. Count Three, they burned a black church, not a white church. Four, 'arson,' there's no doubt. Count Five, the destruction of religious property for reasons of race, that's the so-called 'hate crime.'" Cynthia Tompkins, the imposing black attorney representing the National Church Arson Task Force out of Washington, proposed that Brandy had "willingly" gone to Bay Minette with the agents on July Fourth and given a six-page statement with "a remarkable memory for details about what happened that night, like who was in each car. How would an agent know that? By the process of elimination, it was Brandy who said 'nigger church.'" When Tompkins sat down, she brazenly turned to face the Little River crowd, trying to stare them down, and that was enough for Robert Cumbie. He was already incensed that the judge wouldn't allow the jury to hear the tape of his son denying that he had done anything except put out the first fire at St. Joe, and Tompkins's perceived insolence caused him to snap. He stared back at her and pointed a finger heavenward, mouthing *God will take care of you,* and within seconds a bailiff was taking him by the elbow and escorting him from the room.

Process of elimination? What was a juror to do? Whom to believe? Dennis Knizely, the attorney for Cumbie, reminded them that "reasonable doubt" was enough grounds for acquittal. "The government wants you to believe parts but not all of the statements you've heard," he said, "asking you to turn your head when they stretch the truth. There are inconsistencies all over the place, plenty of reasons for you to have reasonable doubts." Jim Harper, Odom's attorney, tried to hammer home the point that his boy had been drunk, and yielded to peer pressure. "It was a stupid mistake by an eighteen-year-old kid who answered a teenaged dare that went too far. The government has special plans for eighteen-year-olds, you know. He can't vote, can't sit on a jury, can't drink, but he can go to war and he can go to jail."

Richard Yelverton took center stage again, in defense of Brandy and then some. "It was a tragedy. It was *not* okay. Nobody's asking for a 'not guilty' here. Evil lurks out there for young kids these days: the militia, skinheads, drug pushers, cowards with sheets over their heads. Now a church has been burned. Nobody's saying that's all right." He paused to scratch his head, anything for effect. "You know how it is when you buy some clothes and rush home to see how they fit? Well, the government's got itself a new suit and they can't wait to try it on. You don't see racists here, you see eighteen-year-old kids, drunk children. What's the Klan got to do with this case? You've heard testimony that Brandy was scared at the rally, got stuck without a ride and couldn't leave. And here she was, a little girl in a wet bathing suit, hoping to enjoy the Fourth of July with barbecue and some swimming, like everybody else in America, suddenly thrown into a car with three agents. She'd never been out of Little River in her life, and now they were asking her to 'take a little ride' that lasted for hours. And then they conveniently didn't tape her statement." Then he threw his fastball, summoning up the memory of the Klan's bombing of a Birmingham church, in 1963, that had killed four little black girls: "These are the sins of our fathers. Brandy wasn't alive when that church was bombed in Birmingham. Why aren't they trying *that* case under this new law? How long do we have to bear this burden in Alabama? We should be proud of the strides we've made down here." And, finally: "The young lady from Ohio should be sitting in that chair. Not Brandy Boone."

THE LEAD PROSECUTOR, Don Foster, was allowed the final word, countering Yelverton with, "We don't want to send a message that it's okay in Alabama to do anything you want just because you're young and get drunk," thus ending the arguments in the St. Joe Baptist Church phase of the trial. The jury was charged and sent to a room for its deliberations, and a new jury was called to hear the Tate Chapel case. After lunch, while the new jurors were being briefed by Judge Vollmer, there was a hubbub among the lawyers and the prosecutors on the floor of the courtroom. Word had just arrived that Jeremy Boone was pleading guilty to his part in vandalizing Tate and would turn state's evidence against Alan Odom, the only other kid being charged with that crime, and now Odom sat on a bench along the wall behind the defense table, elbows on his knees, head buried in his hands, sobbing audibly. The women of Little River rushed to his side, stroking his hair and kneading his heaving shoulders, trying their best to console him. He had been hung out to dry; refusing to profess his guilt, he was the only one of the kids being charged in both cases.

While the St. Joe jury deliberated elsewhere, the case against Jeremy and Alan was quickly laid out. Armed with Jeremy's guilty plea and his subsequent testimony about how he and Odom had gone on down the road and tried to lay waste to Tate Chapel, there wasn't much doubt about how this one would turn out. There hadn't been enough of the gasoline left to set the second church on fire, he said, so they began slashing at the framed photos hung on the walls. One of them was of the deceased 104-year-old grandmother of Laura Ann Porter and mother of Murray January and George Thomas, a lifetime member of Tate Chapel. "There were tears in my eyes when I saw what had been done to the churches," said Porter. "People come from Milwaukee, Detroit, and New York for homecoming and the holidays. The church means everything to us." With dark coming early these days, both juries were sent home at four o'clock and ordered to return bright and early Monday morning.

Conflicting statements notwithstanding, all five of the kids were found guilty, to one extent or another, when the juries reconvened on Monday. Sentencing would be held sometime in March, but the prosecutors had gotten what they came for: the first conviction in the nation, of Alan Odom, under the new hate-crime statute. They didn't "get" Brandy, as they had so vigorously tried to do, but they would settle for this. And so the news went out over the wires, even though it got swamped by the reams of copy flowing from the more sensational trials taking place in Boston and Denver, and completely overlooked were stirrings that had emanated from Monroeville, the town in Harper Lee's enduring novel of racial injustice, *To Kill a Mockingbird,* on the Friday of the trial. That was Halloween, the date for the big football game between the all-white Monroe Academy, one of those private high schools founded in response to school desegregation thirty years earlier, and the public resegregated all-black Monroe County High. Until adults got wind of the plan and stepped in to head it off, a band of kids from Monroe Academy had been conspiring to celebrate Halloween night by showing up for the game wearing Ku Klux Klan outfits.

ELEVEN

Lives Suspended

––––––––

ALTHOUGH THERE WERE more hunters than usual, thanks to unusually mild weather during the fall and winter in a place where a mere rumor of snow is big news, life in Little River following the trial seemed to be on hold. The kids were out on bail and wouldn't be sentenced until early March, but in the meantime they were being held on a short tether: under dusk-to-dawn house arrest, no associating with each other, obliged to call a certain phone number at seven o'clock every evening to find out whether they would have to go into Bay Minette for a drug test the next morning. They numbered only five, but now that they weren't circulating it seemed as though there were no white teenagers at all left in Little River. Except for stepping up their futile efforts to get such notables as the Fergusons and Murray January and even Joe Dees to say something nice about them in a letter to Judge Vollmer, in hopes of reducing their sentences, they had little to do but sit around and worry about what lay ahead.

Not so at the Boone household on Gantt Road. Susan Boone, her emotional state worsening since her daughter's ordeal, had suffered a stroke almost immediately after the trial and required hospitalization and medication. Soon after her return home she accidentally gave an overdose of Tylenol to her four-year-old daughter, and the child almost died when her systems shut down and she had to be rushed to the high-tech medical center attached to the University of Alabama–Birmingham for a month's stay. Now Susan appeared a decade older than her thirty-seven years, with a twitch in one eye, a nervous mouth, wrinkled skin and droopy eyes, hair falling out, her weight hovering at a skeletal one hundred pounds. She needed all the help she could get from her mother, who fortunately lived in the big house next door, as she tried to get a grip on herself while at the same time consoling Brandy and answering the needs of two girls aged four and nine.

And then, of all things, Brandy got pregnant. Under house arrest, legally barred from seeing the four others, required to be prepared to take a drug test at any time, the femme fatale of the media's dramatic coverage of the trial, surely headed for prison at the age of eighteen, she had managed to slip away in the daylight hours and conceive a child. The father-to-be was Rusty Lilley, a teenage neighbor of Michael Woods in Goodway, one of the boys who had torched the abandoned car near Tensaw in a drunken afternoon caper just days before the night of St. Joe Baptist and Tate Chapel, a kid with a future as a day laborer ahead of him. This was becoming a melodrama, something you might see on the afternoon television soap operas, and the grapevine was thrumming again: "Like mother, like daughter" (for Susan had been a teenager when Brandy was conceived), and "Looking for love in all the wrong places," and "She used to be so pretty." Now, when Susan Boone managed to get out of bed and make the rounds, asking people to sign petitions on behalf of her daughter, she could add that Brandy would have to deliver her baby while in prison. And she, about to become a *grandmother,* for Christ's sake, surely couldn't take care of another kid.

Susan's sister, Darlene, told of a gathering at David Woods's house between the trial and sentencing. The Justice Department was taping material for a documentary aimed at teenagers in high-risk schools all over the country. *Burned: The Consequences of Juvenile Arson* would cost $75,000 and be distributed to 10,000 public schools where students were deemed to be at risk. Although there were no promises or threats, as far as sentencing was concerned, they wanted the kids and their parents to appear in the film. "Alan, Kenneth, and Michael were there, and some of us parents," Darlene said. "I took Susan, but I told 'em they wouldn't get anything out of her. The boys talked about how they'd made a big mistake that was ruining their lives, did it because they got drunk, gave in to peer pressure, all of that. Then some parents talked about the same stuff. Well, then they turned to Susan and she started grabbing at me and begging, 'Don't leave me, don't leave me.' They put her in front of the camera and asked her what she had to say, and she broke down crying. All she said was, 'I don't . . . I don't . . .' and that was all they could get out of her. She's a wreck. This has destroyed her."

THE SENTENCES CAME down during the first week of March, Michael Woods and Jeremy Boone getting the word first because they had pled guilty, and the other three appearing as a group at the same government building in Mobile where the trial had been held. Michael would serve five years for helping destroy St. Joe Baptist, and Jeremy would do three years and ten months for vandalizing Tate Chapel. Brandy and Kenneth Cumbie drew forty-one months each, for their part in the St. Joe arson. Alan Odom had done no more or less than Woods in the torching of Joe Dees's church, the two passing a cigarette lighter back and forth between each other, but he would pay the price for not pleading guilty: fifteen years, ten of it falling under the federal hate-crime statute. Odom would be placed in medium security, but the others would do their time in minimum-security federal facilities that were regarded more as places for drug offenders than as hardcore prisons. Within forty-eight hours of their getting out of prison, they would be required to report to their parole officers and work out a plan for paying restitution, nearly $20,000 apiece, to St. Joe Baptist Church. Alan Odom would immediately file an appeal of the hate-crime judgment, Brandy and Kenneth on the amount of the time to be served. Given the inconsistent testimonies during the trial, when the only thing established about Brandy and Cumbie was that they were running with the crowd and might have stopped the destruction, there was some thinking that their sentences might be reduced.

Even Judge Vollmer seemed to have some misgivings, according to
David Woods, who reported that the judge had said he had "a problem with this case" while he addressed the parents in court that day as
they stood beside their kids, shuffling and looking at the floor, ready
to take their medicine. Still, all things considered, the sentencing
seemed wise. There was no need to make a bad situation worse by
throwing five young people in amongst thieves and killers where they
might become hardened beyond repair. The sensible approach was to
somehow make prison a positive experience; to have it accomplish
what their parents had failed to do, to bring some sort of discipline
and structure to their lives. At the very least, they wouldn't be drinking for quite a while.

Mindful of the nightmare that had developed during the July
Fourth weekend when they were locked up with a passel of losers in
the Mobile Metro jail, the judge agreed to a plan offered by David
Woods. Michael's adoptive father had been talking with some marshals
he knew in the area and had asked them to recommend that the kids
be sent to the jail at Brewton, in nearby Escambia County, less than
seventy miles from Little River, while they awaited their assignments
to federal prisons. That way, Woods argued, they would be separated
from hardened prisoners and could have visits from their friends and
family. Vollmer said yes, good idea, and the moment came for the
kids to be turned over to their new keepers. The last goodbyes had
already taken place back home—John and Debbie Boone, relieved
that Jeremy had gotten off with only a forty-one-month sentence, had
special-ordered from Peanut a dozen ribeye steaks for a going-away
party—so there were few tears as they kissed and hugged and were
taken away. The only thing close to an outburst came when Joe Dees
happened to bump into Doll Boone in the men's room at the government building and asked him, as a matter of courtesy, "How's it going,
Doll?" The old Doll reappeared: "Not so goddam good, Joe, what do
you think? My kid's going to prison for something she didn't do."

As the weeks passed, one by one the kids were moved from the
little county jail in Brewton to a vast holding area in Oklahoma City
to become oriented to prison life and to await assignment to prisons

around the country as space opened up. "I said goodbye to Michael one day in Brewton," said David Woods, "and it seemed like he disappeared for a long time after that. We'd told our little grandson that Michael had gotten on a plane to go to work, and everytime a plane passed over he'd point and say, 'Michael gone to work.' Then one day we got a letter from him, from Lexington, Kentucky." They had placed Michael in a huge minimum-security medical facility there, where he was the youngest of four thousand inmates. Brandy had been dispatched to Marianna, about a three-hour drive across the Florida Panhandle from Little River, where she would stay until she was moved to a halfway house to give birth to her baby (the mother of Rusty Lilley, the father, would raise the child at her home in Goodway until Brandy completed her sentence). Alan Odom was sent to a medium-security prison at Oakdale, Louisiana, 390 miles from Little River but close to where his father worked on dredge boats. Kenneth Cumbie and his new best friend, Jeremy Boone, wound up together in central Florida at a facility near the southbound entrance to Florida's Turnpike at Wildwood. It would be the middle of the summer before any of them would be allowed visits from their parents and friends.

HAD THE ATTACKS on the two churches been racially inspired? The question still hovered in the air like early-morning fog over the marshes, and it was likely that only the kids knew for sure. The two juries' decisions had been unanimous, of course, but there should have been an asterisk beside the vote in the case of St. Joe Baptist. There had been a dramatic moment while Judge Vollmer was polling the jurors about their vote, which had been reached only after fourteen hours of heated deliberations. When he asked Gloria Betts of Monroeville, one of the three black jurors, if she agreed with the verdict against Brandy Boone, she closed her eyes and meditated for a full ten seconds before finally saying, almost under her breath, "Yes." She later would amplify her feelings in an interview with Michael Wilson of the Mobile *Register:* "I felt that race had a lot to do with what was done, and why, and where. I felt that all of those young people were just as guilty on all the counts. I didn't feel Odom was any more guilty than the others." And she believed that Brandy had used the "nigger church" remark. "It was her suggestion. She planted the seed and they carried it out. She just didn't strike a match. But I was the only one who felt that way."

It's probable that Betts's reaction was informed by her being a resident of Monroeville, the town best known for *To Kill a Mockingbird,* where separation of the races has always been much more obvious than in Little River. It's possible that she heard talk of the thwarted Halloween "prank" by the students at the all-white Monroe Academy to dress as Klansmen for the big football game against all-black Monroe County High, just while she was at home for that weekend, trying to make up her mind about how to vote. With a population of about 7,000, Monroeville is a large enough old Southern town to have the "right" and "wrong" side of the tracks, which is to say there are traditionally black and traditionally white neighborhoods and seldom a common ground where the two societies regularly meet. "I went to Monroe County High, and I can tell you that the first time I ever had an honest-to-God conversation with a white person didn't come until I enrolled at Auburn [University]," said Cynthia Tucker, a schoolteacher's daughter who had gone on to become editorial page editor at the newspaper made famous by Ralph McGill, the Atlanta *Constitution.*

Like his father, Joe Witherington is known as an honest man who works hard (as a buyer for one of the smaller timber companies) and is an excellent father to his two young children. He is college educated and eschews using the N word, but as one who has lived his entire life as a resident of Monroeville he now speaks of racial matters in a code that has replaced outright racist talk not only in the South but throughout America. Black people who dress well and take pride in their lawns and houses and vehicles, he reports, are the "light-skinned ones whose ancestors worked in the big house . . . the others' folks were field hands who didn't care much how they lived." Go into a black neighborhood looking for somebody, "nobody ever heard of him, but if you say you've got some money for him they'll say, 'Oh, yeah, *that* one, let me go get him for you.'" A hard worker can earn $600 a week cutting timber, he says, but "they don't keep any of it because they spend it on women and booze and lawyers to keep 'em out of jail." He likes the joke about the faith healer who breezes into Little River, encounters three black men with disabilities, and tells them he can make them whole again. He cures the first man of blindness by merely touching his eyes; the second man dramatically arises from his wheelchair when he simply lays hands on his knees; but when the healer approaches the third man, bent over with back trouble, he is told, "Get away from me, man, I'll lose my checks!"

He explains the success of Cynthia Tucker, the black woman who had left the segregated schools of Monroeville to become a star at the Atlanta *Constitution,* by saying her father "had some white blood in him," and there is a story there. Joe was taking some courses at Alabama Southern Community College in Monroeville, and his English class was taught by Tucker's mother. "One time she asked us to write an essay about Martin Luther King," he says, "so I wrote about his women and all the trouble he'd caused and how I thought he wasn't exactly the man everybody said he was cut out to be. She gave me an 'F' on the paper and implied I was a racist. The way I see it, *she's* the racist."

If you hang around long enough, overhearing conversations at Peanut's store and making note of voting patterns in the various ballot boxes up and down Highway 59 and watching the races interact and picking up on contradictory versions of historical events, certain truths about racial relations in Little River begin to emerge. People of each race, even Peanut Ferguson and Murray January, would swear they are outnumbered by the other; whites vote Republican, blacks, Democrat; the elders of both races commingle, but the young hardly speak to each other; Nigger Lake is known as a pretty good fishing hole to whites, an eerie boneyard to blacks; the Civil War is celebrated as a noble lost cause to whites, but to blacks it is the point in history when everything changed. The two races simply do not know each other and, what's worse, make few attempts to do so. Little wonder, then, that the conversations between blacks and whites—at Peanut's, at the boat launch, at the two diners and the package store and the gas pumps—are about the weather and hunting and where the fish are biting; about anything but a child's schoolwork or an illness in the family or a pay raise or the latest news from a family member who had to leave the South to find work. "We're all stuck down here being poor together" has a lovely democratic ring, but it isn't exactly true.

VIOLENT WEATHER VISITED northern Baldwin County during the first week of April, during this year of El Niño, in the form of gypsy tornadoes and heavy rains spawned by thunderclouds roiling up from the coast. *Red sky at morning, sailor take warning.* The pattern was always the same—a surreal pink blush in the early-morning clouds, temperatures reaching ninety at noon, a suffocating humid stillness in the afternoon, and then a sudden foreboding darkness—before, finally, it came: blinding hailstorms pounding tin roofs, bolts of lightning streaking wildly through the swaying pines, abrupt power outages, dark twisting funnels throwing up swirls of dust from the newly plowed fields of cotton and corn, fallen trees blocking the only main road in and out of Little River, and then the deluge of rainfall that flooded the lowlands and made the bulldozed roads all but impassable, all of that followed by a long, peaceful night of steady rain thoroughly saturating the black earth. Most of the cotton farmers found it necessary to plow under their seedlings and start all over.

"You think they're crazy now, wait'll summer gets here," said Sharon Scott, the clerk at Peanut's store. George Boone, Doll's uncle, had kicked off the season by firing a shotgun blast across the bow of the Boones' Little River Cafe at daybreak on April Fools' Day, trying to draw out a couple of mortal enemies from the *other* Boone clan he knew to be in there sipping coffee and talking bad about him, such impetuosity getting him hauled off to the Baldwin County jail on charges of attempted murder. "He's just trying to get his 'crazy checks,' is all," Sharon said with a shrug. "He's got to show he's as nuts as Joe Dees. He's been working on it a long time. It's become his life's work." He would soon be joined by his son, Tommy, a serious drug user, whose solution to car trouble was to thumb a ride at night on Highway 59 and pull a knife on the poor samaritan who stopped for him, kicking the guy out and going for an all-night joyride. They could hope that conditions at the jail had improved since an unsolved suitcase bombing that had occurred on the morning after the Little River Five's sentencing, said to be not connected, but just the same drawing a $2,500 reward from the governor.

While the kids were away, it seemed, the adults would play. Not long after George's escapade, his brother John—Jeremy's father, Debbie's jealous husband, another of Doll's uncles, the strapping galoot whose modus operandi was to take a construction job only when the money ran out—had a confrontation in the parking lot at Peanut's. John was convinced that his delectable blonde wife was having an affair with a man from Mobile County who had put a trailer near the water, on a dirt road not far from Peanut's, for use as a weekend retreat. The fellow, Larry, was handsome and in his forties and, as far as anyone in Little River knew, unmarried. His trailer sat next to that of a girlfriend of Debbie, who seemed to be spending an inordinate amount of time "visiting my friend" ever since Larry had entered the scene. Now John had begun to stalk the mysterious stranger, and late on a Sunday afternoon in April all hell broke loose. Arriving at Peanut's to gas up his shiny black Chevy pickup, John saw Larry's van parked in the lot while he visited the restroom. A tussle followed when Larry stepped outside—red-faced John bellowing threats, Larry making a move toward his van, John rushing inside to call 911 and say a man was pulling a gun on him—and a crowd had gathered on this otherwise sleepy Sunday afternoon by the time a sheriff's deputy arrived. The deputy made sure there were no guns around, heard the men out, figured he had heard this one before, and advised them to go their separate ways. Debbie wasn't nearly so forgiving, for within days she had filed divorce papers against John. This time, it appeared, she wasn't kidding.

It was a matter of time, it seemed, before poor Joe Dees would join in the madness. This was shaping up to be the worst stretch of ill fortune for him in a lifetime full of it. First, his son Tim was killed. Then his church was destroyed. He had just been forced to deliver his aging parents, unable to care for themselves anymore, to a nursing facility in Mobile, far from the family enclave on Sawmill Road. And now that the story of the kids and the torching of St. Joe Baptist was no longer in the news, contributions had come to a standstill. He had held a ceremony he called "an unearthing of the soil" at the barren site of the church, on a Sunday in mid-April, with a representative of the black Eastern Shore church association there to help shovel some dirt and plant a beribboned stake in the ground, but not a move had been made toward laying a new foundation. Every third Sunday he and his congregation had been trudging off to their temporary quarters at the Mt. Triumph Baptist Church, and every week he had been driving to Bay Minette and Mobile in attempts to raise money, but nothing was happening. Finally, one day in the middle of May, with the temperature already at ninety-five degrees and the area in the midst of a ten-day drought, he walked the four miles from his trailer on Sawmill Road and handed Sharon a $100 bill for a two-dollar Styrofoam cup of Louisiana Pink worms and then turned around to trudge back home in the stultifying heat. *There goes Joe again.* The next day, just as the five white kids were checking into the final destinations where they would serve out their sentences, one of Joe's sons drove him to the VA hospital in Gulfport, Mississippi, for another long process of getting back on his medication.

AND THEN, ALMOST as a prelude to a summer that suddenly didn't look at all promising, the two cultures appeared to be headed on another collision course. On back-to-back Saturdays, the last two weekends in May, there would be the joyous annual black MayFest down at Tensaw followed by another Klan rally on Phil Smith's five-acre spread nearby. "No telling what's gonna happen if he keeps this up," Peanut said with some amazement over Smith's gall. "Doesn't he have any sense at *all*?" The MayFest had been a tradition for longer than anyone could remember in Tensaw, a nearly all-black community. It was, at once, a homecoming and a picnic and a carnival, a celebration of what the sociologists might call "black pride" but what the folks involved would simply call fun: a full day of music, both live and from window-rattling boomboxes; of paper plates loaded with barbecued ribs and fried catfish and beans; of a parade made up of bicycles, horses, antique cars, and fanciful street 'rods with wide racing tires and chrome mufflers and 357-cubic-inch engines that sounded like something out of the Daytona 500 when they were goosed at idle. It was Sunday-after-church multiplied by ten, and there were times when the crowd numbered nearly 3,000.

This year, only four hundred attended. Its promoters could argue that the weather played a part (the latest drought was in its third week) and that the toll of younger blacks migrating to the cities had left northern Baldwin County with a population of aging parents and grandparents who didn't get out so much anymore, but the sad truth was that the Klan's new presence had been felt. "A lot of folks got confused about the date and thought the MayFest and the Klan rally were on the same day," said Murray January. Peanut noted that few of his regular black customers came by the store that day, for the same reason. Sheriff Jimmy Johnson had dispatched a dozen marked patrol cars, ostensibly to control the parade but in fact to be on hand in case any Klansmen showed up with mischief on their minds. The show went on in the suffocating heat, with the general merriment of a carnival or a small county fair, but it seemed as though the participants were looking over their shoulders.

The Alabama White Knights had never taken "credit" for the arson and vandalism that had followed the rally of the previous year, and they wouldn't even mention it during this second rally only eleven months later, but maybe the broad media coverage of the Little River Five had given pause to all but the true believers this time around. The crowd for this rally numbered only forty, about half the number that had attended the one held on the last Saturday night of June in 1997, and fifteen of those were full-fledged Klansmen in their robes. The show went on as before: "Dixie" playing over a public-address system, wafting through the pines, as scattered groups laid out blankets on grassy hillsides to dig into their picnic baskets; Klansmen minding fold-out laundry tables laden with pamphlets, books, T-shirts (Martin Luther King, Jr.'s face in the crosshairs of a rifle scope and the legend, "Our Dream Come True"), and souvenirs (bumper stickers, belt buckles, and Teddy bears dressed in Klan robes); and nearly two and a half hours of thunderous hate-mongering from a series of robed speakers and distinguished heavy breathers. It was followed by a Klan wedding—*hunh?*—and the burning of a cross that had been wrapped in kerosene-soaked burlap.

As before, Baldwin County sheriff's deputies cruised up and down Highway 59 throughout the night to let the Klan know they were paying attention. But this time a lone ATF agent decided to enliven the evening by showing up at the front gate of Phil Smith's property, which was guarded by armed skinheads who stood between the flags of the Confederacy and Nazi Germany, and demanding entrance. David F. Pasqualotto is an imposing sight, a casting director's dream of a stern federal agent, the man who had been in charge of the government's investigation of the fire and vandalism at St. Joe and Tate Chapel. On this night, as the Klansmen and spectators were going through the checkpoint on the road, he simply walked up and identified himself and demanded admittance. It scared the bejesus out of the young underlings manning the gate, causing them to scurry off to tell "Brother Phil" what was up. "Look," Pasqualotto said, glowering and thundering like Moses, or Bear Bryant at the least, "we can do this the easy way or the hard way. It's up to you." If nothing else, it got their attention. "We can drop every mask in this place and do it the hard way, if that's what he wants," one of the speakers would later tell the crowd, hinting that the woods were full of agents and gesturing toward a hangman's noose dangling near the makeshift podium. "We got something for you hangin' from this tree!" All in all, it was a fine night for posturing.

PART THREE

Long, Hot Summer

TWELVE

Dog Days

———

USE ANY SUPERLATIVE FOR the word "hot" and it will describe southern Alabama in the summer: sweaty, sticky, steamy, broiling, sizzling, suffocating, breath-sucking, stultifying, hellish, depleting, numbing, paralyzing. Any one or any combination will do. Baldwin County gets the most annual rainfall of any county in the state, being just far enough away from the Gulf for the rising thunderclouds, driven by ocean breezes, to cool and drop their loads after they have moved about fifty miles inland, but most of the rain comes during the spring tornado season and in early autumns fraught with hurricane warnings. The summers, though, are sheer hell: three weeks of drought, followed by one frightening night of thunderous horizontal rain, followed by two weeks of sopping humidity visibly rising from the spongy swamps. It's damned if it rains, damned if it doesn't.

Except for a new resort development called Arrowhead, in the woods northeast of Little River in the direction of Monroeville, with air-conditioned cottages and manicured ponds and a darkened restaurant wrapped in cooling flagstone, there are few places to hide from the summer's heat and humidity. Dogs and cats make a truce and ride it out together beneath houses, cattle bully each other for space under groves of trees, whole families lug watermelons and sweet iced tea to favored swimming holes, teenaged boys roll down the windows and aimlessly drive around in their pickup trucks with a case of beer on ice in a washtub, and the serious drinkers hole up for drowsy afternoons under the air conditioning at Frosty Acres. There are few people with enough money to afford central air-conditioning, so it's either a window unit or a collection of fans, strategically placed, for most. Sharon Scott and her husband have "the best investment we ever made," she says: a small swimming pool under the trees behind their house, itself outfitted with an even dozen ceiling fans.

The pace of life slows considerably, then, in the summer months. Men who work in the woods begin their days before dawn and knock off at three o'clock in the afternoon. Fishermen go out on the steaming waters either at daybreak or dusk, or else lay out trot lines and fish boxes through the night. Businesses all over the county, following the country tradition, close at noon on Thursdays. Afternoons are the perfect time to get into the car or truck, under air-conditioning, and drive the thirty miles or so to take in an afternoon matinee at the nearest movie house. Although the air conditioner at Peanut's loses its punch with the endless opening and closing of the front door, he notices a lot more people hanging out there when you can see the heat shimmer off Highway 59. Mike Bradley, of the BP station up the road, says his monthly power bill jumps from $450 to $900 with the arrival of summer.

They get bored. "Regarding all these calls about how to get rid of fleas," said a caller to the Mobile paper's message line. "I have found the best solution is bourbon and sand. The fleas get drunk on the bourbon and throw rocks at one another." The *Register's* letters-to-the-editor page sizzled after a woman with a most un-Alabama name, Julia Helgason, had opined that there had been little glory in the Confederacy. "Even after the Confederate States were formed, there were only peaceful intentions," wrote one John Ellis of Mobile. "The South just wanted to be left alone. The South was invaded by Yankees from the North, hence 'The War of Northern Aggression.' Southerners were simply protecting their country and homelands. This just goes to show how the winners of a war get to write the schoolbooks and distort the truth so that even the 'educated majority' are fooled. Once a person learns and understands the truth and has empathy with those who died defending their families and homes from intruders, they, too, will get a lump in their throats when they learn that the flag is to honor those gallant defenders of the homeland. . . ."

They get careless. It was summer, the off-season for hunters, as good a time as any to get the equipment in working order. Down in Perdido, where the feuding clans stare at each other across the interstate, Vincent Lambeth sat in his kitchen, preparing to clean and oil his shotgun. Verlon Dakota Lambeth, his eighteen-month-old son, stood nearby in the doorway, watching Daddy work. *Dang!* There was a No. 8 birdshot cartridge jammed in the gun, ever since the last bird season. Vincent wrestled with it, the gun fired, and little Verlon got it in the head. His vision was going to be all right, the doctors said after surgery in Mobile, but it looked like he might have trouble hearing for a while.

They get pissed. In a community called Hurricane, west of Bay Minette near the banks of the Tensaw River, two law-enforcement helicopters hovered a few yards over John Trough's trailer. They had guessed correctly that he was growing marijuana plants in his yard. Trough grabbed a high-powered rifle from the trailer, which also contained two hand grenades and what the sheriff's office would later call "other small explosives," and commenced to fire five rounds at the helicopters. The choppers left, armed deputies arrived, and he was arrested without a fight. Trough's lawyer said the grenades were disarmed and used for paperweights, the "explosives" were railroad flares brought home by his children, and that his client surely didn't shoot: "If he'd shot, he wouldn't have missed." Said David Whetstone: "Judge, I could swear that a few times when I was out hunting I hit those doves, but I didn't."

They lose it. When his wife mysteriously disappeared from their home in Tennessee, a man named Matthew Sanspree gathered up his two small children and brought them to Baldwin County, where he had been born. There had been no sign of his wife, greatly missed, but he and the kids seemed to be doing all right now. He had a job as a house framer, and they were living with relatives in Loxley. But on a broiling Wednesday, in the middle of the summer, Lt. Hoss Mack and the boys came with a search warrant issued in Tennessee and hauled him off for questioning. There was no evidence that a crime had been committed, and Sanspree wouldn't say anything without a lawyer, so all they could do was impound his car for a forensic search and let him go. His relatives came to get him and took him home, and they didn't see him again until the next night, when they found him in the woods nearby. He had left a note asking his children to forgive him, drawn a map showing precisely where he had buried his wife in a forest in Tennessee, and then hanged himself from a tree.

AFTER ALL OF the excitement they had been through over the last eighteen months, going back to the shotgun killing of Tim Dees in January of '97, life was downright peaceable in Little River as the summer of '98 rolled in like a portable sauna. Peanut drove to the farmer's market in Mobile on the third day of June and returned at midafternoon with the first watermelons of the summer filling the bed of his pickup, a rite of passage in itself for Southerners, and many of his customers bought them directly off the truck. That weekend, some ninety miles away at Georgiana, more than 8,000 fans inundated the little whistle-stop town for the annual Hank Williams Festival, a hootenanny starring the last real country singer—George Jones—and featuring Hank's scrawny grandson, Hank III, and Jett Williams, who had spent years proving that she was Hank's out-of-wedlock daughter, and thus entitled to a large chunk of royalties. The other major entertainment of each summer in the area was the stage production of *To Kill a Mockingbird*, on the grounds of the old courthouse at Monroeville, but few people from Little River had ever seen it and didn't plan to start now. Despite the early drought that had caused many farmers to replant, the cotton crop was on schedule: first blossoms on July 1, first bolls August 1, picking mid-September.

This being an election year, the first piece of business was to hold the Democratic and Republican primaries all across Alabama—the headline issue being whether the state's voters would elect a moderate Democrat as governor for the first time since the Republicans'

Southern Strategy, based on appealing to racial enmities, had been installed in the wake of Lyndon Johnson's liberal civil rights policies in the sixties. The primaries were held on the first Tuesday in June. Sue Ferguson, as proctor for the balloting at what was officially called "The Ferguson Store" precinct in Little River (held in the storage room *cum* tanning salon), came to work that day wearing a somber black pants suit and pearls.

The results easily explained why David Whetstone, running for reelection as the county's district attorney, had switched to the Republican Party in spite of his liberal tendencies. He didn't even have a Democratic opponent this year, and took 72 percent of the vote in the Republican primary to get himself six more years in office. This part of Alabama remained thoroughly conservative—a total of 19,672 Republican voters showed up for the primary throughout Baldwin County, only 2,561 Democrats—and a closer look showed that in Baldwin, as in the rest of the South and the nation, blacks voted Democrat and whites voted Republican. In the nearly all-black Tensaw community, for example, there were 37 Democratic voters and only 12 Republican; but down the road at Stockton, now quickly gentrifying into an enclave for I've-got-mine white commuters and retirees, it was 135 Republicans and just 22 Democrats.

There were two voting places in Little River, at Peanut's store and at the Little River Cafe, and the results there were telling, as well. At Peanut's, the turnout was 21–18, Democrat, mirroring the racial makeup of Little River (although Peanut knew there to be "about twenty-five young coloreds who *should* vote but never do because they work in Bay Minette and they're too tired when they get home to do it"). In contrast, two miles up the road at the café, which served more or less as the two Boone families' personal ballot box, there were sixteen Republican voters and only four Democrats.

WITH THE FIVE white kids off in prison, and their appeals getting nowhere, Little River had settled back into the anonymity that most of its people seemed to choose. There had been an item in the papers listing the students who had made the dean's list at Faulkner Community College in Bay Minette—a school that had traditionally been used by kids from northern Baldwin County as a stepping-stone, remedial education, to get them ready for a four-year college—and there were only two from Little River: a black girl from the Porter family on Sawmill Road and a beautiful Indian girl ("I kid her by calling her Pocahontas," said Peanut) whose family lived on Highway 59. Except for George Boone's intrepid pursuit of "crazy checks" and the attendant publicity it had received, life was returning to normal. The big cotton farmers were regularly weeding and irrigating their fields, the many white itinerant construction workers were off as far away as the Carolinas, the men of Kimberly-Clark were wondering what would happen when that last major paper company pulled out of the area in September '99, and the churches were gussying up for their annual revival meetings and homecomings.

The news of racial ugliness was coming from elsewhere now, in mid-June, and it was so heinous that it brought a feeling of smug satisfaction to the white families of Little River whose kids had been involved in the desecrations at St. Joe Baptist and Tate Chapel. "How 'bout what happened out there in Texas?" said Raymond Cumbie, whose grandson Jeremy Boone was serving time at a minimum-security prison in Florida. "Now *that's* racism." This was the frightening story out of East Texas, mean Klan country in the Big Thicket, wherein three white men had chained a black man to the back of a pickup and dragged him two miles to his decapitation and death. A week later, in Louisiana, the same thing nearly happened when a black man was grabbed by three whites in a car and miraculously survived being dragged two-and-a-half blocks before managing to shake loose. The copycats were reading the papers, for on the same day there was a similar incident as far away as Belleville, Illinois, a town across the Mississippi River from St. Louis. "See?" said Doll Boone. "What Brandy was supposed to have done ain't nothing compared to that stuff."

Their reverie ended on the last day of June, however, when the Mobile *Register* ran a story on its front page under the headline, ONE

YEAR LATER: HAVE FIRES DIED DOWN IN LITTLE RIVER? It was a fairly benign piece, touching all the bases—Tim Dees's killing, Peanut's beating, the Klan rally, the night of wilding, the trial, the sentences, the return to normality—with quotes from Joe Dees's sister ("It was racism"), Peanut ("Everybody thought it was a bad thing"), Murray January ("I've never had any problem with white people"), and Michael Woods's adoptive father, David Woods ("He just wants to get out [of prison] and make a good life for himself").

A young reporter named Joey Bunch had spent the previous weekend in Little River to interview for the article, and on the Tuesday it appeared he was at his desk in the *Register*'s Bay Minette bureau when the first phone call came. It was from a woman named Rose, apparently speaking for her friend Shirley Dees, mother of the deceased Tim Dees. "We don't know why y'all keep bringing it up," she said, "but please, just let the boy rest in peace."

Then came the other. She didn't announce herself, and Bunch was kicking himself for not punching the buttons on the phone that would identify the caller's number, but in an informal poll at Peanut's the next day, with a group that included one of the Boone women, there was unanimous agreement: it sure sounded like Susan Boone, Brandy's mother.

If so, sickly or not, from her heart troubles and her daughter's imprisonment, the caller was furious. "Why do you keep trying to stir this shit up?" she said.

"We didn't stir it up," Bunch told her. "The kids did. It's news."

"Y'all can't get anything right, anyway, can you? Brandy's baby is due in *October,* not December. [This was critical to the Boones, who had heard the gossip that Brandy had purposely gotten pregnant to win sympathy from the judge.] See there? That's why I don't read the paper."

"Sorry, but everybody I talked to told me it was due in December."

She said, "Well, you ought to be writing about that guy in Texas who had his head dragged off, anyway. *That's* racial."

"How'd you know about that?"

"What?"

"The Texas story. It was in the paper, but you say you don't pay any attention to the paper."

"I've got friends who tell me things," she said. "Don't worry. I know what's going on."

They were getting nowhere. They bandied back and forth until she got in the last words—"Fuck you!"—and slammed the phone.

THERE WAS NO question in Joe Dees's mind that 1997 would go down as the worst year of his life, what with the death of his son and the destruction of his church, but he had managed to ride it out with a certain amount of nobility. He hadn't played the race card with any particular fervor, had bitten his lip as the white parents involved audaciously inferred that *they* were the victims of racism, had simply taken the long way around Sawmill Road rather than pass the trailer of his son's killer, and had quietly suffered when donations fell off once the story died. But now, a year later, he seemed to be experiencing a delayed reaction to all of the clamor.

It had begun in May, with the round-trip walk of eight miles, in ninety-five-degree temperatures, to buy a container of worms at Peanut's, resulting in another stay at the VA hospital in Gulfport, Mississippi. Then, not long after he had gotten back on his medication and returned home, he abruptly showed up at the courthouse in Bay Minette one day and began haranguing two circuit judges, demanding that they get his brother Eugene, near blind from diabetes, out of that same mental hospital in Mississippi. Whetstone figured it would be bad timing to have him arrested, saying to the media, "I've known Mister Dees for a while. He's been under a great deal of stress the past few months, and he was very emotional. I realize there may be a problem there."

That's what Sharon Scott was thinking. Joe seemed headed for another fall. "He came in here one day with a wad of bills and asked me for 'eight big ones,' eight one-hundred-dollar bills," she was saying. "Another time, he took a woman by the arm and brought her in the store and told her to buy whatever she wanted, and paid the thirty dollars." He entered the store one day and bought tampons, perfume, panty hose, and "a bunch of other women's stuff like he had a girl-friend or something." On another trip, he bought eight gallons of engine coolant. For a while during the spring, said Peanut, Dees was gathering up empty cardboard boxes from behind the store "like he was gonna be moving or something." And then, once he had returned from his first hospital stay of the year, he began harassing his old black friends, even his godfather, Roger Jones, with late-night threatening phone calls; he had heard that they had "joined the enemy," he told them, by openly questioning his handling of money meant for the St. Joe rebuilding fund.

He finally snapped three days after the Fourth of July. Joe had told his longtime friend and neighbor on Sawmill Road, L. B. "Sylvester" Benjamin, that he was holding a letter that had been inadvertently left in his mailbox. Sylvester, sixty-eight and forced to use a cane to get around now, drove down the dusty road to Joe's trailer around dusk. He stayed in the car, honking the horn, but saw no sign of life. He was about to leave when Joe came around from the rear of the trailer.

"Where you been?" Sylvester said.

"None of your business," Joe told him.

"I was just asking, Joe. I came to get that letter you told me about."

"Come on inside, then."

"Naw, it's getting late."

"The man won't even come into my house."

"Dinner's cooking, Joe, that's all."

"All right, then, I'll go get the thing." Joe stomped into his trailer and soon came back with the letter. It was getting dark, so Sylvester struggled out of the car and got his cane and shuffled over to the streetlight so he could read the letter. He had bent over to read it when—*wham!*—he was cold-cocked by Joe, knocked to the ground, and struck again.

And there was Joe Dees once more, on the front page of the Baldwin County section of the Mobile *Register*: "St. Joe pastor arrested," with one of the photos taken during the aftermath of the church burning. Sylvester had spent the next day at a doctor's office, with a black eye and cuts requiring twenty stitches, and then he signed a warrant for Joe's arrest. Hoss Mack tracked Joe down the next day at the Winn-Dixie in Bay Minette and hauled him in for a misdemeanor, one count of third-degree assault, but he came up with the $150 to make bail and went back home. Early the next morning, Sylvester was awakened by a phone call from Joe. "So, Sylvester," Joe said, sweetly, innocently, "did you sleep well last night?" Six weeks later, Joe's son drove him to Searcy Hospital, across the waters at Mount Vernon, so they could calm him down and get him back on his medication.

IN THE MIDDLE of August, when he had returned home from Searcy and spent his customary week or so in sequestration, making certain he was okay to resume his life, Joe sat at the Formica dinette table in his trailer. The air conditioner was humming, a huge stewpot was bubbling on the stove, and he was shuffling through a pile of papers strewn all over the table. There were phone numbers scribbled on paper napkins, architects' blueprints, newspaper clippings from the past year-and-a-half, sympathy notes, correspondence with various agencies about the rebuilding of the church, memos to himself on the backs of envelopes, a carbon of the typed list of damages that he had read during the trial, even his own crude sketches of a new church layout on sheets of legal paper. On the floor beside the sofa was the electric typewriter he had been using in his ongoing appeals for help.

"The more time passes," he said, holding up the architect's latest rendering, "the smaller the church gets. The one that burned was forty by sixty feet. Now we've cut it to forty by fifty."

"How much will it cost? One time you said well over a hundred thousand dollars."

"We're down to eighty thousand now."

"Well, the kids have to come up with a hundred thousand."

He seemed incredulous. "That'll take forever. First they do their time, and if they don't have jobs when they get out, they don't have to pay but a hundred dollars a month. Half of my congregation might be dead by then."

"There's the grant from the National Council of Churches."

"I'm working on it," he said, curtly. This was a sore spot with Dees. The NCC had passed out $6.6 million in private donations to burned churches since 1996, but it was moving cautiously now after the discovery of fraud here and there; most notably in Florida, where the head of the National Baptist Convention, a black preacher named Henry Lyons, had been caught stealing one-third of the $245,000 in donations from the Anti-Defamation League. Dees's application for $30,000 from the NCC was on hold, for "reasons I'd rather not discuss."

"Now what?" he was asked.

He brightened, happy to change the subject. "We had the 'unearthing of the soil' at the old place, back in the spring, you know, with lots of singing and praying. September the twentieth, we'll celebrate the hundred-and-twelfth anniversary of St. Joe Baptist. Reverend Mark Williams of the Eastern Shore's going to be there to speak. Ought to be a glorious day." His face sagged. The truth was, he had no earthly idea what might happen next. It was up to the Lord to deliver a miracle, he said.

THIRTEEN

Boones, Everywhere

IN THE MONROEVILLE telephone directory, which is where you
find the listings for northern Baldwin County, there are sixteen
Boones with published phone numbers under the 862 prefix denoting Little River. Multiply the sixteen by four, the average number of
adults and children using each phone, and kick in the Boone women
who assumed new surnames after marrying, then add the ones who
don't have phones, and the total number tells you what everybody in
Little River has known for a long time: they are the dominant white
family in the area; and, the way they procreate, they promise to be for
another century. Throw a rock, you'll hit a Boone, goes the saying,
which can be taken either as wry commentary or a suggestion.

There are two strains of Boones in Little River these days,
although the patriarchs of each clan are fourth cousins, the best they
can figure, and both of them claim blood kinship with the Creek
warrior Red Eagle. "What the hell," one of them says in anticipation
of any questions about cousins marrying cousins, "we all come from
Adam and Eve, don't we?" It all began around the turn of the twentieth century when three Boone brothers trudged in from the eastern
colonies and homesteaded along the Little River. From the very
beginning, as now, there were "good" Boones and "bad" Boones.
The big daddy of the three was Bernard *(BER-nerd)*, a farmer and
logger, said to be something of a hell-raiser, who fathered seven boys
and seven girls. His brother Walter had five kids, all of whom went to

college and never returned, one son becoming a professor at Auburn University, another manager of a string of restaurants in Atlanta. The third brother, Arthur, remembered by Peanut Ferguson as "a good man, a Christian man," stayed but never married. Bernard was the biggest landowner, and when he died he left more than enough acreage to ensure that none of his children and grandchildren would ever be land-poor.

Five of Bernard's six living daughters married and left home, for Atmore and Pensacola and the state of Virginia, leaving only their sister June in Little River (disabled with the nervous disorder commonly known as Saint Vitus' dance, married to a construction worker, now living in a trailer rented from her oldest brother on Highway 59). Only two of the seven sons moved away, one becoming a postman in Bay Minette and the other setting up a construction business in the countryside south of Richmond, Virginia, while the others rooted on the land they had inherited. The oldest of them all is Clayton Boone, Sr., who at sixty-eight employs six of his sons, including Clayton "Doll" Boone, Jr., in what is strictly a family logging business; George, disabled in a logging accident nearly forty years ago when he was a teenager; and three others, in their forties, who are gone much of the time on construction jobs: Leroy, now married to his brother George's ex-wife, Betty Cumbie Boone, who runs the Little River Cafe when he is away; John, father of Jeremy Boone and embattled husband of Debbie Cumbie Boone; and Joseph.

The *other* Boones are relative newcomers, having moved from Booneville, not twenty miles away from Little River in neighboring Escambia County, around the time of the Depression. There were two brothers, J.A. and Ray, who stayed on the land they had staked out in the woods about a mile behind Ferguson Grocery, in the direction of the boat launch at Dixie Landing. J.A. died during open-heart surgery and left two sons, Jerry and John Wayne Boone, the latter being the one who got a night-school law degree and began practicing in Mobile. The death of J.A. left as the head of this clan Ray Boone: the grumpy burr-headed sixty-six-year-old father of

Susan and Darlene (whose children, Brandy and Alan Odom, were now in prison), and sons Danny (married to Karen, of Peanut's store, mother of three children) and Roger, both of whom are gone for long stretches as construction workers all over the country.

The two Boone clans hardly speak to each other, something not easily accomplished in a hamlet the size of Little River. When George Boone turned his shotgun on the Little River Cafe that morning, he was trying to flush out Ray and Jerry, who had been saying bad things about him and his two errant children; and he bought himself another week in jail when he phoned the lawyer John Wayne Boone, Jerry's brother and Ray's nephew, respectively, offering to "meet you somewhere so I can whip your ass" simply because John Wayne was representing Ray and Jerry in their case against him for attempted murder. Three of the kids involved in the arson and vandalism were Boones, with Brandy having a mother from one clan and a father from the other, and both sides had been busying themselves since the troubles by poor-mouthing the others in regards to their parenting and other alleged shortcomings. The sniping is particularly keen when it comes to determining who had brought the bad blood to that marriage: Susan from Ray's side, or Doll from Clayton's branch. The debates could rage back and forth, on and on, about which side had the rottenest apples. "Ray and Kathryn raised a couple of beauties, didn't they, between Darlene and Susan?" "Yeah, well, you want to talk about George shootin' for his crazy checks?" "Unh-hanh, how 'bout Rodney damned-near beatin' that nigger to death for tailgatin' his pickup?" "Say, now, you ain't gon' tell me it's somethin' other'n weird when your wife leaves you to marry your damn brother, are you?" Take away the Boones, Little River would have seemed downright placid over the years.

NOT LONG AFTER daybreak on what was shaping up to be another insufferably hot summer's day, Clayton and his six boys were already bent over their work at what they call "the shop," which is actually the acre of yard beside Clayton's oblong gray-painted cinder-block house at the intersection of Highway 59 and Dixie Landing Road. The gravel yard was cluttered with the assortment of vehicles and equipment necessary for them to carry out their business of cutting trees and dragging them from the woods and delivering the stripped timber to various lumberyards: pickups, a dump truck, a bulldozer, a flatbed tractor-trailer rig, axes, ropes, chain saws, a skeletal tubular metal device designed to snap the limbs from a felled tree when it is forced through a five-by-twenty-foot opening by a 'dozer. Rising above the yard was a huge green metal shed, the size of a small warehouse, where Mark, the mechanic of the bunch, was already under the hood of one of the trucks. Wordlessly, for they have been at this routine for many years, the others went about their duties: sharpening blades, hosing the muddy trucks, soldering the limb–stripper, greasing axles, inflating tires.

In the bad days, before Doll cleaned up his act, this is where the party would have begun to unfold at quitting time on Friday afternoons. But a certain somber dedication to duty seemed to have descended upon them all, not just Doll, since the troubles that had resulted in prison sentences for three Boone children. Wearing greasy baseball caps and jeans and muddy work boots, so heavily bearded that it was difficult for a stranger to tell them apart, they labored in the shade of a grove of trees. Clayton, the father and the foreman, quietly walked among them, clenching the plastic filter of a cigar with his teeth, tugging on a red-and-white gimme cap from Huxford Pole & Timber, saying little. The silence was broken from time to time when a blue-and-yellow diesel logging truck, fully loaded and bearing the logo of Kimberly-Clark, would gear down and make the turn onto Dixie Landing Road, blue smoke belching as the driver grabbed another gear and headed toward the company's storage yard towering above the boat launch.

They were between jobs. For nearly a year they had been spot-cutting timber from an 1,100-acre spread just beyond the Little River bridge, back in the deep woods off Smith Lake Landing Road, and they had just finished that job the day before. This day was being used to repair and clean the machinery, for at daybreak the next day they would move their equipment in a caravan to begin another big operation some twenty-five miles away, beyond Uriah at Huxford. Things had been looking up, in fact, ever since Kimberly-Clark's announcement back in May that it was pulling out of northern Baldwin County after decades of domination. That would leave the business to smaller independent outfits like this one, not incorporated but known to all as, simply, "the Boones'." It had been Clayton's dream all along.

"The good Lord has blessed us. My father was a logger, I'm a logger, and so are all of my boys." He had ducked into the house for a respite from the heat and was sitting at the massive oval Formica-topped cedar dining table, tailored to seat seventeen for such occasions as Thanksgiving and Christmas and birthdays, dominating a spacious room crowded with framed family photographs. His wife and the mother of the boys, Jeanette, was finishing putting away the morning's dishes. ("Anybody who marries one of Jeanette's sons will never cook breakfast again," says a Little River woman who didn't.) "I told 'em all to finish high school, and then we'd talk about working for me," Clayton was saying. "It's worked out pretty good. We make enough money to have what we need, but the best thing is that all my boys live within a mile of my house and we're *family*. Even my daughters are close by, one in Atmore and the other two about five miles away from here in southern Monroe County. We've got thirteen grandchildren now, and four great-grandchildren. Mother's Day and Father's Day are pretty big deals around the house here."

Clayton's brood is generally perceived as the "good" Boones, hard workers all, in spite of Doll's slips in the past. Clayton and Jeanette are regulars at Mamie's Chapel, a short walk down Highway 59 from their house, as are son Jeff and his wife and, lately, Doll and his third wife. It was Clayton who had preempted any probings about intermarriage by saying everybody "comes from Adam and Eve," and who blandly says that moonshine whiskey "never hurt nobody. It's good medicine. My grandmother used it like a tonic for the kids when they got colds or fevers. A lot of people got locked up for making it. You know what that was all about. The state wanted that money for themselves, so they started making their own whiskey and selling it in state stores." None of the boys had ever seriously thought of moving away. "For sure," he said, "I wouldn't want to live in a big place like California, Atlanta, or New York, with so much mischief going on. Little River's the same it's always been, except now we've got drugs. Some people have left here and then come back with new ideas, one of 'em being drugs."

Like most of the others whose families had been touched by the crimes against Tate Chapel and St. Joe Baptist, he was still rankling over the media's coverage but was particularly angry at the law. "The stories just tried to stir 'em up on Sawmill Road," he said, using the euphemism for Little River's black community, "and you can't tell me that [St. Joe] was much of a church, anyway. I mean, a tree fell on it once and stayed there for months. Where'd they meet then? And all of that money Joe Dees is getting, it's going to feed Joe Dees and fix his trailer. Look at him. A man who went walking down a road one time, holding a chicken in his arms, whipping it with a switch." He had "prayed a lot" after the arrests, he said, "but it didn't do a whole lot of good. The feds were too eager to arrest somebody, *anybody,* and like that lawyer said about the hate-crime law, they had a new suit and they wanted to try it on. They were way out of bounds, you ask me."

AFTER THE FIVE kids had been shipped out to prisons in the early spring, the story of the church-burning and vandalism disappeared from television and newspaper reports, giving the residents of Little River some hope that they might be able to slide into a peaceable summer of solitude. Such visions didn't last long. "The summer is when they *really* go crazy around here," Sharon Scott had promised more than once, from her stool behind the counter at Peanut's, and sure enough the Little River dateline began reappearing in the Mobile *Register* about the time daily temperatures started reaching the nineties. It was the Boones, again, and for a while one would have thought the father and son, George and Tommy, were in a competition to see which one could get the most ink.

Tommy had gotten a head start on his father three years earlier when he was finally tracked down, asleep in a stolen car loaded with weapons and loot, after a two-day manhunt. He had been sentenced to twenty years for burglarizing fish camps and homes spread over a wide area, from Atmore to Tensaw, but by the summer of '98 he was free and on the prowl again after promising to make full restitution to his victims. Now twenty-seven, he had been hooked on drugs for nearly half of his life, and stealing was the quickest way to feed his habit. In fact, he was in the car that night in the black neighborhood of Clausell, in Monroeville, when the drug dealer was nearly dragged to his death after trying to pass off soap powder as crack cocaine. This time, it looked like Tommy would be locked away for a very long time. There had been a series of stories about a knife-wielding "Masked Bandit" hitting convenience stores in the Atmore area during a spree in early June, and when Tommy was arrested for carjacking, a trail of clues led the cops to finding that he was the Masked Bandit; at the trailer he shared on the Poarch reservation with his common-law wife, an Indian girl, they found a snapshot of her gaily posing in the Halloween mask he had been using.

Enter, Dad. George was in his late fifties now, living alone in an old trailer down a dirt road behind the cafe run by his ex-wife and her common-law husband, his brother Leroy. He hadn't worked since he was injured in a logging-truck accident as a teenager, and spent his days fishing and helping out at the cafe and hanging around Peanut's store. He had made the papers for the first time in the spring of '98 when he lured his daughter Cynthia, who cooked and waited tables at the cafe, into coming by to clean up his trailer; instead, he ambushed her from a closet and slapped her around and spent a week in the Baldwin County jail before bond was posted by a well-off sister who owns a beauty parlor in Virginia. Hearing that Ray and Jerry, of the *other* Boones, had been bad-mouthing him as they loitered around the cafe while he was in jail, he fired on the cafe that morning and was hauled off to jail again. Free once more, thanks to his forgiving sister, he made the threatening call to John Wayne Boone, from a pay phone in Mobile, and it was the same routine: he was booked, the sister made bail for him, and he walked. He had set a record, even for a Boone, by being jailed three times within two months.

"You look at George's record on paper, consider how his kids have turned out and what he's been doing lately," said Joe Witherington, "you'd think he's dirt, the baddest man in town. But if you don't know any of that, just met him on the street, you'd think he's a sweet guy." An affable rogue is probably more like it, a raconteur, Little River's resident bon vivant. He's a ringer for Mickey Rooney, as well: a short, ruddy man with a burr haircut and twinkling eyes and cheeks that puff out like a squirrel with a mouthful of acorns, quick to laugh at his own self-deprecating jokes, stubby arms flailing whether he's lying about the size of a fish he has caught or commenting about Bill Clinton's inability to "keep it in his pants" during the White House scandal that was now in full bloom. For sheer entertainment, truth be known, George Boone wouldn't be a bad choice if someone needed a lively companion on a drive across America.

Out on bail for the third time this year, George stood in the shade of the large tree between the post office and Ferguson's Grocery, toeing the gravel, turning his head to check out every truck or car that zipped by on the highway. To beat the heat on this morning in July, he wore the *de rigueur* mesh baseball cap, unlaced boots that had been razor-cut at the toes to let the air in, and a thin cotton short-sleeved shirt that was left unbuttoned to reveal a scar from his neck to the navel of a belly the size of a pumpkin. He could explain everything, he said. He was eating a banana for breakfast.

"Well, hell, see, I was just tryin' to help Cynthia out."

"You beat her up."

"Aw, naw, it wadn't like that. Didn't leave no bruises or nothin' like that. Just slapped her around a little, is all."

"But she had you arrested."

He glanced at Murray January, who had just rolled up in his pickup and boat trailer to gas up and buy some bait. "Yeah, but when the court date came up eight days later, notice she didn't show up. She loves her daddy. She don't want to see her daddy in jail."

"What happened?"

"Me and Cynthia?" He finished the banana in one chomp and looked around for a place to get rid of the peel. "Drugs. I jumped out on her and said, 'When you gonna quit takin' that stuff?' and she said, 'I try to, Daddy, but it's hell,' and I said, 'I'll show you what hell is,' and I grabbed her and cuffed her up a little bit. Just wanted to slap some sense in her, is all."

The shotgun incident was a natural outgrowth of that, he said. "Ray and Jerry been causing a lot of trouble at the cafe for a long time, sitting around all morning, cussing and running off customers. They're both lazy as hell, don't work or nothing. We'd been trying to make 'em stay away for a long time. Hell, I'd give that land to my damned ex-wife"—he used the term lovingly, with a wink—"so her and Leroy could have something to do. Figured they could pass the store on to the kids when they got tired of playing 'store.' Anyway, Cynthia was waitressing there, and when I got out of jail she told me they'd been bad-mouthing me, so I figured I'd go teach 'em a lesson, too. Had a hell of a rasslin' match after I shot my gun and went on inside."

Ray and his nephew Jerry, the son of Ray's deceased brother J.A., wrestled George to the floor and called the sheriff's deputy Hoss Mack to the scene. Shotgun pellets were dug out of the porch railing, a doorjamb, and the corner of the building. George was delivered to the county jail in Bay Minette on charges of third-degree assault and reckless endangerment and firing into an occupied building, and while he was behind bars he learned that Jerry had hired his brother John Wayne Boone to represent him and that the lawyer's first move was to get the charge upgraded to attempted murder. Out on bond again, thanks to his sister in Virginia, George saw to it that Ray and Jerry got eighty-sixed from the Little River Cafe and then borrowed his ex-wife's faded blue '70 Datsun 210 to drive to Mobile and threaten John Wayne Boone from a pay phone. "Attempted murder? Hell, I was just trying to get their attention."

George was making no excuses about what had become a determined effort to get on the government rolls as mentally defective—to draw his "crazy checks," as it was referred to in Little River—and was, in fact, greatly enjoying his notoriety. "Hey," he said, "I don't know what else I've got to do to show I'm crazier than Joe Dees." He had been drawing disability checks for most of his life, anyway. "I've been pretty much a wreck since I was a kid. This here"—tracing the scar that bisects his body like an exclamation point—"I got that when I wrecked a logging truck and the steering wheel mashed my stomach. It messed up my esophagus, and I still have to chew my food real good to get it down. I'm diabetic and arthritic, on top of that. Ain't worked in years, except to fool around at the cafe."

All of this with a disarming smile. His sister had come up with $5,000 for a lawyer, who had managed to reduce the charge of attempted murder back down to a misdemeanor, the case now scheduled for sometime in the late fall. Cynthia, he said with some pride, had just called the cops on her abusive drug-sharing boyfriend, and had high hopes of getting a job clerking at the County Line Package Store. Tommy, he said, "looks like he's found himself a home and three meals a day down at the jail in Bay Minette." He had been fishing that night when the five kids got drunk and "went crazy," not finding out what had happened until the law and the media rolled into Peanut's parking lot the next morning. "St. Joe wasn't much of a church, but they shouldn't have burned it," he said, walking toward Peanut's and tossing the wilting banana peel into a blue trash barrel. "Beer probably had a lot to do with it, but I think the real problem there was that their folks didn't do a very good job of parenting."

FOURTEEN

Brother Thomas

———

EXCEPT FOR THE THREE aging black couples who have circled their wagons back in Couglan Swamp—the Browns, Marshalls, and Joneses—George and Nellie Thomas live about as deep in the piney woods as one can get in Little River. Pat Haywood Road is denoted by a green street sign where it begins beside Tate Chapel, on Tommy John Earle Road near the Red Eagle gravesite, and the bulldozed road slips past the tidy white church and snakes through the thickets for half a mile until it abruptly ends at a clearing. There are two dwellings there, the Thomases' tilting old frame house and a single-wide trailer belonging to their thirty-one-year-old youngest son. "We raised seven children in this old shack," George likes to say, with some wonderment, as though he still finds that accomplishment difficult to believe.

A shack it is, a "shotgun" affair where it would be possible to fire a shell through the front door and not hit anything as the pellets whistle out the back, and how nine people could occupy the place at one time is a marvel of efficiency and a testimony of not a little love. The paint has long since flaked away and weathered to a streaked gray, leaving no clue of its original color, and the crooked little house perches precariously on cinder blocks. On one side there is a jerry-built chicken coop at the edge of a clump of mimosas and pines, on the other the ubiquitous propane tank and a faded gray Oldsmobile sedan of the eighties muscle-car era, and at the rear there is a hundred-foot-long garden planted in lush, neat rows of sweet potatoes, peanuts, okra, and sugarcane "for the kids to suck on." Cats, his exterminators, have free run of the yard and the house. Walker Evans, whose bleak black-and-white photographs of rural Alabama shocked the world in *Let Us Now Praise Famous Men,* nearly sixty years before, would have loved it.

The rickety screen porch, tacked on as if an afterthought, is a world unto itself, a jumbled storehouse of oil cans and carburetors and tin pails and fishing gear and bald tires and soggy cardboard boxes overflowing with more detritus: crumpled magazines and newspapers, electrical doodads, tools, nails, cookpots, hubcaps, fishing lures, brogans, flatware, thingamajigs, and mousetraps to catch what the cats can't handle. Rising above it all is a giant floor fan, roaring like a helicopter, making a sort of music as it stirs the dust and rebuffs the flies and mosquitoes that have managed to infiltrate the torn screen, bringing some relief from the suffocating air of midsummer in the swamps.

On a Saturday afternoon when the heat index would reach 104, George Thomas was riding it out on one of the two cracked faux-leather chairs that squat beneath the fan on the screened porch. At Tate Chapel, where his name is at the top of a list of stewards and trustees carved in a block of granite planted at the front-door landing, he is known as Brother Thomas, a lifetime member and a main force in the construction of the new building in 1990, but on this day he was just another old man trying to get some respite from the weather Moses had thrown his way. Nellie, his wife, was asleep inside, doubtless on sheets soggy from the humidity. The drought had made the fish sluggish, even stopped the grass from growing, so fishing and mowing the church lawn seemed to be fruitless pursuits. He was staying at home this day, virtually alone, to ponder.

GEORGE THOMAS IS a vision of what the retired basketball star Michael Jordan might look like when he turns seventy-three. Born to a farmer on the eve of the Depression, a man who spent his life working in the fields and the woods and in sawmills around Little River, he is an imposing presence: more than six feet tall, sinewy, bald in an impressive way, with glistening teeth and luminous skin the shade of coal and high cheekbones hinting of Creek or Choctaw blood. He is forceful, articulate, and animated, one of those men whose booming voice can override any conversation and usually does. On this sweltering day, beneath the big floor fan, he was barefoot and shirtless, wearing only the frayed trousers of what must have been a splendid striped charcoal Sunday suit in its prime.

You never know what you're going to find when you pop in on George Thomas; the pensive church elder happy to have some companionship, or the combative old geezer who's been waiting all day for somebody to come along and take a browbeating. Raymond Cumbie had drawn the latter when he called Thomas to offer money as compensation for the damages at Tate Chapel, and what he failed to understand was that such well-meaning offerings reeked of the same old white-to-black paternalism that George, in his fierce pride, simply will not abide. "We don't want to do it like that," he had said, without so much as a thank-you, rallying some of the younger ones in the congregation, rounding up some cash and putting together a workforce, and they had repaired the damage in no time flat. The incident had been further proof of how little the whites in the area really understand about the black psyche.

Today, slightly more than a year since the vandalism of his church, Brother Thomas was in his pensive mode. "Seven kids," he was saying, "and not a one of 'em spent a day in jail unless there's something they didn't tell me about. What'd I *do*? I spanked their asses if they didn't do right, same as my daddy did us. I spent ten minutes in jail one time when I was a kid, for getting in a fistfight with a black boy, and after that Daddy told us if we went to jail, it was up to us to get out. *Hah!* We stayed in line, all right, just like my kids. Every one of mine finished high school and went straight into the military. They all got good jobs now, a nurse, an electrician, and so forth, doing things they learned in the military. Computers and stuff, understand what I'm sayin'? Except for my baby, the one living out back here, and the other one that got his mind messed up in Vietnam, they're off down around Bay Minette and Mobile now. Every one of 'em's still a member of Tate Chapel." One of his grandsons, Marvin Thomas, who had been raised in Bay Minette and attended Troy State University in south Alabama, was currently in the preseason training camp of the National Football League's Detroit Lions.

It was a different time when George was growing up, during the Depression and the heyday of the Klan, and he had gotten "hardly any" formal education. "Back then, if you were a strong young man, they needed you in the fields." Like Henry Brown of Couglan Swamp (something he never knew before), he was drafted during the middle of the Second World War and landed at Omaha Beach the day after D-day with an all-black unit of the Quartermaster Corps. "I was young and full of it, wanted to hit the beach in an LST like John Wayne, shoot some folks, make my mark, but they put me with the quartermasters." He promptly took some shrapnel in the belly, spent a week in a coma, was left with an ugly scar, and by the time he had recovered the European war was over. "We were packing up for the Pacific when they dropped the big bombs, and that one ended, too." He came back to start his family, working mostly in the sawmills, and he proudly reports that he was never injured on the job.

HIS RELIGION RUNS deep and hard, bordering on the fanatical, and when he gets wound up he can sound like a fire-breathing evangelical preacher on doomsday. ("Some folks say I oughta be preachin', but I'd just as soon be one of God's children.") He's an Old Testament man who takes the Bible literally, from the Garden of Eden through the Crucifixion. "It's all right there, if you just read it," he said. "Adam came first, and then the Lord made Eve out of his rib bone, and the minute she got tempted by the serpent to eat that apple, all hell broke loose. What that means is, a woman's place is in the home. Understand what I'm sayin'?" On race: "Red and yellow, black and white. Some people like red cars, some like black cars, some people like Fords, some like Chevys. Out in that yard, you got all kinds of trees, some for fruit, some for shade, some for cats to climb in. But a tree's a tree, a car's a car, a person's a person. They're all different, got their own jobs to do." On the arson and vandalism: "God put Daniel in the lion's den, put Jonah at the bottom of the sea in that whale, put his son up on a cross, to see if they were gonna quit, but he told 'em, 'Don't stop, don't stop, you can get out of this mess.' It's been tried all over, but you can't kill the church. Unh-unh. Can't do it."

People might be questioning the validity of St. Joe Baptist now as they looked back, not only the parents of the kids who had destroyed it but a neutral observer such as the historian Davida Hastie and even some blacks who had seen it shrivel since Joe Dees had taken over, but no one had ever expressed any reservations about the vibrancy of Tate Chapel AME. Like Mamie's Chapel and most of the other small churches in upper Baldwin County, both black and white, Tate uses a visiting preacher when it meets on the second and fourth Sundays, in this case a circuit rider from Mobile, and its membership of twenty-one adults and seven children represents the latest generation of families who, for the most part, have been there from the start, in 1870, when it was founded by freed slaves. Most of them live close by, attending Sunday school and church meetings faithfully, and there are enough wage earners on the rolls for them to tithe and even take care of brothers and sisters who might fall on hard times.

About the only items they had been unable so far to replicate since the vandalism were framed portraits honoring deceased members like Dicie Thomas, the mother of George and his sister Cora January (Murray's wife), who had died a couple of years earlier at the age of 104. Everything else seemed to be in place, though, as George, now shod in unlaced shoes and a pale blue short-sleeved shirt, gave a visitor a tour of the chapel. It's a classic little church in the wildwood, as the hymn goes, with a white bell tower and double doors and some windows paned with stained glass; its interior walls are whitewashed, its floors covered with practical hard-finish gray carpet, its vaulted ceiling hung with seven ornate gilt fans. The first six rows of pews are upholstered in soft gold cushions, the other ten being of shellacked hardwood, and from those pews one sees a raised platform holding a lectern and seats for a choir numbering ten or twelve. There is a hallway behind the choir area, leading to a small kitchen with two oilclothed tables and a stove and a refrigerator, and tacked to a cork bulletin board along the hallway are eight-by-ten photos (slashed by the kids that night, but now replaced) of black icons making up a Wall of Fame: Martin Luther King, Jr., Rosa Parks, Bill Cosby, Malcolm X, Harriet Tubman, Booker T. Washington, Alex Haley, Thurgood Marshall, Jesse Jackson. It is a cool, safe haven, a place to escape the realities of life in Little River, and there is no telling how much hell would have been raised if Tate Chapel, rather than St. Joe Baptist, had been burned to the ground.

George Thomas was no longer in a joking mood as he wandered about the church, flicking dust away with a bandanna wherever he found it. "It's the only church I ever belonged to," he said. "It means everything to me. I ain't over it yet."

"Angry?"

"No time to fool with that. People have said, 'How could they do that to your church?' Well, it ain't *my* church, it's *God's* church. My church is right here"—pounding his breast—"and this is just a building. Understand what I'm sayin'?"

"The kids who did it—"

"I feel sorry for their parents. Like I said, I spanked mine's asses to keep 'em straight, did everything I could to keep 'em out of trouble. Been around that corner, don't you see. You do all you can, but sometimes you can't help what happens. I pray for 'em."

THE LANGUOROUS SUMMER days limp along in Little River. They can be brutal for teenagers—witness the night of destruction in '97—but the older ones learned long ago to make something out of nothing. Murray January can while away an entire morning by driving over to Dixie Landing and watching the fishermen come in with their catches from a night on the water, and pass the afternoon by sitting in a plastic chair under a grove of trees in his yard and processing the information he has received on where the fish are and what they're biting. A housewife can blow three hours by running up to Monroeville and back to wash a load of clothes at a laundromat, even if she has a washer and dryer at the house, just to be around some other people for a while. A retired farmer might drive all the way to the BP station in Stockton to have the oil changed in his pickup, something he has been doing himself in his yard for years, just for something to do. George Thomas always knows that if he sits around on his screened porch long enough, under the whirring floor fan, somebody's sure to come around to enliven his day.

A couple of days after the visit to the church, with a blessed storm on the way to break the drought, he had been joined by an old friend who was just as bored as he: Fred, by name, a wasted fellow of indeterminate age, built like a spider, dressed in khakis and sneakers and a checkered long-sleeved shirt and a camouflage hunting cap. George wore only a pair of ragged suit trousers this time, scissored at the knees to make cutoffs, and his eyes twinkled. Shy, not the least bit combative, his old friend was the perfect straight man.

"Cats hide in trees, waitin' for birds, you know," George was saying.

"Unh-hunh," Fred said.

"Go out on the limbs and wait for 'em."

"Naw. Limbs won't hold 'em."

Bingo. "What you mean? You tellin' me I don't see what I see every day, sittin' on this porch, lookin' straight ahead at that tree, watchin' cats *ambush* birds? That what you're sayin'?"

"Cats too heavy for the limbs, that's all."

"Hah! Snakes, too. They ain't too heavy."

"Snakes, now . . ."

"You believe *that* part, then."

"They not too heavy for the limbs."

"*Evil* ol' things, *sneaky,* right out of the Bible, wonder they ain't tried to talk me into eating an apple. Just like them snipers we had over in France. German snipers." Brother Thomas had an audience. "Whooo! We had 'em on the run after the landing, but they still had their snipers out. It'd be night and I'd hear somebody call my name, real low. 'George Thomas.' Spies had got a-hold of the roster, you know, knew all our names. I didn't hear no password, so I kept my head in the tent. Voice come back again. 'Bill Jones!' Bill Jones stuck his head out and said, 'Yeah?' and *bam!!* Got him in the head. One less GI to feed. But, then, you wouldn't know nothin' 'bout being in battle, would you?"

"Well, I imagine . . ."

"*Imagine?* Hah! You'd have to be there to know what scared is. Shots, smoke, yelling, bombs, people dying all around. 'Medic, medic!' 'Oh, Lord!' 'Mama, Mama!' You're walking along with your buddy and a sniper drops him, you're a goner, won't have time to move before he gets you, too. Got you in his sights already."

"Ain't that somethin'."

"Tell you the truth, Fred, knowing all of that helped me understand things when my boy came back from Vietnam all messed up in the head. Understand where I'm comin' from?" They sat quietly for a few minutes. A rooster crowed from the chicken coop beside the house. Out in the yard, near Fred's old Ford pickup, a cat spied a bird and went into his jungle-cat crouch. "Come on," Brother Thomas said, rising from his chair and pulling a paring knife from his pocket. "Let's find a pail and go cut you some okra. Ain't no way me and Nellie can eat all this stuff."

FIFTEEN

Mom

Darlene Boone Odom Middleton would turn forty on her next birthday, a freckled redhead who's a bit thick in the middle, twice divorced and not eager to try marriage again anytime soon. Her only concession along that line was to allow her current boyfriend to permanently camp his bullet-shaped travel trailer about fifty paces through the trampled grass from her hundred-foot-long single-wide, on a high ridge off a county road some ten miles north of Ferguson's Grocery. Close, but not *too* close. The only one of her three kids still living at home, in this summer of 1998, was twelve-year-old Tommy, a bulky fullback on the junior varsity team at J. U. Blacksher High in Uriah. Her oldest son, Alan, was in prison in Louisiana, a 390-mile drive from Little River, and he won't be eligible for parole until the year 2010, when he is thirty-two. Her only daughter, Wendy, was spending the summer between her junior and senior years of high school going through Army National Guard basic training at Fort Jackson, in South Carolina. In the meantime, Mom was working eight hours a day during the week at the Medline plant up the road in Frisco City, sewing together surgical gowns beside Doll Boone's wife, Teresa, and on weekends tending the counter at the County Line Package Store.

Let others laugh and say she was cruising for a date when she went to the Klan rally at Tensaw, the one that preceded the night of wilding forty-eight hours later in 1997, but this is a hard world for a woman to live in. It was a Saturday night and she was lonesome, and she went where she thought she might find a certain guy she was seeing at the time. He wasn't there, so she borrowed her niece Brandy's little blue Toyota, left her at the rally with her young friends, and drove on to Frosty Acres, the second most likely place he might be, and there he was. "Susan [her sister, Brandy's mother] is still technically married to her third husband, but they haven't lived together since their four-year-old was, like, six weeks old," she said. "As far as a single unmarried woman that doesn't live with a man"—ignoring the boyfriend living in her yard—"I'm the only one in Little River. It's not a good place to be single, I can tell you." She paused and laughed. "Single, and working at a liquor store, at that."

On a wall in the front room of the well-appointed trailer, where Tommy slouched on the sofa, aimlessly surfing the cartoon channels with the remote, there was a framed glamor photograph of Wendy wearing a cowgirl hat—a pretty girl, passing for a country singer, Darlene's hope. Barefoot, wearing cutoffs and a T-shirt, she padded down the hallway and returned from a back room with a recent letter from Wendy. "All of her letters sound like, 'I'm growing up, Mama,'" Darlene said. "She'll finish high school and do her time in the army, and then she'll be able to go to any college she wants to, anywhere. She'd like to be a lawyer, something like that." She read from the letter. "Says, 'I want to be a good role model for Tommy. I feel like if he sees what I do it'll inspire him to do well, also. Life is full of choices, and I want him to make good ones. I love him and I want to see him succeed. Alan has already made a mistake, but he can use it to his advantage . . . '"

Like any parent, Darlene wanted her children to avoid the mistakes she had made and to do better. She had gotten married right out of high school, to a local man named Ted Odom, a "good provider," and was proud to say that all three of her kids had been fathered by the same man. But he was gone all the time, making good money on dredge boats far from Little River, and they had divorced after fourteen years. Soon after, she married a man named Greg Middleton, who worked for the local power company, but that turned out to be a mistake vis-à-vis her children. "The kids flat didn't like Greg," she said, and so both Alan and Wendy spent more time four miles down the road living with their father when he was home, in a frame house he had built on stilts, or next door at his parents' house. When she divorced Middleton after only three years, she found this trailer and moved in with young Tommy. Alone again.

"Don't get me wrong," she said, "but the men that are from Little River, they're all Boones or Deans or Cumbies, and I wouldn't want to marry or be with any of 'em. They don't have any ambition. They don't want to succeed, do better, don't have any—what's the word?— they don't have any *expectations*. There's a lot that's 'disabled' that ain't disabled, you know? A lot of the men don't work because they don't *want* to work. Everybody here got raised the same, stayed home, married each other, never changed anything. It's especially rough on girls, like I was, where it's a sort of male society, you know? Hopefully, Wendy'll be different. I always drummed it into her head: 'Go somewhere, do something. You're pretty and smart, *do* something.' Basically, that's why she joined the National Guard. The discipline keeps her on the straight and narrow, for sure, and I don't see her coming back to live the same old life in Little River. You can see where it led Alan."

WHAT HAPPENED THAT night and during the following days? As she began to reconstruct the events, from the morning of Murray January's discovery of the fire and destruction to the five kids' arrest, it became clear just how little control the parents had over their own children's comings and goings. "I was cooking at the Boones' cafe then, and the first I heard about it was at work that morning after the fire. You know how gossip spreads: 'Guess what, guess what . . .' When they said a nigger church had burned down, I asked if it was the one down at Red Eagle's or that little piece-of-junk church [St. Joe Baptist]. They said it was the one that was just about all the way in and I said, 'Well, somebody just come by and set it on fire.' It never registered with me that it was a church. I mean, it used to be a church, years ago when I was a kid, but it was just a piece of junk. It was not a church anymore. It just wasn't."

Then she had a call at the cafe from her sister, Susan, imploring her to come over to her house the minute she got off work, "and I knew then that something was wrong. I knew. I just knew. See, Susan told me she'd asked Brandy that morning, soon as she got up, 'Brandy, did you hear about the nigger church burning down?' And Brandy said, 'Which one?' And she said, 'The one down there on Red Eagle's road,' and Brandy said, 'I've got to call Jeremy.' She tried, but Jeremy wasn't home. Brandy didn't say nothing right then, but then she said, 'Now, Mama, we was all down there but we didn't burn no church down.' Susan said, 'What do you mean?' and Brandy said, 'Let me go find Jeremy.' She went to Jeremy's and she come back and she says, 'Do you know what Jeremy told me, Mama?' Jeremy had told her the whole story. See, Brandy didn't know that the church had burnt down until the next day. The child *did . . . not . . . know!* She was not even there!"

Darlene began to repeat the now-familiar story of that night, as Brandy told it to the two sisters, her mother and her aunt: of the three cars, of the flat tire on Alan's pickup, of how most of them had returned to the Gentry house, where the party had begun, but "Alan, Michael and Jessica whatever [Perry, the visitor from Ohio], they didn't see them no more because they went the other way, to turn around, supposedly. And that's when those three went back to St. Joe and stopped and set it on fire. Jeremy didn't even find out the church was on fire until later on, when him and Alan got back in Alan's truck and they passed the church on the way to the Tate church, where *that* happened. Brandy was getting in her car about that time and going home. See, she didn't know anything. I mean, Brandy knew *nothing.* So that's how I found out. I said, 'Brandy, what is *wrong* with you young 'uns?' you know, that's all I could think about. I didn't know nothin' about no law. I didn't think they'd wind up in prison for just burnin' an old piece of junk. That's the way everybody in this community, generally, looked at it. Now if they had come over here and burnt the [Little River] Baptist church, or if they had burnt the other church [Tate Chapel] down, or they had went to Tensaw and burnt one of them churches down, one that somebody was actually *goin'* to . . . I mean, I ain't seen nobody [at St. Joe] in years, and I've lived here all my life. I thought it was abandoned. That was a bunch of bull, about it being a real church."

Unable to track down her son on that day when it seemed the world had come crashing down on Little River, she finally caught up with him on Wednesday, the next day. She had taken Wendy and Tommy to the house of Kenneth Lambert, the crippled man tended by Susan Boone, to go swimming in his pool, and found that Alan and Michael Woods were there. "By then," Darlene said, "I'd done heard about the law and stuff on tee-vee the night before when they up and said, 'Whoever done it could be charged,' and blah-blah-blah and all this, and I said, 'Say *what?*' So when I'd got to Kenneth's I went out there on the back porch and I said, 'Alan, what in the world do y'all mean by burning that church down?' He said, 'Mama, that ain't no church,' and I said, 'Alan, y'all are in some bad trouble.' And whatever else I said must have made him mad, and I knew then that that was it. I believe the law had already talked to him, just some general questions, and either scared him or made him mad. Anyway, he said, 'Mama, I don't want to talk about it,' and I said, 'Well, whatever, but I'm telling you . . .' And I turned and looked at Michael, because I knew he was in on it, too, and I said, 'Bud, you're in trouble just as much as the rest of 'em. Y'all are *all* in trouble.' I told 'em, 'I don't know who done what and I ain't asked you and I ain't *going* to ask you, but I'm telling you y'all are all in trouble.' They got mad at me because I was the bearer of bad news."

The kids were in denial, stonewalling even their parents, up to the moment they cracked under interrogation and were locked up. Darlene had a visit at the cafe on Thursday from Mickey Pumphrey, who worked alongside her second husband, Greg Middleton, at the power company, and had loaned Alan his tools to change to the donut spare during that long Monday night of caterwauling. "He come to the back where I was cooking and said I ought to know that the ATF and the fire marshals was wanting to know all about that flat tire, and he was wondering if they were trying to say those young 'uns was mixed up in that church burning. I didn't let on what I knew, but after the lunch rush was over I called over at Kenneth's and asked him to call Alan to the phone. I told him what Mickey had just told me, and all he said was, '*Bye!*' and slammed the phone. It was one o'clock then and I was hurting, wishing two o'clock would come, because I didn't know what was fixin' to happen." When she passed Ted Odom's house and "saw the ATF agents all over the yard," talking to Alan and Michael, she stopped and was told that they wanted to take the boys to Bay Minette to "ask 'em a few questions." That was when Alan assured her that the agents wanted to "talk to us for a while and they're gonna bring us back." Darlene told him "if he needed me, I'd be at Kenneth's pool with Wendy and Tommy. He just never came back home."

That her two older children had been living in their father's mostly empty house or at his parents' home next door to it, and that she didn't even have Ted Odom's phone number on the job in Louisiana, would lead one to believe that she had been effectively excommunicated from the Odom family after the divorce six years earlier. On the Friday, when Alan and the others were in jail and incommunicado, she called Odom's parents to find out how to reach him—"He was on a lake near Morgan City and you had to use a marine operator to get him"—and learned that Ted's sister had already reached him and he was on his way home. On Tuesday, Darlene and Wendy rode with Ted to Bay Minette, where Ted made bond for Alan, and they brought him back to Little River. "It was pretty quiet in the car," she said. "We were all still kinda stunned."

ON THIS AFTERNOON, slightly more than a year later, she left Tommy in front of the television set with his cartoons and stepped outside for a cigarette. The cicadas had cranked up their scratchety evening serenade in earnest as the blistering orange sun began to drop below the pines. Her boyfriend's empty silver trailer—he was out of town again, on a construction job—caught the last glints of sunlight.

A single cow lowed inside the barbed-wire enclosure in the front yard, head bent, working her way through the high blue-green grass. Still barefoot, sitting on the concrete steps at the door to the trailer, Darlene lit up.

"I'm assuming they got so drunk they didn't know what they was doing," she said, "and that they was on a little marijuana, too. I'm sure they every one of 'em would've tested positive. Lord! They're not like mean young 'uns. They hadn't never hurt nobody, you know, like gettin' in fights and things. Now Michael, I think he had a scuffle or two at school, but the rest of 'em . . . *nothing*."

She had made the long drive to visit Alan in Louisiana once so far, she said, and he had told her it "wadn't all that bad, just the fact that he can't leave. They've got their own little world in there. There's twelve hundred inmates, mostly Mexicans, Jamaicans, and Colombians, in for drugs and immigration. He's in medium security, not minimum like the other kids, meaning he's sleeping behind bars every night. We're appealing Count Five, the hate-crime thing, but the way it is now he'll have to serve eighty-five percent of his fifteen years. If he'd done like Michael [Woods] and gone ahead and pleaded guilty, he'd be home before you know it. I don't know what that was all about, the stuff betwen him and his lawyer. Anyway. The poor kid, he'll be middle-aged before he gets out and has to start his life over again."

Flipping the cigarette into the weeds, she stood, flexed her hands and winced. "Two hundred women at that shop, and I bet every one of 'em's had that carpal tunnel syndrome at one time or another. Today, the sewing plant. Tomorrow, the liquor store. Some life, huh?"

SIXTEEN

Shootout at Butterfork Hill

————

THE FATHER OF THEM all was a farmer named Tom Cumbie, who arrived in Little River toward the end of the nineteenth century and died in 1968. He had sired five sons, only two of them still living at the approach of the millennium in 1998: Bill, the eighty-two-year old, riding out the remainder of his days with his wife, Hannis, in the tin-roofed house beneath cedars just beyond the Little River bridge; and Dennis, seventy-eight, deaf since birth, briefly married once (to a woman who very nearly scammed him of his meager land inheritance), who now spent his days hanging out at Peanut's store just to escape the loneliness of his small trailer beside the All-Seeing Eyes Holiness Church's fanciful sign on the highway. One of the deceased sons of Tom Cumbie was Farish, who died in the eighties, leaving six heirs: daughters Betty (who had married George Boone and then left him to marry his brother Leroy) and Mary (married to the lawyer John Wayne Boone); and sons Raymond, Willard, Harold, and another who died years ago. There had been so much commingling between the Cumbies and the Boones over the generations that each seemed like an extended family of the other. In terms of sheer numbers, those two had become the dominant families in Little River.

Raymond Cumbie, like his uncles Bill and Dennis and his brothers Willard and Harold, had decided early on to get a union card and hire out as a freelance construction worker rather than to risk his life on a dead-end job in the forests. Maintaining his home in Little

River, and having only one child to support, Debbie, he had made a lot of money from those high-paying Teamsters jobs all over the country, but that had never fully satisfied him. "Raymond's father made him what he is," said Joe Phillips, Raymond's next-door neighbor on Highway 59, just south of Peanut's place. "Farish wanted the easy dollar—moonshine, marijuana, whatever." Said James Witherington: "Raymond could've been something better, but he was raised into an outlaw family. A lawyer wanted me to say something nice about one of 'em one time and I said, 'Not for *that* bunch.'" Raymond himself would vehemently disagree with these assessments— "Anybody that says anything bad about my daddy is lyin'"—but the fact remains that Raymond has experienced more than a little excitement during his sixty-four years.

"Anybody that's had dealings with the law knows it's rotten from top to bottom," he was saying on a late-summer morning in '98, in the voice of a man who feels he has been wronged at every turn. There was his being blocked for a beer license at a place he owned in the sixties on Sawmill Road ("I was going to be in competition with Jim Dees [Joe's father], but he was fronting for [big white landowner] Cleveland Gantt, who was buddies with the sheriff at that time"). There was his killing of Ralph Dees in 1975, at what is now the County Line Package Store ("I was framed by the new sheriff, charged with first-degree murder, but they"—an all-white jury—"finally let me off on self-defense"). There was the law's refusal to investigate the "kidnapping" of his daughter, Deborah Cumbie Boone, then a teenager, by a "hippie" at a motel in Colorado. There was the long soap-opera marriage to Carol, and then her mysterious hit-and-run death only a year after her taking up with a ne'er-do-well half her age ("They was both on drugs, so I guess she didn't count"). There was the arrest and imprisonment of his only grandson, Jeremy Boone, in the vandalism of Tate Chapel ("Why didn't they get that Jessica Perry? She's the one behind everything"). And, most famously, there was the Shootout at Butterfork Hill.

AFTER YEARS OF sharing the brick house he had built in 1982, with Debbie or John or Jeremy or all three, during the tumultuous years of his marriage, Raymond was living alone now. He and John had just been laid off after a summer on a pipeline construction job in Linden, Alabama, near the Mississippi line, and he was biding his time until another one opened up. Wearing the usual workingman's uniform of jeans, boots, and long-sleeved shirt, speaking in a gentle high-pitched voice that belied his physical strength, Raymond seemed to have reached that point in life where he was eager to set his stories straight, of making amends, perhaps, which had been the impetus for his trying to help Joe Dees and the men of Tate Chapel in the wake of the church desecrations.

Due to its isolation and relative poverty, northern Baldwin County and southern Monroe had been classic moonshine country in the earliest years of the twentieth century. "My daddy used to say bootleggers ought to wear badges to identify themselves so they wouldn't try to sell moonshine to each other," said Bill Cumbie, born in 1916. Little River was so far back in the woods, extremely difficult to reach before the completion of Highway 59 during the Second World War, that the sheriffs of Baldwin and Monroe didn't have much time to track down bootleggers. A man and his sons could work their land or even hold fulltime jobs in the factories or fields and still have plenty of time to nurse moonshine stills. There was ample corn for the mash, streams everywhere for the water they needed, and a maze of dirt back roads leading to the legally "dry" markets in Monroeville and Bay Minette. Although the occasional cat-and-mouse chases involving moonshine runners and lawmen were more famously connected to the Appalachian hollows, leading to the birth of the Southern sport of stock-car racing, there was plenty of that in the swamps and forests of south Alabama: good old boys in souped-up hot rods, loaded to the roof with jars of contraband whiskey, dust flying in their wake as they roared through the piney woods, hotly pursued by revenuers, in their dash toward town. It was regarded not only as the most economical use of corn, whose bulk presented transportation problems, but also as a thrilling way to break the monotony and maybe even gain a little local notoriety.

Then, in the seventies, the men discovered an even easier way to make money on the side, and lots more of it: growing and selling marijuana. Several factors had conspired against homemade whiskey—publicity about poisonous batches, better law enforcement due to surveillance helicopters and new paved roads, the legalization of liquor sales in the old Bible Belt, a new generation of kids who preferred "dope" over alcohol—and the bootleggers simply shifted from one crop to another. The humid land was just as suitable for growing marijuana plants as corn, and a hundred times more profitable, so by the early seventies the stuff was growing like kudzu in the rich black loam of the swamps. Raymond Cumbie and his father, Farish, decided to go into business.

"I HAD GOT a-holt of some marijuana seeds while I was working up at Claiborne," Raymond said, referring to the lock and dam at U.S. Highway 84, where it crosses the Alabama River west of Monroeville. "There was this white nigger from Atmore who worked with us and was a dealer in marijuana. Me and my daddy was trying to learn to grow it, but we found out that was the hardest stuff to grow you ever seen. You'd plant the seeds, but everything had to be just right. I reckon the rats would come and bite it off, and if you didn't keep your eyes on it all the time it'd just sit there and die on you. We'd go out in the woods and clean us up some spot—didn't put any on *our* land, mind you, but somebody else's, because if the Feds caught you, there went your land—find us a little swag with good topsoil and dig it up just like you was gonna plant a garden. Daddy, he kept fooling with it, and it got to where in the second or third year it was doing fine. We made these cylinders out of screen wire to go around the plants and keep the rats out. We even tried putting a few in seedbeds at home, like starting tomato plants, and when they come up we'd transplant 'em into cups, and that worked pretty good."

Then, in the fall of 1976, a year after he had been cleared in the killing of Joe Dees's brother, Raymond and his father saw the chance to make a big score. "After the law done me the way they did, costing me close to ten thousand dollars' worth of money defending myself, I decided I was gonna get my money back. They didn't nobody know about the marijuana but Mama and Daddy and [his wife] Carol. We'd been going all day and night for a long time, cleaning and working and watering the plants, and we figured we might make maybe fifty or seventy thousand dollars apiece. Then Daddy and Mother came to see me one day. Mama said, 'Raymond, Willard [his brother] ain't making much money, so why don't y'all help him out some so he can pay on his house?' I said, 'Mama, Willard talks too much. Him and his wife do, both of 'em, and in six months they'll do us in.' She said, 'Well, we'll talk to him, tell him to keep his mouth shut.' And I said, 'I know both of 'em, and I'm not gon' fool with it.' I told Daddy, 'If you want to fool with it, go ahead, but I'm not gon' do it.'"

Raymond had his hands full at that time, running the County Line Package Store, working all day at the Claiborne lock-and-dam project, and trying to keep up with his capricious wife, Carol. He had already tried to help Willard, in the mid-sixties, by lending him $12,000 to start up a drive-in dairy bar in Uriah, but after the place was up and running Willard refused to repay the loan. "He told me that Daddy had built me a place one time, that store down on Sawmill and Dixie Landing roads, and he figured it was time *he* got something. I had to hire a lawyer to get my money back from my own brother. The dairy bar's still there, but Willard don't own it because they let it go to hell. You just couldn't trust Willard, neither him or his wife, Ezerlee."

NOW, IN 1976, Willard was doing construction work at a paper mill in Brewton, and he came to visit Raymond one day with the news that there was a coworker at the plant in Brewton who had a cousin in Atlanta who was interested in buying a lot of marijuana. "I was skittish," said Raymond, "and I told Daddy I was afraid to fool with it. But me and Daddy got Willard and set him down and said, 'Now, Willard, we'll take a chance on this guy. We want him to come at such-and-such evening, and y'all be at the store, you and him, at six o'clock.' In the meantime, me and Daddy got what little we had and brought it to his house, and he and Willard got what they had. All told, we had about a hundred and sixty pounds of it in brown paper sacks, hid away from the house. The evening they was supposed to come, it got to be six o'clock and they didn't show up. I stayed in the store 'til eight o'clock, and when they still hadn't come I closed up and me and Carol went to the trailer out back, where we was living then, when pretty soon here come Willard."

Raymond's instincts told him to walk away from the deal. "Willard said, 'All right, I got him out there in his van. Everything's set.' I said, 'Yeah, but look at the time.' 'Oh, he says he had some kind of car trouble or something.' I said, 'Let's don't fool with him, Willard, if he can't do what he's told to do.' 'Naw, I'm gon' take him on down to Daddy's, and you can come if you want to.' So he turned and got into the man's van and went on to Daddy's house, the one where Debbie's living now. I waited fifteen to twenty minutes before I told Carol, 'Let's go see what they're doing.' I had me a little old 'seventy-three Volkswagen, and I had a pistol."

When Raymond and his wife arrived at Farish's house on Highway 59, not far from where Raymond now lives, they first saw the buyer's old Chevy panel truck and then "here come Willard and Daddy, and the man with 'em. When I told Daddy I still didn't want to fool with it, he told me it was too late, there was another man already in the van sampling the stuff. The men hadn't brought no money, and we were gon' have to go up the road to get it. I told Daddy I wouldn't go from here to the road with those guys. We didn't know who they were, nothing but what Willard had told us, and they were late and didn't have the money and now we had to go way up the highway late at night to close the deal. I just suspected something wadn't right about this whole thing. Anyway, we finally agreed that Daddy and Willard would ride along in the truck with the marijuana and the two guys, and I'd be right behind 'em in my VW, to meet the payoff man up at Butterfork Hill."

NO ONE ALIVE seems to know the origin of the name, except that a large swatch of the area around Uriah once was known as Butterfork, but Butterfork Hill is the last rise along a roller-coaster portion of Highway 59 before the road ends at Uriah. It is a spooky stretch of asphalt, just beyond a silver water tank, bounded by thick stands of pines. Lagging behind the panel truck by two or three hundred yards, just close enough to keep it in sight, Raymond felt queasier than ever. He felt like a cowboy running into a box canyon, with no way out. The van passed the water tank, slowed at Butterfork Hill, then turned right and disappeared down into the woods. "I pulled off on the left shoulder, the other side of the road, and turned my lights off and sat there for a minute or two. I knew Daddy had a nine-millimeter gun on him and Willard had a pistol stuck in his boot, and then, all of a sudden, it was *Pow-pow-pow!* I figured, *Yeah, that's what I thought.* I hit the starter, cranked up, and got the hell out of there."

Whatever had happened down there in the woods, this was no time for Raymond to go and investigate. The chase was on. He went sailing toward Uriah and, seeing headlights rushing up in his rearview mirror, spun left at the dairy bar he had once financed for Willard, then took a quick right for another block, slowing long enough to toss his own pistol into some high weeds in a vacant lot. When he turned right again, making it back to the intersection that is Uriah's town square, he realized he had been hemmed in by two police cruisers. "So I stopped, naturally. They had me in their lights, blocked in, and I got out real easy, so they'd see I wasn't armed. Three agents had their guns drawn, and I noticed one of 'em was this ABI [Alabama Bureau of Investigation] agent I didn't have much use for. He kept yelling, 'Watch him, watch him, he's got a gun and he'll kill you.' I said, 'I ain't got nothing.' He hated my guts, see, and he was just trying to get 'em to shoot me."

Willard had sung, all right, because a virtual platoon of lawmen had been waiting in the woods at Butterfork Hill—thirty-one of them, by count. "Shoot 'em, shoot 'em!" Farish had shouted when he saw them, but it was the cops who fired. Willard took a slug from a powerful .357 magnum, through the chest and out the back, prompting Farish to drop his pistol, and that was that. The officers, most of them drug enforcement agents, hauled Willard to the hospital in Atmore, where Raymond and his father were escorted. All three were arrested on drug charges.

"Well, hell," Raymond said, finishing his tale, "I knew Willard and his wife couldn't keep their mouths shut. The [informer] had a real job at the mill. There were about five or six union guys like that working in the mill, all of 'em informers. They'd been caught for other things, see, so they'd made a deal with the Feds to stay out of jail. Happens all the time, I reckon. Anyway, not having much choice, we all plead guilty. We all got four years. Daddy and Willard both served two years, and I didn't do but six months, since I wasn't actually on the scene and I didn't have a gun on me that they knew about. Mama stayed with Willard's wife while he was in jail, paying their bills, and I'll be damned if Willard and his wife kept saying I was the one that got us caught. Me and Daddy both knew we were breaking the law, if they caught us we'd have to do time. You take your chances."

Two years later, when the three Cumbies had served their time and were back home again (Willard, due to his injuries, disabled for life), there came a splendid opportunity for a sequel to the Shootout at Butterfork Hill. They had been particularly incensed that they had gotten no breaks from the district attorney who had vigorously pursued their case, one James Hendrix. "Other than me being tried for murder that time, we'd never been into nothing, but we got the maximum sentences." Then the news broke, two years after Butterfork Hill, that Hendrix himself was going on trial in Mobile for dealing in marijuana. *Well, well, now.* Raymond and Farish got up before daybreak every day, spiffed themselves up, and drove into town early so they could get front-row seats. "We'd sit there and grin and wave at Hendrix all day, and then catch him on breaks. 'Aw, Mister Hendrix, this is just awful. Fine man like you, you couldn't 'o done this. They just out to get you. We're behind you all the way.' Playing with his mind, see. About drove him crazy. He was found guilty as hell and they sent his ass away for five years."

IT WAS PROBABLY nothing more than coincidence, but most of the pivotal events during Raymond Cumbie's lifetime had occurred in the waning days of summer, right around Labor Day. He had been judged not guilty of murdering Ralph Dees in late August of 1975. The shootout at Butterfork Hill had taken place in September of '76. The hit-and-run death of his ex-wife Carol was discovered in August of '86. And his only grandson, Jeremy Boone, had been born on the eighth day of September in '77. Now, in the days leading up to Labor Day of 1998, with his grandson in prison and the marriage of his daughter to John Boone apparently nearing its end, it was time for more adjustments in his life.

The relationship between him and John had been an odd one. "One time while I was running the liquor store," he said, "John drove up and wanted some gas for his truck. He was pissed off at me because I wouldn't let Debbie marry him. So while I was bent over, pumping gas, he up and cold-cocked me." When they went ahead and married, anyway, Raymond grudgingly accepted it, and over the years he and John worked side-by-side on construction jobs; and, because John didn't hold on to his money, there were long periods when all three—John, Debbie, and Jeremy—lived with him and Carol after he had built his house on the highway in 1982. Then, after Raymond's parents died, he bought their old house down the road: "One of the Bradleys wanted it to put a family of niggers in, so I bought it for Debbie and them."

Even now, with the breakup of the marriage seeming to be a sure thing, something he had been wanting for a long time, Raymond was counseling John as he would a son. "One evening this spring, right before Jeremy went away, about the time John jumped Debbie's boyfriend up at Peanut's, I had 'em all three at my house. Debbie wanted John out, and he wanted to move in with me. I said I didn't want nobody living with me, I wanted my privacy. I said, 'Look, you're working six twelves, and bringing in a thousand dollars a week [on the pipeline job at Linden]. Why don't you save up and go get yourself a trailer? That way, you'll have a home, a place for Jeremy to call you when he's gone.' Debbie'd already told Jeremy about this other fellow. I told John, 'You can't *make* a woman live with you. Look what I went through. Go on and make a life for yourself.'"

Debbie was certainly doing that for herself now. The prettiest woman around, still in her thirties and with a job that gave her independence, she had found the perfect time to make the break she had been threatening for years. She had executed papers to keep John out of the house, after he had tried to break down the door to get in one night, and their son wouldn't be out of prison for two or three years. Her beau, this Larry, wasn't exactly rich but he was from outside of Little River and available and, obviously, had proven to be interesting during their trysts at his cabin.

Then, on that very afternoon while Raymond sat and reminisced about his life, the news swept through Little River that Larry's cabin on the water near Peanut's had been burned to the ground. Raymond heard about it when Debbie called him from the courthouse where she worked in Bay Minette, and asked him to come to the house when she got home around six o'clock.

She was in the kitchen, wearing white Capri pants and a T-shirt, when he came in. Dinner was simmering on the stove, and she was sitting at the Formica dining table, having an animated conversation on the phone, when her father entered the room. "They're pretty sure it's arson," she was saying, twirling her blonde hair with her fingers. "Well, you know . . . Everything, I guess . . . Sure . . . I'll be there. . . ."

When she hung up, she seemed to be happy more than anything else. *That ought to do it, by God.* To Raymond, who thought he had seen everything, this was a hell of a turn of events. He and John had just returned home, laid off from the pipeline job in Linden, and he had no idea where he was staying these days. He said to his daughter, "Larry?"

"Uh-hunh. He's coming up."

"Who do you think done it?"

Debbie was incredulous. "Who else?" she said. "My soon-to-be ex-husband. That sonofabitch."

They chatted for a few more minutes, about Jeremy and her job and Larry and the trailer, and soon a shadow began to fall over Raymond's lined face. Was he hearing what he thought he was hearing? There was nothing more she could do for Jeremy, she said, not for a good while. John was history now, she said. The drive to Bay Minette every day was getting old, she said. There was nothing to keep her in Little River anymore, she said. In Mobile, say, a girl could take a long hot bath and put on a pretty dress and go out to a fancy restaurant. Have *fun*. When Raymond asked her if she might be thinking about leaving Little River and she said, with only a slight hesitation, "Maybe," he was struck dumb. He had only *thought* he wanted his privacy.

SEVENTEEN

It Takes a Village

OF ALL THE PARENTS whose kids had gotten into such trouble, David Woods was the one most entitled to ask, "Why me?" It had never made sense that his adopted son, Michael, would have done such a thing because in many ways David was the most substantial of the parents. He had willingly adopted Michael, a bruised and under-nourished infant, when he married the boy's aunt and adoptive mother. When that marriage failed so Patricia Williams could try to regain her teenage years, he took on their two young daughters. Two more kids joined the brood when he married Mary Shepherd, who had two boys from a previous marriage. A burly dark-skinned truck driver and mechanic with a mild demeanor (except, everyone agreed, when riled), he was a proud man with a deep, forceful drawl, quite a catch for the women of the area during the two-and-a-half years between his marriages: both a gentle man and a "good provider," a rare combination in those parts.

None of the others could make a better case that the arson and vandalism of two black churches had not been racially motivated, at least on the part of his stepson. David himself was three-fourths Choctaw-Creek (on the rolls at the Poarch Indian reservation and thus eligible for college-loan assistance, ironic because Michael had hated school so much that he had dropped out of high school in his freshman year). And now he and Mary were the proud grandparents of a black baby boy, the result of her son Jason's marriage to a serene young black woman who was already pregnant with another man's child. David was respected—greatly admired, even—in both the black and white communities clustered along Highway 59 between Stockton and Uriah, where he could be seen every day wheeling the company's trucks from job to job ("I'll drive anything yellow and green"). It was he who had helped the crew from Kimberly-Clark clean up the mess at St. Joe Baptist, he who had counseled his step-son to tell the truth and take the consequences, and he who had pulled strings to have the kids held at the county jail in Brewton for reasons of their own safety.

About the time Michael was being sent to Kentucky to begin serving his five-year sentence, David and Mary and their children moved into the new house he had built at the community of Good-way, deep in the piney woods some five miles beyond Uriah, across the road from the house they had been renting. It was an airy place, carpeted, with central heat and air-conditioning and four bedrooms, and he had added a blue-tiled oval swimming pool just off the flag-stoned patio. Through the patio doors, you could see the large steel shed he had built, with Michael's help, where he could "piddle with engines and stuff" or even open his own machine shop in the event he was laid off in the imminent closing of Kimberly-Clark's opera-tions in the Mobile district. He had enough confidence to feel it would never come to that. "The papers are full of hundreds of jobs for truck drivers every day, so I'm not worried," he said. "I'm a good worker, and everybody knows it."

LATE ONE SATURDAY afternoon toward the end of August, with shadows growing long on the knoll where his big new house sits like a workingman's castle, David Woods was presiding over his brood. The sort of man who says not that he *has* to work overtime but that he'll "be working Saturday"—*Sairdie*—he had put in a full day, show-ered and changed into jeans and a clean T-shirt, and now sat at a din-ing table just off the den so he could look through the patio's sliding glass doors and watch Mary and her black daughter-in-law splash in the pool with his new grandson. The large den was dominated by a hulking television cabinet with a fifty-two-inch screen, silent now, for a couple of the other kids were in a back bedroom watching cartoons on another set. One of the two daughters from that first marriage— Nicole, the bright and pretty majorette, his pet, who appeared headed for the University of Alabama when she graduated high school a year hence—passed by for a kiss on the cheek as she headed off for a friend's wedding. The king was in his parlor.

"They don't call it God's country for nothing," he was saying. "There's peace and quiet here. Nobody bothers you. You don't have to hustle and drive just to be somewhere in an hour. We don't need a picture-show because my wife manages a movie gallery in Monroeville and we get free movies before they even get to the theaters. This is the life. It don't get any better. I see that every time we go to Jacksonville to visit her folks. If I had to fight traffic like those people do, I'd be like those people at the post office who grab machine guns and go crazy. What do they call it? 'Go postal.' If you was raised there and that's all you knew, I guess *that* would be the life. But my brother-in-law's from Jacksonville and he just built himself a house there on the hill." He was interrupted by a phone call, from the daughter of that brother-in-law, wanting to know how to broil corn on a grill ("Just butter it up, wrap it in foil, and let it go for a while . . . What? Aw, you know, a *while*").

Although he is not the sort of man to bitch and moan about things beyond his control, or to snipe at others, he was still rankling over what he perceived as the law's overly zealous prosecution of the case. "I'd like to talk to the judge, just to tell him I think they got railroaded, but I don't guess that'll happen. The one I'd *really* love to talk to is that woman in Washington [Cynthia Tompkins] that's in charge of 'hate crimes.' The prosecutors just stood there and outright lied, no matter what the kids and their lawyers said. I mean, Michael did *not* say Brandy said 'nigger church.' He told 'em he couldn't even say whether it was a male or a female voice that said it. And I tell you, maybe I can't vote for David Whetstone in Monroe County but I know a lot of people in Baldwin that do, and I've done everything I could to keep him out of office. He *needed* this to be a racial thing so he could go after the Klan and make a hero out of hisself. The police, now, that's different. They was just doing what they had to do. They even stopped and bought something for Michael and Alan [Odom] to eat when they was taking them to the jail in Bay Minette."

Like all of the other parents, he reserved special scorn for Rev. Joe Dees. "Doll [Boone] called me once, about two weeks after the sentencing, and we got to talking about what had happened and how we were gonna manage to pay all of these bills for lawyers and such. [Woods had paid $7,500 for Michael's lawyer to plead guilty on his behalf; money well spent, as it turned out.] Seventy-two hours after they get out of prison they have to report to their parole officer and make out a plan to pay nearly twenty thousand dollars apiece to Dees. They'll have to pay at least a hundred dollars a month if they don't even have a job. Me and Doll agreed that it looks like the money Dees has gotten so far has gone to fix up his trailer. That's what he's calling his 'church' now. I've got nothing to say for him. Everybody has his day, and his day's coming." In response to remarks about Dees's continuing emotional problems: "He had three wrecks and got fired at Scott, before they got bought out by Kimberly-Clark. He ever tell you about the time he was walking down the road with a chicken and a switch to whup it with?"

HIS FOCUS THESE days was on the absent Michael, anyway, and his thinking was that the boy's stint in prison might turn out to be a good thing in the long run. Sometimes it happened like that, he said, aware of the story about Merle Haggard, the country singer and songwriter, whose juvenile indiscretions had finally led him to a three-year stretch at San Quentin; after a stay in "the hole," isolation, for a moonshine whiskey scheme, he volunteered for "the hardest job y'all got," working in the laundry, and came out of it with grotesquely gnarled fingernails but a new lease on life. "I don't know how often that happens," Woods was saying, "but I think Michael's learning some things up there that he never got before."

One plus, of course, was the lack of alcohol. "I think the number of beers they was said to have drank was exaggerated during the trial," he said, "but they drank a pile of it. Michael's a good kid, like the rest of 'em, but they got to drinking. I think this Tyler Burgess started the whole thing when he walked through the door [of the Gentrys' house] while they were watching television and said, 'There's a car down there, let's go burn it.' If he hadn't come in, they'd probably gone ahead and watched the movie. But one thing led to another, you know, and pretty soon they was setting fire to a church. The beer had a lot to do with it, no doubt about it, and Michael knows that. Between the trial and lockup day, when they was on curfew, Michael volunteered to go up to Monroeville two days a week for six weeks to this drug school they had."

They'd had to be content with phone calls from Michael for the first three months of his imprisonment, while he went through orientation and got settled into the regimen, working KP all of that time, but David and Mary hightailed it to Kentucky the moment their visitation papers arrived around the Fourth of July. They were back again a month later. It's a 640-mile drive from Goodway to the Federal Medical Center in Lexington, and visiting was easier now that Mary's father had bought a house that happened to be less than a two-hour drive from the prison. The boy seemed happier and more involved in projects, *any* project, than at any other time in his life.

"He's doing great," David said. "There's more'n four thousand inmates there, and the others look out for him because he's the baby. It's not a hard lockup place, like a real prison, but more of a drug rehabilitation center. He eats all he wants to, works out with weights, runs around the track they've got, does five hundred push-ups and sit-ups a day. When he finished with the kitchen duty, they let him start taking art classes. That boy could always draw. Put a piece of paper in front of him, he could flat draw anything. So now all he can talk about is putting on weight, getting his GED diploma, taking all the courses he can, and drawing things. He said, 'I'm sorry I hurt y'all, but when I get out I'm gonna make y'all proud.'" With time off for good behavior, David figures he will be released in the early part of the year 2001, assigned either to a military-style "boot camp" or a halfway house.

MICHAEL SHOULD BE returning to the Little River area just before his twenty-second birthday, about the time in life when many others across America are coming home from college, and in a sense prison will have been his college. (His accomplice, Alan Odom, will be in his early thirties when he returns, and Brandy Boone will be coming home to a two- or three-year-old child she will have barely had time to get to know.) It's a high price to pay, but one of the side benefits of his time away will be his mingling with other people from other places who, most likely, have sadder tales than he of their earliest years in life. "Yeah," said his stepfather, "ol' Hard Knocks U." If it works like it is supposed to, returning a man who is sober and wiser and stronger than when he went in, then congratulations will be due the judge and the jury and the entire system. Only time will tell.

There are fuzzy sentiments in an old adage, "It takes a village to raise a child"—the first phrase was the title of a book published around this time by the president's wife, Hillary Rodham Clinton— and one would like to think that the saying had its very origins in just such a place as Little River and its environs. Given the smallness of the area, and the fact that everybody knows everything about everybody else's daily doings, it would seem that a kid wouldn't be able to get away with anything; if he'd been seen drunk at one o'clock in the afternoon, or was spotted fishtailing up and down Sawmill Road, or had been caught stealing a tire from somebody's garage, that his parents would get a call. That's the way it goes in the more prosperous communities, where there is an active parent-teacher organization at school and a centralized town center and a thriving church life, but it doesn't seem to work like that in Little River. Rather than forming a united front to ensure that *all* of the children do the right thing, the parents seem preoccupied with defending their own to the extent that a whistleblower would get no thanks. *Yeah, well let me tell you what* your *kid did the other day.* It is a village divided, not united.

Neighborhoods in the big cities are more close-knit than these sparsely populated rural communities. Kenneth Cumbie's father lives more than sixty miles away from the quarreling parents of Jeremy Boone, and the Woodses live halfway between the two. Both of the Boone clans have isolated themselves from each other and the rest of the Little River community for generations. Old animosities are not forgotten, and sniping is rampant. Nobody asked her, but when Patricia Williams, Michael Woods's exiled adoptive mother, heard of Brandy Boone's pregnancy, she went around telling anyone who would listen that "the baby ought to be named 'Target.' You know, 'open twenty-four hours, everybody welcome.'" Even David Woods wasn't exempt: of Alan Odom's mother he said "looking for a boyfriend at a Klan rally will tell you what kind of person Darlene is"; and of Jeremy Boone he allowed as how he didn't know much about him except that he's "pretty much a daddy-mama's boy who thinks he's better than the rest of 'em." The parents were spread all over the place, pursuing disparate vocations, from Ted Odom dredging in the Louisiana marshes to Robert Cumbie teaching in Evergreen classrooms, and in almost every case they were repeating the same errors of their own parents when it came to child-raising: when kids got their own cars, they were on their own. The notion of a caring village had turned out to be a myth.

The parents' own words showed that there was little trust and communication between them and their children. Alan Odom had said "Bye!" and slammed the phone on his mother, Darlene, when she inquired about the events of that night, prompting her to say that she "don't know who done what and I ain't asked you and I ain't going to." Brandy wouldn't say anything to her mother until she had conferred with her cousin Jeremy, who found it easier to talk to his grandfather, Raymond Cumbie, than to his wandering father. The only things the parents of the five seemed to have in common were their denial that the trouble had been racially inspired, a feeling that the law had gone overboard in its prosecution, and that Joe Dees and his church didn't count.

Even David Woods, the good father, had been unable to get through to his adopted son. He had his theories about what had caused Michael to torch St. Joe Baptist that night, but he had heard many of the details during the week-long trial in Mobile, not from Michael, and more than a year later he was still hoping to learn what had really happened. "A lot of it didn't come out [in the trial]," he was saying on this Saturday as night fell over Old Stage Road in Goodway. "I'll know more about what happened when Michael gets out. I want to talk to him, see if I can get out of him what happened, what he had on his mind, what he was doing, *why*. I've got a lot of questions I don't have the answers to. Me and him are gonna take a long ride when he gets home. Then I'll know."

EIGHTEEN

Murray January

————

During the summer months, when the Baldwin County grand jury is out and he's not needed to serve as sergeant-at-arms at the courthouse in Bay Minette, the only way to find Murray January is to go looking for his old black pickup truck with FORD spelled out in block white letters across the top of the windshield. He took semiretirement as a Baldwin County deputy sheriff in January 1996, when he turned sixty-one, after sixteen years on the force, opting to work during the nineteen weeks each year when the courts are in session. "We used to call the house if we had a drunk or something," says Peanut Ferguson, "but now we just call direct to the sheriff's office in Bay Minette. Murray isn't home most times, and if you give the details to his wife, she'll either forget to tell him or just won't bother." Most likely, Murray is fishing somewhere on the river. He has found it much more rewarding, at this point in his life, to pursue the noble largemouth bass rather than mess with drunks or run down petty thieves fleeing through the swamps and brambles in the woods.

You'll get an entirely different opinion about Murray from some of the stubborn older whites of Little River, who still find it hard to deal with the fact that a black man actually has the power to arrest them, but to blacks he is something of a hero, one of theirs who has made it in a white world. As it is with Jews in the rural South, who traditionally had to go into business for themselves because whites wouldn't hire them, those blacks who have succeeded had to farm, preach, teach, or take jobs in law enforcement, one of the first equal-opportunity employers. It wasn't easy for Murray, who had put in his share of time cutting trees and working on production lines, but he had lived an honorable life. He had the respect of the sheriff and the district attorney down in Bay Minette, who regarded him as their main man in the distant reaches of northern Baldwin County, and all six of his and Cora's daughters had turned out splendidly. Murray was, arguably, the most successful black man still living in Little River.

As a teenaged high school dropout, one of four boys born to a farmer in Evergreen, some sixty miles away to the east, Murray followed his older brother Jesse to Little River in the fall of 1952. He would spend the week with a logging company at Bon Secour, near the mouth of Mobile Bay, coming home on weekends to stay at Jesse's ramshackle frame house stuck in the woods a mile south of Ferguson's Grocery. Soon he married George Thomas's sister, Cora, and built a house next door to Jesse on what amounts to a country cul-de-sac just off of Cumbie Road. "I even logged for a while with Bernard Boone and Clayton, senior," he says, with a rueful shrug, for the Boones are not among his fans. Then, needing more security and benefits as the kids started coming along, he took a job on the line at Standard Furniture in Bay Minette.

Many men enter law enforcement by way of the military, but Murray had been too young for the Second World War and Korea, and too old and burdened with family to make Vietnam, thus never serving in the armed forces. The door to law enforcement cracked open for him in 1971, not that he had initiated it, when he was first approached by Taylor Wilkins, the Baldwin County sheriff at the time. "There were some black guys making moonshine up here, and he tried to get me to help out. I knew where one of their stills was, but I wouldn't tell him." He was given a deputy's card anyway, this being at a time when governments were under pressure to add blacks to their rolls, but there was no pay and he wouldn't have the power to arrest unless he attended the police academy. At the end of the decade, with another sheriff in office, Murray became a full-time salaried deputy. He finally graduated from the police academy in 1993, at the age of fifty-eight, and was empowered to make arrests.

We aren't talking about Wyatt Earp or Bat Masterson here. Even his strongest supporters, from his black neighbors in Little River to his bosses at the county courthouse, don't argue that he is anything more than a fair and competent backwoods deputy. "Yeah, you tell him where there's some trouble and he'll run the other way," says James Witherington, but that's a minority sentiment representing the embittered older whites. Murray has the laid-back temperament of a patient fisherman—where the fish are, what they're biting, and whether they're worth messing with—traits that serve him well as a lawman. "We'll have these family arguments, with people calling and saying we'd better get up there before somebody starts shooting," says David Whetstone, "but Murray knows who's who and what's what in Little River. The good guys, the bad guys, who's likely to do something serious, all of that. Spread out as we are, we need somebody like that." It was Murray, of course, who discovered the smoking shell of St. Joe Baptist and the sprung front door of Tate Chapel on that morning in July '97 and "had a pretty good idea about who might've done it" to pass on to the deputies and federal agents when they arrived. Had he not been on duty at the courthouse that morning of the following spring, he would have been the man to arrest George Boone for firing a shotgun on the family restaurant.

MURRAY JANUARY IS another of those people in Little River who looks as though he has been dispatched from Central Casting. Broad-chested, well over six feet tall even in his slouch, with a pot belly being supported by a wide silver-buckled belt, he is a ringer for the actor Paul Winfield: a laconic, slow-moving man with coal-black skin, chewing on Beechnut tobacco most of the time, any kid's idea of a good grandpa. His idea of a great good time is to sit on a white plastic chair under the trees in front of his house in the woods, after a day of fishing, and debate his skittish brother Jesse, a seventy-two-year-old retired sawyer, on matters ranging from Ford versus Chevrolet trucks to whether it's best to fish from the riverbank or from a boat. Their hope is that the arguments never get settled.

And he is yet another of those black parents in Little River who have done a remarkable job raising their children. "Black parents *do* have to try harder," he says. "There's no future for [black] kids here. If you're born black in Alabama, you've got two strikes against you right there." Like the Marshalls and George Thomas and even Joe Dees, he set the ground rules early for his children: Get an education, and leave Little River. "It wasn't easy, raising six girls. I told 'em, 'There's nothing here for you unless you want to wind up in some-body's kitchen. You get your high school education, and if you want to go to college I'll help out. There ain't nothing here for black peo-ple.'" Figuring that he'd better get a high school diploma himself if he intended to enforce those rules, he got his GED at the age of thirty-three by attending classes three nights a week at Faulkner Community College in Bay Minette after working all day at the Standard Furniture plant. Cora, in the meantime, bent over vats bub-bling with oil to fry chicken and catfish all day at the Dixie Landing Cafe, finally quitting after twenty years when she developed heart trouble, a sufficient reminder to the girls of what could happen to them if they didn't study and leave.

Only one of the daughters chose to stay in Little River: Laura Ann, thirty-three, married to Elijah "PeeWee" Porter, a foreman at the Kimberly-Clark lumberyard at Dixie Landing. Mother of three ranging from five to eighteen years old, keeper of a neat frame house on Sawmill Road with the legend THE PORTERS proudly burnished on a wooden slab posted in the yard, she works at a carpet outlet in Atmore and serves as the church secretary at Tate Chapel while not administering to her children. It was she, tastefully dressed in a dark suit embellished with a gold crucifix necklace, who turned out to be the most articulate of the witnesses for the prosecution during the trial in Mobile, a fervent church lady reverently describing the black Wall of Fame and telling of what the church had meant to her grandmother before her death, the year before the vandalism, at the age of 104.

The other girls went to college and left at the first opportunity. The oldest is planning to retire soon—in Atlanta, not Little River—after putting in twenty years as a hospital nurse on Long Island, New York. The second oldest graduated from Auburn University in eastern Alabama and now teaches in the Atlanta public school system. One was doing home health care before she took a job as a nurse at the hospital in Bay Minette. Another spent two years attending Faulkner Community College, worked at the state women's prison near Montgomery, and now is a superintendent with the state board of corrections. But the star of them all is Angela, only twenty-six, who graduated summa cum laude in education at Auburn (only eleven in her class of 220 did so) and in 1998 was named assistant principal at a highly regarded middle school in a suburb of Atlanta, where she is the only black teacher in a school that is 85 percent white. On top of all that, when she married she carefully chose a hyphenated surname to celebrate her liberated role as a modern woman, Angela January-Moton, which sort of tickled Murray. That's a long, long way from a crowded little frame house in the piney woods of Little River, Alabama, at the end of a dirt turnaround.

ON ANOTHER STEAMY morning in the summer of '98, Murray was found observing the fishermen coming in with their catches at Dixie Landing. The men had been out on the water all night, black and white, young and old, and they were dragging their boats up the sandy slope. His dented pickup parked haphazardly under a grove of trees, he was admiring the mounds of fish in Styrofoam coolers, congratulating the men, and getting the skinny—"Where they at?" "What's your bait?" "Nice mess you got there"—while, in the meantime, a caravan of logging trucks lined up to drop their loads of ragged pinepoles at the Kimberly-Clark yard, where his son-in-law PeeWee Porter worked.

"Maybe we're from slaves, maybe not, I don't care." He had taken refuge from the blistering sun by moving to the roofed side entrance of the Dixie Landing Cafe, closed on this day, a Tuesday. "I got something in the mail one day saying if I sent fifteen dollars they'd send me a form to fill out about my family tree, and then if I sent 'em another fifty dollars they'd send me a book that'd tell me all about the Januarys." He was amused. He spat some tobacco juice over the railing and said, "All I care about is right now."

In spite of the racism that he knew to exist, deep in the bones of people like the Boones and Cumbies, he had about decided that the torching of St. Joe and the vandalism at Tate Chapel had not been racially inspired. "Looks to me like they just got so drunk they didn't know *where* they were. It's their upbringing more than anything. If they had to do it over again, though, I can guarantee they wouldn't burn anybody's church. They've had a lot of time to think about it lately." He wouldn't go beyond that by naming names or casting stones. He was a father and a law officer, not a preacher or a judge. Besides, he felt it worth pointing out, Alabama didn't have a corner on racism. "My oldest, the one about to retire from the hospital in New York, says it's gotten as bad up there as it is here."

He freshened his chaw and laughed at a memory of what could be construed as the only thing resembling a civil rights meeting in the history of Little River. "Must've been twenty years ago," he said. "One of the Marshall boys came back home from up North. Might've been Alexander Hampshire, Elizabeth's son, the one that played football in college in D.C. Anyway, he had this idea. Printed up fliers, handed 'em out at the churches, Peanut's, some of the other places on the road. Said for a ten-dollar donation there was gon' be a meeting at the Tate Creek Missionary Baptist Church. He was gon' give a talk called 'How to Get Along with White Folks.' He'd been up *Nawth*, see. He *knew*. Gon' teach the brothers and the sisters how to get along with the Boones and them." He was laughing at the very idea.

"Anybody go?"

"Doubt it. Ain't nobody got the money."

"You weren't curious yourself?"

Murray had been having fun with the story, but now his eyes went cold. "Ain't nobody got to tell me how to get along with white folks," he said. He chewed and squinted for a full minute before delivering the one line that might say it all about race relations in Little River, at least from the black standpoint. "I can get along with a polecat," he said, "long as he don't piss on me." He spat over the railing and allowed as how he might run up to Peanut's and buy some Louisiana Pinks. Things were looking good on the river today.

NINETEEN

Deliverance

———

IT WAS PEANUT'S NATURE to keep his troubles to himself, but everybody knew that he was still suffering from the beating that had nearly taken his life in June '97. There was dizziness, a knot in his head where he wore a steel plate, an eye that fluttered, numbness in the entire right side of his body, and blood clots in one leg that would require surgery when he could get around to it. That hadn't kept him from joining in all of the fun with the twins when the family took a week's vacation to Florida in July, where, against doctors' orders, he delighted Shane and Christie by taking on every hellish ride Disney World had to offer. Still, haunted by nightmares and hobbled during the day, he was obsessed by memories of that bloody morning and determined to see that justice was delivered to his attacker.

Twice he and Sue had dressed up and driven to the courthouse in Bay Minette for the trial of Ronald Hines, but both times there had been a last-minute snag and they had to turn around and go back home to Little River. He would gladly do that for as long as he had to, he said, because he wanted to see this guy put away forever. "It's a wonder he didn't kill me. He's crazy, and sooner or later he *is* going to kill somebody. I don't know, this generation of coloreds . . ." Peanut's voice trailed off. Hines had kept delaying the trial by feigning illness or firing his court-appointed attorneys, and the judges were getting tired of it. But for David Whetstone, the district attorney, the delays gave him more time to find a *third* attack somewhere

in Hines's record that could put him away for good. "So far, the best
we can get is thirty years, out in eight, and he'd still be only about
forty years old," said Whetstone. "Some of these little places don't
keep very good records. We're trying to find some incident like this
one, something that they might not have put in the computer, so we
can put him away for so long that he'll be too old to raise hell when
he gets out."

The weather hadn't exactly turned cool, at the approach of the
Labor Day weekend, but at least it had become bearable, with highs
in the mid-eighties during the middle of the day and in the sixties at
night. On the second day of September, young father-to-be Rusty
Lilley had left his parents' house in Goodway to fetch Brandy from
the prison in Marianna and drive her to the facility in West Virginia,
where she was expected to give birth in another six weeks or so. The
first bolls of cotton had appeared around the first of August, like pop-
corn on Christmas trees, and as the leaves curled and died the cotton
farmers were seen backing their John Deere pickers out of the barns
in preparation for the harvest. With Joe Dees off again to the mental
hospital in Mount Vernon, the black friends he had pestered for hinting that he was stealing funds for his church were sleeping through
nights uninterrupted by his angry phone calls. At Ferguson's Grocery,
small knots of old men and little boys had begun to gather in the
parking lot every day simply to watch a crew of masons raising an
add-on that would become the new location of Peanut's package
liquor store.

ONCE AGAIN, ON the morning of the day after Labor Day, Peanut
and Sue dressed for court and drove into Bay Minette for the trial of
Ronald Hines. (The first person they happened to see at the courthouse was L. B. "Sylvester" Benjamin, who had come in to quietly
drop the charges against Dees for the unprovoked beating he took
that night while reading his mail under the streetlight on Sawmill
Road. "I figure Joe's suffered enough," he said.) They checked in
with Whetstone, who promised there would be no more delays,

walked past a half-dozen witnesses from Little River, sitting on benches in the hallway, ready to be called, and then entered the courtroom and took seats on the hard pews toward the back. Peanut was dressed like the simple country grocer he is, in slacks and a checkered short-sleeved shirt, but Sue wore a more decorous turquoise pants suit. Peanut's daughter, Bridget, in a white linen suit, joined them after she had driven in from her home in Daphne.

The morning session was to be a "suppression hearing," an attempt by Hines's lawyer to keep some of the evidence away from the jury, but it got off to a rowdy start the moment Hines was brought in by four guards. He was a menacing sight, a large black man with bulging shoulders and hard eyes, and for fifteen minutes he raged about his lawyer and the judge and the justice system in general. "I'm being railroaded," he said, "so you might as well go ahead and send me straight to jail." Saying his lawyer was fired, he threw back his chair, stood up, and announced he was leaving. The guards descended on him. "Why you keep touchin' on me?" he yelled at one, trying to stare him down. The judge was Lyn Stuart, one of the two who had been threatened earlier in the year by Joe Dees, a middle-aged mother known to the county's habitual prisoners as "Ninety-Nine" for her tough sentences. "You'll stay here and have your day in court," she said, "even if I have to have you shackled, handcuffed, and gagged." Hines was already wired with a remote-controlled shock device. Watching this from his pew, Peanut whispered: "There he is. That's him. He'd do it again." Murray January, on his first day of duty since summer's end, slipped into the room—difficult to recognize at first glance, dressed now in his brown deputy's uniform—to help the guards keep order.

For the rest of the morning, Whetstone and Lt. Hoss Mack engaged in a dog and pony show they have been performing for years. Whetstone, in a rumpled brown suit, raking his hand through hair that was barely there anymore, adjusting his silver-rimmed glasses, fed the lines, and Hoss—pleasant, chubby, balding, also wearing glasses and a brown suit—gave the answers that established Little River and Ferguson's Grocery and the story line of that day, then toting up the evidence his men had found: fingerprints, Hines's bloody shirt, cigarette cartons he had stolen, DNA. A couple of witnesses were questioned by Whetstone—the black man who had happened on the beating-in-progress, and a white employee of County Line Package Store who had refused to barter a dollar's worth of gas for a pack of cigarettes with Hines—before the judge called for a lunch recess. None of the evidence would be suppressed, she said. She advised the hapless court-appointed lawyer, Wayne Doerr, to try patching things up with Hines during the lunch break.

WHETSTONE WANTED JUDGMENTS of attempted murder and first-degree robbery from the jury that had been assembled by midafternoon (five white males, five white females, and two black females), and from the evidence he and Hoss Mack had assembled, it appeared to be a cakewalk. But veteran lawyers never take anything for granted, and the district attorney had some reasons to fidget. It had to be a unanimous decision, of course, and Whetstone saw a couple of problems. One of the jurors was a dour middle-aged black woman who wore dreadlocks and was a nurse at the Baldwin County hospital ("She'll know all about the Klan rally and the church burning"). And he had to prove that Hines had gone into the store that morning with murder on his mind. The burden of proof was on the state, and Doerr, who had made up with Hines, had only to come down hard on whether the jury had reasonable doubt that his man's murderous fit had been premeditated.

Every trial tends to have one moment that becomes its signature, that will stand out forever, and Whetstone maneuvered that one early on. Sue Ferguson had just spent ten minutes on the stand, telling about their marriage and the store and giving her version of the events, when Peanut took her place. He was seven minutes into his testimony ("I didn't pass out completely. . . . He must've hit me about forty times. . . .") when Whetstone flashed onto a television screen a photograph taken of Peanut at the hospital. The jury members were visibly upset when they saw the gory closeup of Peanut, his head wrapped in a bloody turban, looking like a prune, eyes barely visible. Peanut fell apart the moment he saw it: sobbing, shoulders jerking, reaching for Kleenex to stanch the tears, his wife and daughter in the back pews recoiling and weeping at the sight. He looked like a monster from a horror movie. "I'm not the same man . . ." Peanut said, trailing off into another fit of uncontrollable crying.

There would be other moments during that first day and into the next as Whetstone paraded his experts and witnesses for the jury's edification. One of the witnesses was Jerry Boone, who identified himself as a "disabled construction worker" who is "dog kin" to Clayton Boone, Sr., and from his perch on a stool at the Little River Cafe that morning of the attack had seen Hines run across Clayton's yard after he had abandoned his car. Hoss Mack testified that he had radioed to the deputies taking Hines to the county jail not to let him wash his hands, still spattered with Peanut's blood. Whetstone found another opportunity to show the photo of Peanut's bloody turbaned head, which looked even worse upon a second viewing and brought another spasm of crying from Peanut, and he was called to the bench for a sidebar reprimand—too late—after he went theatrical: "Ka-boom! I wish I had a hammer and a watermelon to give you an idea . . ." He ended his closing argument by saying, simply, that Hines had "ruined this man's life."

The public defender, Wayne Doerr, did what he could with what little he had. "Why didn't he plan an escape, bring a gun, if he went in there with the intent to murder Mister Ferguson?" he said. "The only question is *intent*. We're not arguing about the robbery, but the other charge. This wasn't an attempted murder, ladies and gentlemen, it was a robbery gone bad." Hines had cussed and raised hell all day and night, when not in the courtroom, causing the jailers to move him from one cell to another, but he was morose and silent when the jury returned after only an hour's deliberation. The photo of Peanut had been enough to outweigh any questions about premeditated murder. Guilty, they said, of robbery in the first degree *and* attempted murder. The judge scheduled sentencing for two weeks hence, but Whetstone knew that this time it was the prosecution that would be allowed to dawdle until, he hoped, he could find the third incident that would allow him to take Hines out of circulation for a long, long time.

AS A FURTHER measure of how vigorously the grapevine thrums in northern Baldwin County, news of the verdict had reached Little River before Peanut and Sue could make it back to the store. (That, and more. A former clerk at Ferguson's Grocery, Denise Reed, had been subpoenaed but never called to testify as an eyewitness. While idling away the hours at the courthouse, reading anything at hand, she had come across a juicy item in the county's law journal that seemed worth sharing with the folks back home. John Wayne Boone, of the night-school law degree, had just been reprimanded by the district bar association, for the second time that year, for "unethical behavior." As with Hines, three strikes and he would be out.) Peanut thought that maybe the crowd on hand at the store when he and Sue returned was meant for him, that everybody was there to celebrate and offer congratulations and replay the day of the attack, but he was dismayed to learn that they had gathered merely to await the mail and to watch the masons begin framing for the roof of the new package store. The most traumatic moment of his life had already become old news.

The coming of fall marked a time of deliverance, of renewal, in a way. Hurricanes were brewing out in the Gulf, first the tropical storm Frances and then Hurricane Georges, bringing their mixed blessings to the inland communities—too far away to cause severe damage, but close enough for the high winds and rain to clear the fetid air. The cotton farmers were being forced to rush the harvest now, lest their crops be damaged in the coming storms, and the fields were clouded with swirls of dust as the men feverishly operated their pickers into the night, headlights ablaze, like Erwin Rommel's tanks hightailing it across the North African desert. From the little high school football fields in Uriah and Monroeville and Bay Minette, all through the dark stretches of southwestern Alabama, came the tootlings of marching bands and the eager implorations of leggy cheerleaders: "Y'all yell, now!"

George Wallace finally passed away after years of hanging on, a near-deaf cripple since the failed assassination attempt of 1972, prompting acerbic commentaries throughout the world about the sincerity of the old governor's late-in-life apology and taking that particular monkey off Alabama's back, a renewal in itself. Joe Dees showed up at Ferguson's Grocery a couple of days later, telling Peanut he'd "been away" and wanted to settle up his bill, though he feared he "might have to go to jail," learning only then that Sylvester Benjamin had dropped the charges against him. The torching of Debbie Boone's new love's trailer had been officially ruled an arson, just as suspected, and now it was up to Larry to make the next move. Doves and turkey and deer, working without calendars that would advise them the holocaust was upon them, boldly fluttered and poked about the killing fields on the cooler days leading up to hunting season. An item in the Baldwin County *Times* announced that George Boone's ex-wife, Betty, was now officially married to his brother, Leroy, after all of those years together. Far away in bustling Atlanta, the heartbeat of the self-proclaimed New South, three hundred miles from the tumbledown house where she had been raised, Angela January-Moton was assuming her duties as assistant principal of the majority-white Lilburn Middle School. And still farther away, in West Virginia and Florida and Louisiana and Kentucky, the five white kids whose drunken indiscretions on the night of a full moon over the swamps had changed their lives and the history of Little River forever sat and pondered a future that had never seemed promising to begin with.

NEARLY A YEAR had passed since the weeklong trial of the five kids in Mobile, but to Virginia Rasco it might as well have been yesterday. A sweet white church lady nearing her seventies, from the community of Mexia, five miles west of Monroeville, where she once worked in the Vanity Fair plant, she had served on the jury during that last week of October and still recalled it as "the worst ordeal of my life. I couldn't sleep at all at night, and I'm still confused about what happened." Like the black female juror from Monroeville, who had admitted she "couldn't get past the 'nigger church' remark," Rasco had bought the prosecution's view that Brandy was the one who had said it ("All those boyfriends were protecting her"); but, on the other hand, she couldn't understand why "that girl from Ohio"—Jessica Perry—had been granted immunity from prosecution because "she was right in the middle of everything, egging 'em on, just like Brandy."

Every morning at daybreak, she and her retired husband, Roy, had left home for the hundred-mile drive to Mobile and what turned out to be the greatest adventure of her life ("I'm putting together a scrapbook of my notes, newspaper clippings, affidavits, everything, for my grandchildren"). She was frightened from the very first. "The judge had said he wanted to 'protect' us, so we'd meet every morning in some big old building down toward the docks. They had two agents to watch our cars all day. Then we'd get in a van together and they'd drive us on some side streets to the government building and then escort us through a secret back door. To tell the truth, I expected to see a bunch of Klansmen out front, threatening us." And finally, once they had been seated in the jury box, "I looked out and saw all those rough-looking people from Little River staring back at us." Like most people in the region, she knew the stories about the general lawlessness of the place.

It is not unusual for a group of randomly selected average American citizens, a "jury of peers," to be confused by the legalese dropped in their laps once they are sequestered in a room to pass judgment, but that was more pronounced in this case due to the conflicting testimony and the varying degrees of guilt (or innocence) the jury was expected to weigh. From the very beginning, when the jurors retired to begin their deliberations, there was every possibility of a hung jury. "Those lawyers have a language all their own," Virginia Rasco was saying now, a year later. "We had forty-two sheets of paper in front of us, and I couldn't make heads or tails of half of it. We sat there scratching our heads for an hour before we sent word to the judge that we needed a dictionary. He sent back word, 'No.' Then we asked if he could send somebody in to explain some things to us. 'No,' again. He was real nice, understand, sent us food and drinks, bought some cigarettes one time for a girl that smoked, even stood up every time we entered the courtroom. But we needed help, and he said he just couldn't give it to us. It was too late."

In spite of the standard admonition from a judge to a jury to weigh only the evidence they have heard, everyone knows that jurors are human beings who can be swayed by such peripheral matters as a lawyer's performance or a defendant's mien or a convincing witness. This jury, according to Virginia Rasco, was "only human . . . We did the best we could." They liked the styles of Brandy's Richard Yelverton and Cumbie's Dennis Knizely, but ridiculed Odom's James Harper ("He wore a new wig, you know; when we were being asked if we knew any of the lawyers, one lady said, 'Oh, Mister Harper, I didn't recognize you with all that hair'"). They thought that Brandy looked a little too "sassy" during the trial; noticed that Alan Odom "never looked up from the table once, like he knew he was guilty"; felt intimidated by the intense crowd attending every day from Little River; couldn't figure why Cumbie was even there, since he had "put the first fire out and never went back"; regarded Joe Dees as a bumbling "half-preacher with a church that wasn't a real church." If there was any levity during the deliberations, Rasco said, it came when they brought up the N word. "A white girl asked a black woman, 'But don't y'all call each *other* "nigger"?' The woman said, 'Sure, but we just don't want *y'all* calling us that.' Then the white girl said, 'I was just wondering, but what do y'all call *us* when you're by yourselves?' The black woman said, '*Honkies.*' I swear. I never knew that. Isn't that something? 'Honkies.' Where'd that come from?"

Confused to the end, they soldiered on. "There wasn't much doubt that Woods and Odom set the church on fire, with Brandy and that Jessica egging 'em on, like there wasn't any doubt that Cumbie hadn't done *anything* bad except be someplace he shouldn't be, but I didn't want to see anybody get ten years for burning that church down, not *that* one. Don't get me wrong. Nobody's got a right to burn *anything* down, even an outhouse, but this wasn't a real church. It was abandoned, didn't have electricity or water, and hardly ever met as far as we knew. If it had been a big, active church, black or white, that would've been something else." She left the impression that the jurors were as shocked as anyone in Little River when the judge announced the sentences some five months later. "I've felt bad about it ever since," Virginia Rasco said.

Then she told of a chance meeting in Birmingham only two weeks after the trial had ended. "My husband and I had gone up to the medical center in Birmingham for checkups, and while we were sitting in the waiting room he whispered to me, said, 'Whatever you do, don't turn around.' Well, you know how that goes. I couldn't help myself, so I looked behind us and there was about five or six of those rough-looking Boone men from Little River, the ones I'd seen staring at us every day in the courtroom. I guess they were up there getting checkups to prove they were still disabled so they could keep getting their checks. It liked to scared me to death, thinking they'd recognize me. I was all nerves until we got back home. Still am. You won't catch me going down to Little River like I used to."

No Church Today

———

ON THE THIRD SATURDAY of September, with storms swirling out on the Gulf as the hurricane season neared its peak, I drove down Sawmill Road in hopes of finding Joe Dees at his trailer. Ever since our first meeting, in July 1997, not long after his church had been destroyed, he had seemed to be fairly candid with me on the rare occasions when I could track him down. Certainly, he had never before discussed in such depth his emotional problems with anyone beyond his family and closest friends—even Peanut seemed surprised when I shared some of the details—and I tried to keep those troubles in mind as the evidence began to build that, alas, Joe Dees wasn't much of a preacher and St. Joe Baptist hadn't been much of a church. Davida Hastie's assessment seemed a bit harsh ("If they wanted to pick a church to burn down, they picked the right one [because] that one doesn't do much"), but it had been a church, after all, and attention must be paid. The real issue was that a bunch of white kids could commit such an indignity and feel it was okay simply because the building was, in Darlene Middleton's assessment, "just an old piece of junk."

Joe was standing beside the mailbox on the road in front of his trailer, a batch of letters stuck under one arm while he held an envelope that had just arrived by priority mail. Whatever it held, the news wasn't good. He mumbled a greeting without looking up, and continued to flip back and forth through the pages, frowning, reading with his lips, as though he were translating from the Greek.

"Not good?"

"I'm not sure."

"I'm guessing National Council of Churches," I said. Since 1996, when the rash of church burnings had begun, the NCC out of New York had dispensed more than $6 million of its private donations in the form of grants to a total of 149 churches around the country, three-fourths of the grants going to churches in the South. Joe Dees had applied for whatever he could get, at least enough to start rebuilding, and he had been sweating the mail ever since.

All he would say now was, "I'd rather not discuss it at this time."

"Well, anyway," I said, "I was just wanting to see if the hundred-and-twelfth anniversary is still on for tomorrow."

"Oh." He folded the sheets and tucked them back into the envelope. "Not as I'd originally planned. We won't have a ceremony. But I'll certainly make reference to it."

"Okay if I come?"

"Sure. Sunday school at nine, church at eleven."

"White boy like me?"

"God knows no color," he said.

There had been another of those torrential storms during the night, like a laser show, with every flash of lightning revealing wind and rain lashing through the pines, and when day broke on Sunday the storm had settled into a steady rain. Not a creature was stirring, not even at Peanut's store, and the slickened dirt roads were virtually impassable. Time had stopped, it seemed, in Little River.

At a few minutes past nine o'clock, Joe sat beneath the pines at Mt. Triumph Baptist Church in a borrowed sedan, the rain spitting on the roof, music from a distant gospel station crackling from the car radio. He wore his Sunday best, the same outfit from the trial in Mobile: a striped charcoal double-breasted suit, a white dress shirt and subdued tie, gray socks and black tasseled loafers. No one else was in sight. When I squished onto the grass in my old Chevy Blazer and stopped beside the car, we rolled down our windows and spoke through the mist. "I was going to talk about faith this morning," he said, with some embarrassment. "Looks like some of my people need to hear it." The weather was rotten, hard to get around in, he said, and some of his congregants were sick, one of them in the hospital having a toe amputated as we spoke, and his mother was on the brink of death at the nursing home in Mobile, but that was no excuse for this. Some anniversary.

Grabbing umbrellas, dashing through the misty rain past the half-completed shell of a rising new Mt. Triumph church (work had stopped while they awaited a loan), we worked our way past neat stacks of cinder block and lumber to reach the tumbledown frame shack that had been Mt. Triumph Baptist Church for more than a century. This was where the members of St. Joe, in their diaspora, had been meeting for more than a year. The place looked more like a storage room than a place of worship. Rusty cookpots caught water dripping through the leaky roof. Cobwebs and filthy windowpanes and sawdust and a busted piano with yellowing ivory keys gave the impression of an abandoned warehouse. The creaky board floors sagged under a jumble of chairs and pews piled upon each other like discards.

"We might as well get started," the Rev. Joe Dees said. I took a handkerchief and dusted off one of the more stable pews. He produced copies of a quarterly magazine from the National Baptist Publishing Board in Nashville, Tennessee, opening them to the lesson for September 20, 1998, passing one to me and then stepping back behind the rickety lectern he had salvaged from the pile of musty old furniture. "We'll be reading from Deuteronomy today. The lesson is, 'What Is the Law?' I'll read first, then you read the next paragraph." He cleared his throat, the sound echoing as though he were crying from the bottom of a well. "I am the Lord thy God," he began, "which brought thee out of the land of Egypt, from the house of bondage." He nodded toward me to continue the reading.

"Thou shalt have none other gods before me.

"Thou shalt not make thee any graven image, or any likeness of any thing that is in heaven above, or that is in the earth beneath, or that is in the waters beneath the earth.

"Thou shalt not bow down thyself unto them, nor serve them; for I the Lord thy God am a jealous God, visiting the iniquity of the fathers upon the children unto the third and fourth generation of them that hate me. . . ."

FALL PASSED, AND then winter, and in the spring I went back to see what had transpired since I had closed out the cabin on the last day of September. The mice and the dust and cobwebs had reclaimed the place since the end of another hunting season, and the mere sight of it brought back memories that were not altogether pleasant. Six months alone, cooking for one, trying to work and sleep through insufferable heat broken only by brief, chaotic thunderstorms and harassing middle-of-the-night phone calls, had brought new meaning to my friend's observation about "parachuting into strange towns, looking for bad news." Those phone calls had likely been made by the same person who had sneaked onto the land one night in late August as I slept and neatly punctured two tires on my Blazer. "Ain't you got that book wrote yet?" was the jocular greeting I had gotten one morning at Peanut's, back when I was a mere curiosity. But now, upon my return, I heard a menacing, "What the hell you doin' back down here again?" and turned in time to see John Boone's black Chevy pickup spin away from the gas pumps. John had reason to be surly, as it turned out, because Debbie had married the lover, Larry Kiper, and moved to Mobile, leaving moot the question of who set fire to the trailer. "It's the smartest move Debbie ever made," Peanut said, "but John ain't so happy these days."

Most of the news, in fact, had involved Boones. Brandy had given birth on the first of November, to a boy she named Logan, while in the halfway house in West Virginia. She had talked the authorities into letting her keep the child for the first four months of his life, bringing him home before returning to prison in Marianna to finish out her sentence, and she wasn't a good-time girl anymore. "I was behind the counter, making change," Peanut said, "when this woman came in, holding a baby, and everybody was talking about how cute he was. I honestly didn't recognize Brandy. She was fatter and older, just didn't look like herself. She'd changed."

So had her father, Doll, whose transformation from bounder to born-again Christian continued. He had decided in the fall that he wanted to get baptized in a favored washhole down at the river, but when the water turned cold he settled on being dunked in the above-ground children's wading pool in the yard behind his brother Mark's trailer. And now the man who'd had little time for his daughter as she grew up was turning out to be a doting grandfather beyond anyone's belief. "There were eighteen Boones at Mamie's Chapel on Easter Sunday, including Doll and Teresa and her daughter and Brandy's baby," reported Edith Cox (who now, incidentally, had retired as postmistress), "and after church they drove to Marianna with the baby to visit Brandy."

• George Boone's carefully orchestrated pursuit of "crazy checks" didn't turn out as he had envisioned it. He had caught the Feds' attention, all right. It had taken a lot of energy and disingenuousness for a "disabled" man to cuff up his daughter and fire a shotgun at the family restaurant and then haul ass to Mobile to threaten his cousin, the lawyer. Upon a closer look at his condition, both physical and mental, they took away his food stamps and ordered him to get a job. George had driven a truck for a while and now worked nights as a security guard in Atmore during the week, coming home to his trailer in Little River on weekends.

• Peanut might be winning the county-line liquor wars now that his package store was housed out front, for all to see, but he was downright gleeful about the fate of the man who had nearly killed him with a hammer. Not for nothing was Judge Lyn Stuart known as "Ninety-Nine," for that's how many years she had given Ronald Hines, so heinous had been his attack, and he won't be eligible for parole until he turns sixty-eight.

• More wedding bells! Jessica Perry, the notorious "Jessica from Ohio," the other femme fatale from that disastrous night of the full moon, had agreed to a marriage proposal from Daniel Gentry, whose father's house had been the site of the drinking party that greased the proceedings, but with a codicil that they would leave Little River. The couple now resides in Dayton, Ohio, where Mr. Gentry is employed in the construction industry.

• Susan Rena "Wild Child" Smith, the star of the show at Jerry's Cabaret until she got put away for selling drugs, was let out on probation for a second time and rejoined her husband, Phil Smith, the Klansman, at their place on the road near Tensaw. It turned out to be a brief reunion when she got caught again—same crime, same place, same result—and was returned to prison for a very long time.

EXCEPT FOR THE occasional success stories emanating from the black communities (Joe Dees's son Michael, for instance, had been hired full-time as a psychologist at Holman Prison after graduating from USA), the news from Little River had been relentlessly depressing since the first of the Klan rallies. Any fantasies I might have held about one day buying a place in the country, far from the clamor of cities, had quickly dissipated. Being a witness to the crumbling of the civilization that had been Little River, Alabama, shot through now with suspicions and backbiting and open animosities, had been like being the beat reporter traveling with a losing ball club. "Nothing's gonna change," Peanut was telling me one day, "until they start branching out, meeting other people, getting educated, and leaving." It sounded like a blueprint for the future he and Sue had in mind for their twins and, once the kids were gone, for themselves.

One of the few white teenagers in the area who had seemed to have prospects was Nicole Woods, the lissome daughter of David Woods. Bright and pretty, she had dutifully attended each day of the trial in Mobile, standing by her men, as it were: her stepbrother Michael and her boyfriend Alan Odom, the two who had passed the cigarette lighter back and forth that night. Once they had been shuffled off to prison, the boyfriend for nearly fifteen years, she had bent to her studies at J. U. Blacksher High in Uriah in hopes of going off to the University of Alabama, the first in her immediate family to attend college. Her grades were there, she knew the drawbacks of hanging around, and her father had his checkbook out. There was hope for a bright future after all, a chance to fly away and catch a ride on a star, to break away from all of this, find a new world, lead the way into a bright new century. But no. She had taken up with a fellow named Alex Baggett, a boy who had attended the first Klan rally and was last seen pouring concrete for a living; and now, in the spring of 1999, they had found a piece of land in Little River and were looking for a double-wide trailer to put on it so they could set up housekeeping. "She'll be pregnant soon," Peanut said, shaking his head. End of story.

As he turned fifty, during the last spring of the twentieth century, Joe Dees found himself in the deepest hole of his life. He had managed to spring his brother Eugene from the mental hospital on the Gulf Coast and bring him back home to Sawmill Road, but his mother had died and his father remained in the nursing home in Mobile. The National Council of Churches finally had told him no, sorry, there were no more funds available at this time. The coffers finally bare, he and his sister Margaret had quit writing checks on the St. Joe Baptist Church account. Now and then Joe would come into Peanut's to cash a check for twenty-five or fifty dollars, made out to him, for preaching at some church in the area. Meanwhile, the rows of donated pews lay rotting in the weeds behind his trailer and the ragged remnants of his congregation were trouping, disconsolately, to their borrowed home on every third Sunday. About twenty-five dollars was being deducted from the monthly prison pay of each of the five white kids, and deposited in the St. Joe Rebuilding Fund at a bank in Bay Minette, but by the time they were paroled and began paying restitution in earnest, he said, "three-fourths of my people will be dead" and it would be too late. He was a preacher without a church, a man without a country, a lost soul with every right to sing a sad song, a mournful ballad, for a life that might have been.